BULL'S EYE

THE ASSASSINATION
AND LIFE
OF SUPERGUN INVENTOR
GERALD BULL

JAMES ADAMS

TIMES T BOOKS

All rights reserved under International and Pan-American Copyright Coventions. Published in the United States by Times Books, a division of Random House, Inc., New York, and simultaneously in Canada by Random House of Canada Limited, Toronto.

Library of Congress Cataloging-in-Publication Data

Adams, James
  Bull's eye : the assassination and life of supergun inventor Gerald Bull / James Adams.—1st ed.
      p.   cm.
  Includes bibliographical references and index.
  ISBN- 0-8129-2009-0
  1. Bull, G. V. (Gerald V.)—Assassination.   2. Military engineers—Canada—Biography   3. Firearms designers—Canada—Biography.   4. Illegal arms transfers—History—20th century.   5. Ordnance—Design and construction—History—20th century.   6. Artillery, Field and mountain—History—20th century.   I. Title.
UG128.B85A33   1992
623'.092—dc20
[B]   91-30274

Design by Robert Bull Design

Manufactured in the United States of America

9 8 7 6 5 4 3 2

First Edition

To Ella

"War will never occur until a nation planning aggression thinks it can win. As long as the nations desiring peace can maintain better weapons than the nations desiring war, there will be a deterrent to aggression. Then they are not weapons of war, but weapons of peace." —JERRY BULL, 1953

ACKNOWLEDGMENTS

A number of people took a great deal of time and trouble to help in the preparation of this book. First, I must thank Geoff Ritts, who did much of the early research. A Yale law student, Geoff showed an outstanding talent for interviewing and for following a trail wherever it might lead. He opened doors I thought were shut and found answers where I thought there were none. I am not sure what the legal profession will make of his talents, but I know he would make a fine reporter.

Jerry Bull's family, bruised by his killing and constant harassment by the media, still took the trouble to see me and answer my questions.

Dr. Charles Murphy of the U.S. Army's Ballistics Research Laboratory was Jerry Bull's oldest friend, and he was unfailingly helpful and courteous. Jean de Valpine and Reed Johnston, who worked at the Memorial Drive Trust and at Arthur D. Little respectively, and were also close friends with Bull, helped me as well. I am grateful to Harland Riker for his trust in giving me access to the files of Arthur D. Little.

The Gulf war interrupted both the research and the writing of this book. The result was considerable pressure to complete the task and meet the deadlines. Kathleen Herron assisted me in this regard and was always good-humored in the face of increasingly unreasonable requests.

I am especially grateful to my wife, René, for being so patient, and allowing me time, which we should have been spending together, to finish the book. She is a source of tremendous encouragement, and her absolute faith that I could meet the schedule gave me the confidence to do so.

PROLOGUE

WHEN JERRY BULL was shot dead by a professional assassin in March 1990, few mourned his passing and little more than the fact of his death was recorded.

It appeared to be simply a brutal, clinical killing, with Bull the arms dealer paying the ultimate price in a business that does not tolerate the amateur. Yet a month later, when the first reports of Iraq's plan to develop a supergun surfaced, it was Jerry Bull who emerged as one of the keys to Saddam Hussein's plan to create one of the most powerful armed forces in the world.

For those of us who had followed the career of Jerry Bull over the previous ten years, his involvement with Saddam Hussein came as no surprise. I had first come across Bull at the beginning of the 1980s when researching *The Unnatural Alliance,* a book that examined the relations between Israel and South Africa. Bull was relevant because he had recently been jailed as a result of his involvement in a complex smuggling operation by which South Africa, with Israel's assistance, had been able to obtain the most modern and powerful howitzer in the world. At the time, there was a full United Nations arms embargo in force against South Africa. Bull was a perfect example of the amoral arms dealer prepared to turn a profit whatever the circumstances.

Over the next few years he surfaced occasionally in articles on artillery or discussions of new trends in the arms business. My file had him in China one year, in Spain the next, in Iraq the next. His guns were spreading all over the world, testimony to his talent as a weapons designer and to his reputation as a man who would sell his designs to anyone with the cash to pay.

I began the research for this book believing that I was investigating the low life of an arms dealer that would graphically illustrate the personal and professional corruption of the business. But, as the work progressed and Bull's family and friends were persuaded to talk, a very different picture of Jerry Bull emerged. This was a man desperate to belong. He had been rejected by the country of his birth and his country of adoption and spurned as a pariah by many of his fellow scientists. While there was disagreement about his motives and personality, there was no conflict about his talent. He was without doubt one of the most brilliant weapons designers of this century.

Arms dealers and designers live in a closed world where meetings, travel plans, and deals are shrouded in secrecy, kept hidden from jealous competitors and governments eager to stop the spread of arms. Not surprisingly, arms dealers are incessant gossips, lying about one another and themselves as a matter of routine.

Penetrating this world is always difficult for an author, but I approached the problem having already written *Engines of War*, a book about the arms business, and a number of other books dealing with terrorism, intelligence, and warfare, all of which gave me excellent contacts among Bull's former competitors.

Four other factors helped unlock some doors for me. As an eminent scientist, Bull had worked with a number of respected academics, and I was pleased to discover that many of these men and women are hoarders who throw nothing away. The result in some cases was a treasure trove of documents, photographs, and personal contemporary records that helped build a picture of Bull personally and professionally.

The customs officials who investigated Bull's involvement in the smuggling of arms to South Africa and the lawyers who both defended and prosecuted him all kept meticulous records.

These did not simply cover the case, but ranged over Bull's early life and included previously undisclosed information about his character. Bull's death made it easier for many of those people to talk to me, and I am grateful for their help.

The supergun affair prompted a number of Western intelligence agencies to devote great efforts over several months to try to understand just what Saddam Hussein was trying to build in northern Iraq. My contacts in that field have allowed me to develop the most complete account of how Western intelligence organizations learned about the supergun project and what they did about it.

Finally, while Bull's reputation has suffered at the hands of the media since his death, his children have remained fiercely loyal and utterly convinced of their father's innocence. They cooperated with me in the research for this book, but the results can in no way be said to be an authorized biography. On the contrary, they disagree strongly with some of my conclusions, preferring to stand by their own narrow views of events rather than accept the overwhelming evidence that suggests Jerry Bull was not just a victim.

The picture of Jerry Bull that appears in this book was completed with material gathered in talks with colleagues and other arms dealers, with the spies who hung on his coattails and used him, with the police and intelligence officers who tracked his travels around the world. Interviews with family, friends, customs agents, spies, government officials, and colleagues took place in Brussels, Montreal, Washington, Tel Aviv, Pretoria, London, and Cambridge, Massachusetts.

Where possible, sources have been identified in the text and in the notes that appear at the end of the text. Some sources spoke only on the basis that their names not appear, and in every case I have respected their wishes. I have not tried to reconstruct conversations unless a contemporaneous note was taken and I have seen the note. Sourced information has been checked to make sure that I have made no mistakes in transcribing my notes.

Despite such care, sifting fact from rumor and fiction has been difficult. Bull provoked fierce loyalty from his friends, antagonized large numbers of people, and was the subject of a great deal of speculation by the media. It would be unrealistic to expect that this is the full story of the man who lived so long in the shadows. But every part of this story has been checked, and the full manuscript has been read by seven people, all of whom were intimately involved with his life, including family, friends, business partners, investigators, and intelligence agents.

This is the story of Jerry Bull, who claimed he lived under a good star and who died because he was a guilty man who continued to believe in his own innocence.

CONTENTS

I N T R O D U C T I O N

THE MARCH TO WAR
AND MURDER

WHEN PRESIDENT Saddam Hussein's army marched over the border from Iraq into neighboring Kuwait in the early morning of August 2, 1990, the tiny Arab emirate was overwhelmed almost immediately. Within a month, Saddam had reinforced his invasion troops with an occupying force that would eventually total 590,000 men.

While the invasion may have come as a shock to Kuwait and her allies, its outcome was predictable. Over the previous decade, Saddam had built the fourth-largest military force in the world after China, India, and the Soviet Union. He had control of over a million men under arms, 955,000 of them in the army. He could field 5,500 tanks, 6,000 armored personnel carriers (APCs), and 689 combat aircraft. Kuwait, on the other hand, had only 20,300 men, and her armory included 245 tanks, 200 APCs, and 23 fighters. Even Saudi Arabia's armed strength was not much more impressive, consisting of 67,500 men, 550 tanks, 1,100 APCs, and 189 combat aircraft. Clearly, Iraq's two southern neighbors were hopelessly outnumbered and outgunned.[1]

That fact that Iraq was able to develop such enormous military capability is a tribute to the single-minded vision of Saddam Hussein—and a result of the greed of the international arms manufacturers who rushed to feed at his trough.

. . .

The Iraqi arms buildup began in 1971, when Saddam Hussein was vice-president, but the de facto leader of the country. His quest for military superiority was designed to ensure that Iraq would dominate—by threat or action—Israel and the surrounding Arab countries to become the major power in the Middle East. To accomplish this task, Saddam established a secret underground network of agents, brokers, and illegal traders to find and buy arms. They were paid through Swiss bank accounts funded by 5 percent of the country's oil revenues. By the time the Iran-Iraq war began on September 22, 1980, Saddam was in an excellent position to strengthen his military base on the back of the conflict.

Before the Ayatollah Khomeini was brought to power, Iran had been a staunch Western ally, the shah a close friend of the United States. Iraq, on the other hand, had been isolated by Western governments as a supporter of terrorism and a client state of the Soviet Union. But the 1979 Iranian revolution, and the war that followed between the two countries, produced a dramatic shift in Iraq's relationship to the rest of the world.

Serious concern existed among many nations about the spread of Muslim fundamentalism from Iran to other Middle Eastern countries, perhaps even to North Africa and the Soviet Union. Instability in a region already troubled by the presence of Israel and the Palestinian problem would threaten the security of oil supplies to the West, and possibly Japan. Iraq was considered the lesser of two evils, and there was a ground swell of private support for an Iraqi victory over Iran, despite public declarations of neutrality.

Howard Teicher, a former member of Reagan's National Security Council, recalled a meeting with Egyptian president Hosni Mubarak in April 1982. "Mubarak gave me a fifteen-minute lecture about how much Iraq had changed," he said.[2]

" 'You have to do everything you can to help Iraq survive the war. You have to tell President Reagan.'

"He kept shaking my hand and wouldn't let go."

Ten years later, Mubarak became one of the strongest advocates in the allied coalition for a decisive victory against Iraq, even arguing for Saddam Hussein's assassination.

While this policy may not have been articulated publicly, the world understood the game that was being played, and no one understood it better than the arms manufacturers and their salesmen. There had been signs of a shift in direction, however. In 1982, Iraq was taken off the State Department's list of countries supporting terrorism, despite the fact that two major terrorist leaders—Abul Abbas from the Palestine Liberation Front, and Abu Nidal of the Abu Nidal Organization—were regular visitors to Baghdad. A year later, the U.S. launched Operation Staunch, a multiagency project designed to stop the illegal flow of arms to Iran. While this was a laudable effort, no comparable attempt was made to stop weapons from reaching Iraq.[3]

Once Iraq was off the list of terrorist sponsors, the U.S. could reestablish diplomatic relations. By 1984, trade at all levels was considered acceptable. Between 1983 and 1989, trade between the U.S. and Iraq grew from $571 million to $3.6 billion. During the same period, using loans from American banks, many of them guaranteed by the federal government, the Iraqis spent $5.2 billion on American food, technology, and industrial goods.[4]

Moreover, from 1985 to 1990, the U.S. Commerce Department approved the sale of $1.5 billion of high-technology exports to Iraq, equipment that was supposed to be for civilian use but that in fact had military applications. Much of this equipment was used to set up a military research and development center called Saad 16 in the mountains near Mosul, north of Baghdad.

The Iraqis described the use of the Saad 16 complex as entirely peaceful, claiming it would be used for "the development and modernization of scientific instruments and apparatuses." However, some in the U.S. government thought the project was entirely defense related. The Pentagon objected to the export of a new computer that was identical to the one being used at the U.S. government's White Sands Missile Range in New Mexico. They were also concerned about exports of electronic instruments for rocket testing, computer-graphic terminals for rocket research, flight-test laboratory equipment, microwave technology, and a computer mapping system. In all cases, the Commerce Department overruled Pentagon objections and granted export licenses to the U.S. manufacturers. But the Pentagon demonstrated the strength of its convictions by bombing the Saad 16 complex in the first week of the 1991 allied air offensive in order to destroy Saddam's military capability.

According to the Stockholm International Peace Research Institute (SIPRI), Iraq may have spent as much as $80 billion on arms during the 1980s. The spending reached a peak of $33.3 billion in 1984, when military spending accounted for 30 percent of the country's total budget. Even as late as 1989, arms spending totaled $15 billion.[5]

In addition, between 1980 and 1989, 80 percent of Iraq's major weapons systems were procured from three of the five permanent members of the United Nations Security Council: France, China, and the Soviet Union. Moscow alone supplied 53 percent of Iraq's weaponry.

France was perhaps Iraq's second-biggest supplier. The French provided the Iraqis with the nuclear technology and scientific training that was instrumental in the development of their first nuclear reactor at Osiraq, which was destroyed by the Israelis in 1981. Dassault, the French aircraft manufacturer, sold them 130 advanced Mirage fighters—the same fighters the French would use against the Iraqis in the Gulf war—while Matra and Thomson sold them missiles and radar systems. Bouygues, the French construction company, was responsible for building much of Iraq's road network.[6]

Even the British, who are happy to criticize France's amoral attitude toward the arms business, jumped on the Iraqi bandwagon. Despite an embargo on arms sales imposed in 1984, British companies were allowed to sell a wide range of defense-related goods to Saddam. Many of the deals were for the raw materials to manufacture defense equipment rather than for the equipment itself. This is a common loophole exploited by arms manufacturers and governments, allowing them to protest their innocence while knowing the ultimate purpose of the materials they're selling.[7]

At the Taji Industrial Plant, just south of Baghdad, for instance, inside Shed C stood row upon row of computer-controlled lathes, which make the casings, fins, and nose cones for mortar shells. The equipment was supplied by a British company named Wickman Bennett, which argued that the lathes themselves were perfectly innocent. It was the Japanese-supplied software that turned the machinery into tools for the Iraqi arms business.

Saddam also bought rocket propellant from British Aerospace, UHF and HF battlefield radios from Racal Radio, and the Cymbeline radar system—the British army's state-of-the-art service—from Thorn EMI. It wasn't surprising, then, to discover that during the war British and Iraqi artillery gunners were spotting each other's fire with the same radar system; only the superior training of the British made the Iraqi artillery ineffective. Ironically, when the Gulf crisis began, the British found they had no desert camouflage uniforms to give the troops—all of them had been sold to the Iraqis some years earlier.

Meanwhile, West German companies such as MANN and H&H Metalform, with full knowledge and support of their government, were assisting on both nuclear and chemical projects, supplying equipment and training that would enable Iraq to become a powerful threat, not only in the Middle East but to the world at large.

March 1988: The Kurdish town of Halabja in northeastern Iraq, population sixty thousand, is captured by Iranian troops. A week later, Iraqi aircraft fly over the town and drop a lethal cocktail of nerve and chemical agents on the Iranian troops, as well as the Kurdish citizens.[8]

Bodies lie in the dirt streets, sprawled in rooms and courtyards of deserted villas, preserved at the moment of death in a modern version of the disaster that struck Pompeii. A father dies in the dust trying to protect his child from the white clouds of cyanide vapor. A mother cradles her infant next to a minibus that lies sideways across the road. The carcass of a cow lies tethered to a gatepost. Yards away, an entire family is spread side by side—mother, father, daughter. Families crouch together in cellars; shoes and clothes are scattered outside their homes.

Possession of weapons does not necessarily mean a commitment to using them; however, in his war with Iran, Saddam showed his willingness to use every weapon in his arsenal—on innocent people as well as the enemy. Approximately five thousand people died in the attack, but even this did not stop the U.S. government and other Western nations from considering Saddam a reasonable man. The State Department publicly condemned the act but privately sent a note of conciliation to Baghdad. The U.S. Senate passed tough unilateral sanctions by an 87–0 vote, but the Reagan administration lobbied against the move, and the motion, which the president had watered down, was eventually killed.

Even while the Senate was attacking Iraq, the U.S. was continuing a covert relationship with Saddam that had begun shortly before the resumption of diplomatic relations. The Central Intelligence Agency had provided Iraq with information about the disposition of Iranian forces, as well as their plans and capabilities. In return, the U.S. received very little information of value on terrorists and the Soviet Union.

Such a relationship, combined with the feeble response to the chemical attack on the Kurds, undoubtedly convinced Saddam—a tough and ruthless street fighter who by now was a veteran in the application of war—that no matter what he did, the West would continue to need him and his oil. Consequently, the invasion of Kuwait was a clear calculation based on his belief that neither the West nor the Soviet Union would act openly against his country, either passively or by force.

In fact, less than a year before the invasion, Saddam had tested America's resolve and found it perfectly pliant. On February 15, 1990, the Voice of America broadcast an editorial entitled "No More Secret Police," which praised the move toward democracy in a number of Eastern European countries. It also reported that secret police were still widely present in China, North Korea, Iran, Syria, Libya, Cuba, Albania, and Iraq.

On February 16, 1990, April Glaspie, the U.S. ambassador to

Iraq, was summoned to see the foreign minister in Baghdad, who protested America's flagrant interference in Iraq's internal affairs. Glaspie replied in equivocating terms: "It is absolutely not United States policy to question the legitimacy of the government of Iraq, nor to interfere in any way with the domestic concerns of the Iraqi people and government. My government regrets that the wording of the editorial left it open to incorrect interpretation. . . . President Bush wants good relations with Iraq, relations built on confidence and trust."[9]

This conciliatory approach must have reassured Saddam and made him feel that he had nothing to fear from the West. On the contrary, he'd been given every indication that the U.S. wanted a strong Iraq and that U.S. talk of arms embargoes was nothing but bluff.

Saddam appeared to receive further encouragement of his territorial ambitions from the U.S. State Department at a meeting with Ambassador Glaspie on July 25, 1990. The conversation, which was tape-recorded by the Iraqis (who later released a transcript), has not been disputed by the State Department. Saddam had introduced the subject of Kuwait, declaring that the emir had been undermining Iraq by controlling the production and, therefore, the price of oil. He hinted that he might have to take some action to curb his troublesome neighbor.

"We have no opinion on the Arab-Arab conflicts, such as your border agreement with Kuwait," Glaspie had replied. "I worked at the American embassy in Kuwait during the late 1960s, and our instructions during that time were to express no opinion on this issue, which is not associated with America."

And so, encouraged by such attitudes, instead of building a defensive military designed to protect Iraq from surrounding countries, Saddam decided to establish a fearsome offensive capability.

SS-1 missiles, commonly known as Scuds, were bought from the Soviet Union and North Korea and then modified by the Iraqis to increase their range from 190 to 560 miles. To accomplish this, Iraq was forced to reduce the missiles' explosive payload in order to increase their fuel capacity. As a result, the

Scuds tended to be very inaccurate at greater ranges, rarely landing within 6,500 feet of their main target. Nonetheless, they were a potent weapon in Saddam's armory during the Gulf war.[10]

After the invasion of Kuwait, the CIA claimed that the North Koreans were shipping Scud spares to Iraq. A meeting was held in early February 1991 to confront them with the American evidence. The North Koreans denied all knowledge of the shipments.

China, too, was reportedly trying to find a country prepared to smuggle its weapons to Iraq. The country's arms export business had shrunk from $4.7 billion in 1987 to $1.1 billion in 1989. Obviously, the Chinese government was attempting to capitalize on the war. Before the invasion, China had supplied Iraq with T-69 tanks, infantry weapons, and Silkworm missiles, and then had turned right around and sold a longer-range missile to Saudi Arabia. Fortunately, the U.S. managed to persuade the Chinese that an arms-smuggling operation would not be in their best interests.

And yet, if the history of arms sales to Iraq is filled with corruption and the most deadly of ironies—American, French, and British weapons being used to kill American, French, and British soldiers—there is one story that rises above the others. It is the cautionary tale of one man who found a home for his talents in a corrupt nation, and a dictator who was rich enough to reward Jerry Bull handsomely for betraying his dreams.

When Jerry Bull left the University of Toronto at the age of twenty, one of the youngest graduates with a Bachelor of Science degree in aeronautical engineering, he was determined to conquer the final frontier of space. At the start of his career, he was one of the few elite scientists in North America performing pioneering work on rockets and missile technology. His aim, as he put it, was to design "weapons of peace." But contracts with the U.S. Army and NASA rapidly twisted his ideal, and soon he was among the first to develop antiballistic missile systems—the forerunners of today's Strategic Defense Initiative (SDI), or Star Wars program.

His true dream, however, was to put satellites into space

using guns instead of rockets, an ambition that was thwarted by personality clashes and bureaucratic infighting in the Canadian and American governments. Gradually, he became a designer of guns and shells. Instead of ushering peace into the world, Jerry Bull created a legacy of weapons and ammunition with awesome destructive might.

Partly responsible for bringing China, Chile, and South Africa into the arms business, he helped them earn billions of dollars in valuable foreign exchange. He also facilitated Iraq's acquisition of weapons, which would prove more sophisticated and effective than any comparable systems used by the allied armies in the Saudi desert during 1990 and 1991.

Saddam's three hundred 155-mm howitzers, for example, were designed by Jerry Bull. Saddam had bought one hundred of them from Armscor, the South African arms company, which had bought the original weapons and their ammunition from Bull's operation, the Space Research Corporation International (SRCI) in Brussels, Belgium. Financed by Armscor, the actual shipment was arranged by Israel and the CIA, which smuggled the equipment to South Africa via Canada and the U.S. The South Africans then built their own version of the gun, known as the G-5, with a range of twenty-five miles, which can be towed into battle at speeds up to fifty-five miles per hour. Its eight-man crew can set up and begin shooting within four minutes, firing between two and three shells a minute, each carrying one hundred pounds of high explosive. On impact, each casing produces about forty-five hundred pieces of shrapnel. This gun has been the foundation of the South African arms business that, ten years ago, was in its infancy. Today, South Africa is among the top ten arms exporters in the world.[11]

The other two hundred howitzers Saddam bought were manufactured by NORICUM, an Austrian company, and sold to Iraq as the GH N-45. Austria purchased a license to manufacture the gun from SRC. The deal was brokered by the Canadian Commercial Corporation, a government body that acts as the prime contractor in arms sales. The gun that Bull actually designed was known as the GC-45, which stands for Gun Caliber 45, meaning the length of the gun barrel is forty-five times its interior diameter of 155 millimeters.

Then, in February 1988, Jerry Bull was invited to Iraq to discuss new defense opportunities. He flew to Baghdad with two of his sons, Michel and Stephen. They were told that the war with Iran would end soon (a cease-fire would be declared in July 1988, five months later) and that Iraq would need help rebuilding its armed forces. In particular, the Iraqis, while satisfied with the GH N-45, wanted to make it mobile. A contract, worth approximately $5 million a year, was signed on June 6, 1988, covering the development of 155-mm and 210-mm self-propelled guns, as well as providing for enhanced ammunition and ballistic training courses, which would be given to Iraqi personnel by SRC.[12]

The result of this collaboration was two new artillery systems, the 210-mm Al Fao and the 155-mm Majnoon. Prototypes of both weapons were built by Trebelan, a Spanish company, using components bought from France, Germany, and Spain. When the Iraqi government wanted to unveil the two new guns at the Baghdad Arms Fair in April and May 1989, Saddam arranged for the weapons to be flown to Iraq in a Soviet Antonov An-124 military transport.

If the statistics supplied by the Iraqis are correct, the Al Fao, with a range of 34 miles, is the most powerful piece of artillery in the world. Weighing fifty-three tons on a six-wheeled armored chassis, it is self-propelled and has a 560-hp Mercedes diesel engine. It can travel at speeds of forty-five miles an hour over rough ground, fifty-five miles an hour over paved roads, and can fire four three-hundred-pound shells a minute from its thirty-six-foot barrel. The Majnoon runs a close second, weighing forty-three tons and having a range of twenty-three miles. If the Al Fao and the Majnoon ever enter full-scale production, Iraq will have not only the most destructive guns known to man but also a major product for arms export.

Jerry Bull's relationship with the Iraqis was not over at the time of his death. He was working with them on a gun even more powerful than either the Al Fao or the Majnoon, one that could fire a shell more than a thousand miles. This supergun, Bull's special brainchild, would have a barrel two hundred feet long, be supported in a fixed position by steel scaffolding, and fire a massive rocket-assisted shell.

And yet, even as he worked on these weapons of war, Bull tried to maintain the image of a peaceful scientist at work, insisting that the supergun would be used to launch satellites into space. But most dealers believed that its real purpose was to allow Saddam Hussein to blast shells carrying chemical or nuclear charges at any country in the Middle East, including Israel.

March 22, 1990: A cold, gray early spring Thursday in Brussels. Dr. Jerry Bull had spent the afternoon doing what he did best: selling his genius as a weapons designer to a fellow arms dealer, Christopher Gumbley. At the end of a productive day, he telephoned Helen Gregoire, a family friend, to confirm their arrangements for dinner at seven-thirty. They would meet at his Uccle apartment at 28 avenue François Folie.[13]

Home to the European Commission, Brussels is the political headquarters of NATO, the North Atlantic Treaty Organization. Since 1982, it had been Jerry Bull's primary home. When Bull moved to Brussels after serving his jail sentence in the U.S., he left behind his wife, Mimi, and the rest of his family. Mimi refused to come with him because her daughter was still in school; the couple agreed that they would meet either in Canada or Mimi would fly over to Europe a number of times a year. This may have seemed a strange relationship to an outsider, but family and friends agree that the two remained very much in love, despite the distance that separated them. Later, two of Jerry's sons, Stephen and Michel, joined him in Brussels, the former to help with the engineering and design of artillery systems, the latter to handle the company's administration. Another son, Philippe, became a heart surgeon and moved to Vienna.

For eight years, Bull had been running Space Research International, a company that had been shifting its focus from the frontiers of space to conventional earthbound artillery. SRI's headquarters, located in Uccle, a southern suburb of Brussels, was Bull's center of operations, where he leased eighteen thousand square feet on two floors. The first floor housed the design and production staff; the second floor held the administration section and his office. Other branches of SRI operated in Geneva, Athens, and Montreal.

Bull had left work shortly after six-thirty. He was driven home by Monique Jamine, SRC's purchasing officer and Jerry's friend for fifteen years and personal assistant for the past ten. Monique had just told him that one of his female employees had asked her out on a date, and he found this very amusing. His bearlike shoulders were rolling with laughter as he walked through the gate to his apartment building.

Number 20 was on the sixth floor, overlooking a park. The apartment complex was actually four connected apartment buildings. A single key fitted all four entrances. Bull rode the elevator to his floor, took three paces, turned left and then left again to face the yellow front door of his apartment. As his right hand fumbled with the key in the lock, his left hand gripped the packed briefcase under his arm. He heard a footfall behind him. It was a busy building, so he didn't bother to turn around. Then he noticed that the footsteps had stopped.

A man drew a 7.65-mm automatic pistol with a long, bulbous silencer from his pocket. The killer leveled it smoothly and began firing, making almost no noise. Only the metallic sound of the pistol slide, ejecting one round and chambering the next, echoed softly down the corridor.

Three shots entered Bull's back, driving his body forward against the door frame. The impact of the bullets was so strong, the aim so precise, that he was dead before he hit the ground. To be sure the job was done, however, the gunman placed the pistol against the back of Bull's head and pulled the trigger twice more. These two bullets completed the bloody assassination, spraying blood and bone fragments onto the hall carpet.

Ten minutes later, at 6:45 P.M., Helen Gregoire discovered the body.

Later that evening, Bull's second son, Michel, received a phone call from the Brussels police at his home near Montreal. In a short, even brusque, conversation, the Brussels policeman told Michel of his father's death. Michel immediately drove to his mother's house in Charny, Quebec, where she lived with her daughter, Naomi-Jane. Michel's mother, Noemie, known to the family as Mimi, broke down on hearing the news.

The next day, Bull's eldest son, Philippe, known to his father as Pilpot, was informed of the killing. He immediately flew from Vienna to Brussels and identified his father's body.

According to Christopher Foss, the editor of the authoritative *Jane's Armour and Artillery*, Bull was "perhaps the greatest gun designer of the century." But other obituaries insinuated there was more to Jerry Bull than simple gun designs. According to Dr. Charles Murphy, his lifelong friend and head of the Launch and Flight Division of the U.S. Army Ballistic Research Laboratory at Aberdeen Proving Ground in Maryland, the U.S. government did "zero point zero" to help transport Bull's body back to Canada for burial, even though he was an American citizen who had been murdered overseas and had made significant contributions to the U.S. Army in the past. Canada, his birthplace and the permanent home of his family, and a country that had also benefited greatly from Bull's designs and research, never even bothered to inquire about the matter with the Brussels police.

In fact, from the moment of Bull's killing, family and friends were shocked at the response of the media and the U.S., Canadian, and Belgian governments. The Belgian police made their feelings obvious—when Michel flew to Brussels to collect his father's body and belongings two days after the shooting, he discovered the hallway to be just as the police had found it the night Bull was shot: blood splattered all over the walls, the carpet in the hallway stained rust red. As far as the Brussels police were concerned, Bull was a victim of his own profession.

When Mimi arrived in Brussels a month later to close the apartment, the bloodstains were still on the hall rug, and blood remained on the door and walls. Immediately after Bull's death, the media began hounding the family, calling at all times of the day and night. The family realized that no matter what anyone said, the man they knew as a loving husband and father would be portrayed as a monster, selling death to some of the most evil regimes in the world. The family remained genuinely baffled, insisting that Jerry Bull was only a scientist.

By the time Bull was buried on March 31, 1990, at the Church of St. Bruno outside Montreal, he had become an enigma whom no one seemed to know.

The church was filled to capacity with nearly six hundred people, some of whom had not seen Bull for thirty years, some traveling long distances to pay their final respects. It seemed odd that Bull's funeral would draw such a large congregation. He was disliked, if not vilified, by Western intelligence agencies, and the media consistently wrote about him as a ruthless and amoral arms dealer. Yet, clearly, a large number of people had great affection for him.

The family's glowing tribute described a paragon, a perfect father, a Samaritan, a gentleman in the true sense of the word.[14] But to others he was a convicted criminal, a sanctions buster who smuggled arms illegally to South Africa, and, possibly, a rogue agent for the CIA.

These apparent contradictions made for some confusion in the investigation by the Brussels police. In the weeks following Bull's death, they visited every apartment in the complex, seeking witnesses. No one had noticed anything unusual on the day of the shooting. The only slender clue they uncovered came from the owner of one of the four buildings. He told them that the previous December, two men had rented an apartment from him at 265 avenue François Folie. The two men, described by neighbors as Mediterranean in appearance, paid three months' rent in advance. They stayed ten days and then vanished without a trace.[15]

However, in order to get the electricity connected, they had to appear in person at the offices of UNERG, the Brussels utility company, where one of them had to show proof of identity. As a routine precaution, the company made a copy of the identity card, owned by a Casablanca-born French citizen. Using this clue, the Belgian police then checked back with immigration records and discovered that the two men had arrived together. The second man was traveling on a false passport, and the "French citizen" had a criminal record. Further inquiries suggested that the man traveling on the false passport was an Israeli national.

In itself, this did not mean very much. The men might have been from Mossad, the Israeli intelligence agency. But if that was the case, they had left a fairly clear trail, which was not Mossad's style. The Belgian police were well aware that Israelis now made up a number of the freelance hit squads roaming the world. In fact, Israelis had largely replaced the British, French, and South Africans as the mercenaries of the underworld. Israelis were also prominent players in the international arms market, and Israeli intelligence was known to be active in Europe in its constant hunt for Palestinian terrorists planning attacks on Jewish targets.

At the very least, the police were certain that the killing had been carried out by a professional assassin. Bull had died from five bullets—including a two-shot *coup de grâce* in the back of the neck—fired from a silenced gun, all of which suggested a well-trained killer. But professionals rarely engage in three months of planning for a contract that is so simple to fulfill. Why rent the apartment? If the men had intended to be that thorough, they would not have left behind such obvious clues. Also, the killer apparently made no attempt to take the twenty thousand dollars in cash that Bull had in his briefcase at the time of the murder. Robbery, therefore, was not a motive, and this was no casual slaying.

Still, the police could not understand why the two men would have wanted to rent that particular apartment, if Bull was their target. The apartment complex is in a single row with number 26 and number 28 on the same side of the street. Consequently, anyone in number 26 would be unable to keep watch on someone in number 28. True, renting an apartment would have provided them with a key to both buildings, but Bull could have been assassinated outside the gate. Probably, the police conjectured, their initial visit in December was a very preliminary reconnaissance.

And yet, determining that it had been a professional hit gave the police no definitive leads as to who might have paid for the killing. The investigation centered on five possible suspects.

. . .

At the top of the list were the Israelis. Immediately after Bull's death, an Israeli radio broadcast remarked that Bull's killing had set back Iraq's nuclear program by several years, which led Michel, Bull's second son, to speculate that the murder was paid for by the Israelis.

"My father told me that a friend of his who had contact with the Mossad had warned him that they were after him," Michel said. "If one accepts the theory that my father was killed because we deal with Iraq, then I would have to think that Israel is the primary suspect."[16]

In fact, the March issue of *Middle East*, the London-based magazine, revealed—the same month Bull was murdered—that he had been developing a new arms system that would allow the Iraqis to shoot satellites into space.[17] The article alleged that Iraq was showing interest in reviving a twenty-year-old project to produce a supergun capable of firing satellites or weapons into low earth orbit. During the 1960s, Bull had been the motivating force behind the High Altitude Research Project (HARP), designing an enormous gun that eventually pushed shells over 111 miles up into the atmosphere. At the time, HARP was hailed as a possible alternative to the use of expensive rockets for space research. But there was no hard evidence, the article concluded, that Iraq's interest had moved beyond Bull's initial discussions to actual procurement. Nevertheless, the article may have prompted a swift investigation by the Israelis, assuming it was not their men who had rented the Brussels apartment earlier. Clearly, HARP's massive guns could be used to hit targets all over the Middle East with shells containing chemicals or conventional explosives. Israel may have decided to eliminate the threat by killing the only person capable of re-creating the project.

Bull's murder had striking similarities to the death of Yahya El Meshad, a fifty-year-old Egyptian-born scientist, who was a central figure in Saddam Hussein's efforts to develop a nuclear bomb. In 1980, Meshad was found dead in a Paris hotel room. The police believed that the scientist was murdered soon after a prostitute had left his room at the Hôtel Méridien, whereupon

Mossad agents had entered and cut his throat. During the initial interrogation, however, the prostitute—known to her clients as Marie Express—claimed that Meshad had refused her advances and they had parted at his door. Unfortunately, she was run over by a car and killed before the police could ask any more questions.

As in Bull's case, Meshad's murder was obviously a professional hit: the scientist was a key figure in an Iraqi arms program that might have threatened Israel; nothing was stolen from the body, including fourteen hundred francs; no trace was ever found of the murderers. In the minds of the Belgian police, Israel had an established reputation for ruthlessness and a willingness to kill anyone who contributed to Iraq's armament. The difference between the two cases is that within days of the Meshad killing, the Israelis privately admitted to their colleagues in British and American intelligence that they were responsible, although publicly, of course, they said nothing.

And yet, such admissions mean very little. Mossad is a master of disinformation and propaganda. It would have been in Israel's best interests to claim responsibility for Bull's murder, even if they had not carried it out. To acknowledge an assassination privately costs nothing and would have helped foster Israel's reputation as an uncompromising hunter of anyone it considered a danger to the state, which in turn might have discouraged others from following in the footsteps of people like Jerry Bull.

The second suspects in the slaying were the Iraqis themselves, possibly because of some falling out between them and SRCI. Similar killings had occurred in Brussels during 1989: an Arab Muslim religious leader and his daughter had been shot, followed by the murder of a Jewish doctor. Belgian police believed that both killings had been carried out by assassins working for the Iraqi government. In addition, 7.65-mm weapons had been used in all four slayings. But the caliber of the weapon was not particularly convincing evidence that the deaths were related. The 7.65-mm gun had been the standard weapon of the Belgian police for several years. Large numbers of the

pistols circulated through the Belgian underworld, and a significant percentage of murders were carried out with the weapon
each year.

A similar argument applied to the Iranian government, the third
suspect. Although Bull's gun designs had been sold to both sides
in the eight-year Iran-Iraq war, he had only done business directly with the Iraqis. He did not deal with the government in
Tehran, not because of any moral principles, but because the
Iraqis had the cash and were prepared to pay.

Perhaps the Iranians feared that Bull might have been further
along in developing the supergun for Saddam Hussein and took
action, partly as punishment for the betrayal and partly to stop
the project.

Israel, Iraq, and Iran might have been the prime suspects, but
there were others as well. The murder could have been the result of bad blood between arms dealers; it could, as some newspapers speculated, have been carried out by the CIA. This
argument, in particular, was advanced by his family.

In 1980, Bull had received a six-month jail sentence in the
United States for smuggling arms to South Africa. On the advice
of his lawyers, he had pleaded guilty at the trial, but he always
maintained that he had been set up by the U.S. government and
betrayed by his friends in the CIA. Bull was certain that the
arms smuggling operation had taken place with the full approval
of American officials and that the operation was actually representative of a general U.S. policy to support the Pretoria government in its fight against communists in Angola. After his
release from jail and self-imposed exile in Belgium, Bull became
obsessed with proving his innocence and receiving a pardon
from the president of the United States.

In the ten years after his release from prison, he had amassed
a great volume of evidence in his own defense. He had persuaded
three colleagues to write a detailed dossier and was planning to
send this document to President Bush.

But simple documentary evidence was not enough to overturn his conviction. He needed hard information. He kept searching for the final lever to force action from the Bush administration. In January 1990, he told his son Stephen that he was "that close" to finding out the full details of the CIA's involvement in the smuggling of arms to South Africa.

Bull flew to the United States in February 1990, one month before his assassination. He had told his family that he was following a lead in his investigation of the CIA, but he would not tell them whom he intended to see. He met Mimi at Mardi Gras in New Orleans. They then flew to Washington, D.C., where they stayed for three days. Later investigations show that he saw a number of people who were central to SRC's involvement with South Africa in the late 1970s, including one of South Africa's key contacts in the U.S. government.

When he returned to Brussels, he seemed satisfied, even elated, at the way the trip had gone, but he still refused to reveal whom he had seen or what he had learned. All he would tell Stephen was that he had eaten a meal with someone in Washington who had told him that if he had not pleaded guilty at his trial ten years earlier, orders had been given to assassinate him. He was shocked, he said, but the news confirmed to him that he had been used as a scapegoat.

Bull was killed on the third day after his return to Brussels from the American trip.

In the first hours of the investigation, the Belgian police were surprised to discover just how closely the U.S. embassy in Brussels had been monitoring Bull's case. The embassy was officially notified of his death four hours after the body was discovered. At five o'clock the following morning, when the police arrived at the embassy to speak with officials, the consulate had a copy of Bull's security file, which appeared to be six inches thick. Normally, such files take weeks, not hours, to arrive from Washington.

Even the British Secret Intelligence Service, also known as MI6, was a suspect in Bull's assassination. Bull knew all the details of Britain's involvement in illegal arms dealing with Iraq. According to this theory, British intelligence had full knowledge of Bull's development of a supergun for the Iraqis but took no overt action. The reasons for this passivity were unclear. Perhaps British intelligence wanted to observe the spread of Iraq's underground arms-purchasing network. Maybe the British were content to ignore the supergun in the same way they had been content to sell the Iraqis a wide range of military equipment while officially enforcing an embargo.

When the article in *Middle East* magazine appeared, British intelligence may have feared that their knowledge of the project would be exposed along with their willingness to allow it to proceed. The British had no desire to be caught in the same trap in which the CIA had found themselves ten years earlier, regarding the smuggling of arms to South Africa. They didn't want to risk the publicity of an unwelcome trial, which would potentially involve some of the most prominent arms manufacturers in Britain.

The final candidate for the role of assassin was any of the arms dealers working with Bull. For many years, Bull had operated in the murky world of the arms business, where subterfuge and double-dealing are common practice. Bull had an unusually good reputation in the business as an honest man who delivered the goods on time and to specification. He did not actually sell the hardware—fighters, rifles, artillery, or tanks—but he did market the design of weapons. So, to some extent, he was one step removed from the really grubby end of the business, where competition is particularly cutthroat and the practitioners are often only too happy to get rid of the competition.

Even so, Bull was a forceful personality who made many enemies by saying what he felt about individuals or their products. He had alienated a number of important people in Belgium, the country he had chosen for his home.

In the 1970s, SRC had formed a business partnership with a Belgian arms manufacturer, Poudrières Réunies de Belgique (PRB). Bull designed the guns and shells; PRB did some of the manufacturing and marketing. While Bull was in jail, the relationship between the two companies collapsed amid Bull's allegations that PRB had stolen much of his work without paying for it.

PRB was owned by one of Belgium's biggest multinational corporations, Sociéte Générale de Belgique (SGB). In the mid-1980s, Bull had tried to buy PRB from SGB but had been turned down. On the surface, this might have been just an ordinary business deal gone wrong, but Bull thought that officials at SGB were responsible for the murder of Joseph Severin, a close friend and former head of PRB, who had died in 1978 after falling down a flight of stairs in his Brussels home. Bull believed that Severin had been killed because he was about to expose corruption on a vast scale at PRB. However, there is no evidence to support the assertion that Severin was murdered.

In 1989, PRB was taken over by a British company called Astra Holdings. Immediately after the takeover, Astra's board of directors found that, in fact, they had bought a worthless shell, which meant that Astra was likely to go bankrupt. If so, the directors of the company would be under investigation by a number of British government departments.

On the day he died, Jerry Bull had played host to Christopher Gumbley, the former managing director of Astra. The two men had never met, but Gumbley had received a call from Bull earlier in the week and had agreed to a meeting in which affairs of mutual interest would be discussed. Gumbley flew to Brussels and went to SRC's offices, where he spent most of the day. To Gumbley's amazement, Bull suggested that he had enough evidence of corruption at PRB and SGB to ensure that Astra could win a legal action for fraud (no evidence has been found to support Bull's allegation). He offered to fund Astra's litigation for as much as it cost and as long as it took. Gumbley flew back to London, astonished at his good fortune. However, even before his plane had taken off, Bull was dead.

Since the killing, Gumbley has lived in fear for his life. An ordinary, modestly successful businessman, he has been propelled into the world of murderers, spies, and criminals that he does not understand. He is certain that Bull's assassination was related to their meeting and is terrified of becoming the next target.

. . .

In the year following Bull's death, the Brussels police investigators traveled to Britain, Canada, and the United States. But the information they gathered was open to a nightmare of conflicting interpretations: Bull, the brilliant egotist and ballistics genius who would sell his talents to anyone; Bull, the arms dealer who had links to arms manufacturers in China, South Africa, Austria, Israel, Iran, and Iraq; Bull, the man who his family claims was an innocent libeled by the press and the U.S. government; Bull, the man accused of being a criminal with his finger in hundreds of dirty arms deals. And yet, the one thing the Brussels police did not learn was who killed Gerald Bull.

O N E

VELVET GLOVE AND
THE NEW SCIENCE OF
SUPERSONICS

BORN ON March 9, 1928, in North Bay, Ontario, Jerry Bull was the second youngest of ten children in a prosperous middle-class family. His father, Bull believed, was a prominent Canadian criminal lawyer, and a member of the elite King's Counsel, which placed him at the top of his profession. In fact, when George Bull died, his family learned that two George Bulls practiced law in Canada. Jerry Bull's father was the less successful of the two.[1]

His mother, Gertrude LaBrosse, was also born in North Bay, in 1893, the daughter of one of the town's original settlers. Despite his mother's French Canadian surname, Jerry was actually an English Canadian. The LaBrosse side of the family emerged when a French Canadian prospector named Napoleon LaBrosse married Isabel Parker, Gertrude's mother, an English Canadian. Shortly after the marriage was consummated, however, the prospector headed back into the wilderness, where he died. Mrs. LaBrosse raised her children in Vancouver, British Columbia, before moving to Ontario.

When Gertrude was in her early teens, the family moved back to North Bay. When she was fifteen, Gertrude went to work in the law offices of George Bull. For the unmarried thirty-five-year-old lawyer, the young and virginal Gertrude must have appeared attractive, easy prey. Seduced by his charms, Gertrude married the lawyer in 1909 when she was only sixteen, an arrangement that scandalized the small conservative community. Over the next eighteen years, Gertrude had seven children, six boys and a girl. Then on March 9, 1928, the youngest, Gerald Vincent Bull, was born.

When Jerry was three years old, his family moved to Toronto and his father established a new law practice. Tragedy struck when his mother died of complications following the birth of her youngest son, Gordon, in 1931, just three months after the move. The death had a crushing effect on Bull's fifty-seven-year-old father, who became consumed by grief. In later life, Bull came to believe that the shock of his mother's death may have caused his father to suffer a mild stroke, which could explain, in part, the radical change in his personality. Certainly, George Bull went through some kind of breakdown, abandoning his profitable law practice and taking his family to live in his parents' old mansion in Trenton, east of Toronto. One daughter had married by then, so nine children were left to support. He received some help from his unmarried sister, Laura Bull, a retired nurse, who moved into the house and tried to become Jerry's surrogate mother.

Laura, unfortunately, knew little about the cares and needs of little children, so George Bull continued to dominate the household. He was a stern and unbending man, full of moral certainty and the pomposity of those brought up in the English tradition, without the softening influence of England itself. He imposed a strict and humorless regime. In 1932, Laura died of cancer. Once again, a warm, loving influence was removed from Bull's life.

In his quiet country home, George Bull must have found a kind of stability, because he soon fell in love and remarried. Unfortunately, his new wife had no interest in taking responsibility for his offspring from the earlier marriage. They were not invited to the wedding, and from that day on, George Bull effectively abandoned his children. He moved back to Toronto, his confidence restored, and started practicing law once more. But

Jerry, who was then just seven years old, and three of his brothers did not move with him. They were taken in by one of their married sisters, Bernice, who lived in Sharbot Lake, north of Kingston.

When Jerry turned seven, he spent his summer vacation with Philip LaBrosse, his mother's younger brother, and his wife, Edith. They lived on a sixty-eight-acre farm east of Kingston. A warm and happy couple, they treated Jerry like the son they never had. He loved the rural existence, and when the time came to return to school at Sharbot Lake, he did not want to go.

In those days, Jerry was shy and unwilling or unable to express himself, so he couldn't admit to Edith and Philip that he wanted to stay. Only when his aunt and uncle drove him back to Sharbot Lake and were about to help him unpack did they discover that his suitcase was empty. Jerry had deliberately left all of his school clothes at the farm, in the hope that the subterfuge would extend the holiday.

His ploy worked, and seven-year-old Jerry moved in with his new family. For nearly three years he lived an idyllic, if lonely, existence. He went to the small village school and worked hard to meet the demands of Edith, who was determined that Jerry would meet the high standards she set and thus break away from what she saw as the scandalous and corrupting influence of the rest of the Bull family.

When Jerry was ten the LaBrosses planned to spend the winter in Florida, so they enrolled Jerry at Regiopolis College, a private Jesuit boarding school in Kingston. The headmaster was reluctant to take him at first—he looked and acted so young and was indeed two years younger than the other new arrivals. However, when the LaBrosses arrived to pick him up at the end of the term, the headmaster had changed his attitude. Jerry had blossomed under the teachings of the Jesuits and was beginning to demonstrate his brilliance. He spent the next six years at the college, where he would develop the love of poetry that remained with him for the rest of his life. His two favorite poets were Thomas Gray and Henry Wadsworth Longfellow; his favorite poem was Gray's "Elegy Written in a Country Churchyard," its gentle cadences evoking the beauty and simplicity of country life.

> *The Curfew tolls the knell of parting day,*
> *The lowing herd wind slowly o'er the lea,*
> *The ploughman homeward plods his weary way,*
> *And leaves the world to darkness and to me.*
>
> *Now fades the glimmering landscape on the sight,*
> *And all the air a solemn stillness holds,*
> *Save where the beetle wheels his droning flight,*
> *And drowsy tinklings lull the distant folds.*

During his first year at Regiopolis, Jerry spent Christmas with his adopted parents, which was memorable for two reasons. Jerry had a visit from Santa Claus, who left him two model aircraft kits. Understanding the complicated instructions, then building the aircraft and making them fly presented a real challenge. The thrill of those flights and the struggles with the basic principles of aerodynamics became his first sources of inspiration.

"When I went shopping after that," recalled Edith LaBrosse, "he insisted on coming along to make sure I bought the breakfast cereal with the plane designs on the box. It didn't matter whether the cereal was eaten or not."

Three years after Jerry arrived at the farm, Edith won the Irish Sweepstakes and traveled to Dublin to collect the prize money. Although this helped with the family's finances, it actually made little difference in Jerry's life. Uncle Phil and Aunt Edith were quiet, sensible, middle-class Canadians. Winning the Irish Sweepstakes was just a small diversion that wasn't about to upset the steady tenor of their lives.

In the summer of 1944, at the age of sixteen, Jerry told his aunt and uncle that he wanted to become a doctor. This was a curious choice, because he hated the sight of blood and routinely fainted during injections. But the decision was soon thwarted, because he couldn't find a medical school that would accept him at his age. The only faculty that would agree to teach him was in the Department of Aeronautical Engineering at the University of Toronto. Tommy Loudon, one of the faculty members, saw Jerry's promise immediately and even detected a nascent talent for design. Jerry was the youngest student in the new department; once again, his enthusiasm and intelligence carried him past the prejudices of the authorities who had been reluctant to admit him.

He graduated four years later with a Bachelor of Applied Science in aeronautical engineering. During the same year, his father died. By that time, however, there was little affection or contact between the two men, though Jerry was beginning to gain some understanding of his father's almost total rejection. The remote figure who had been incapable of giving love and had been subject to violent mood swings was, in fact, an alcoholic. Like many children of alcoholics, Jerry Bull would be tempted to drink as he grew older.

Bull's first job was as a draftsman for the A. V. Roe aircraft company near Toronto. From the beginning of his interest in aeronautics, Bull had been a visionary, one of the few with the energy and imagination to travel to the outer reaches of science. During his studies at the University of Toronto, he'd become fascinated by the possibility of driving objects through air and space faster than the speed of sound. Breaking the sound barrier was an entirely new theoretical concept, but scientists all over the world recognized the importance of conquering supersonics before any major advances in aircraft and rocket design could take place.

"We are learning that supersonic aerodynamics can have many civilian applications," Bull said in 1953. "It can provide us with safer and faster air travel. It will help us conquer space, man's last frontier. Someday guided missiles will carry mail instead of a warhead, and a letter mailed in Vancouver will be in Halifax an hour later."

Bull made this remark in the course of an interview with

Fred Bodsworth of the Canadian magazine *Maclean's,* which resulted in a very flattering profile that appeared on March 1, 1953. Unfortunately for Bull, the article was headlined "Jerry Bull, Boy Rocket Scientist," a description that was to haunt him for the rest of his career. In the Canadian scientific community, where politics and jealousy play significant parts, the profile of a twenty-four-year-old engineer who seemed willing to comment with apparent confidence and certitude on a large number of subjects caused considerable resentment. To other scientists and to some government officials, Bull was nothing but an upstart, an ambitious young man who needed to be taught the value of age and experience. Bull, of course, had no idea of the stir the article caused, and he was immensely flattered to have been taken so seriously by *Maclean's.*

In 1948, Dr. Gordon N. Patterson had established the Institute of Aerophysics for the research and teaching of supersonic dynamics at the University of Toronto. The institute was funded largely by Canada's Defence Research Board (DRB). Because the science of supersonics was so poorly understood, little teaching could be accomplished, however. Instead, the DRB offered grants of two thousand dollars, on average, which allowed students to conduct their own research in a university setting as part of their graduate work toward an M.A. or Ph.D. degree.

The institute could support only twelve students at any one time or accept up to four new students a year. Jerry applied when he was twenty. Again, he was much younger than the other students, most of whom were married, some of whom were veterans of the war. Although his age was working against him, once more Jerry impressed the faculty enough to be admitted.

Fifteen students from Bull's undergraduate class applied for one vacancy in the supersonic dynamics program; Bull was selected. And so began a relationship between Patterson and Bull, marked by the considerable fortitude of the older man in the face of the younger's exuberant approach to research, which would continue for the rest of Patterson's life.

Bull's first idea was to create a supersonic wind tunnel,

which Patterson unfortunately agreed should be set up in room 36, the office next to his. The tunnel was seven feet long, and nearly all the parts had to be manufactured elsewhere and put together on-site. When the first tunnel was delivered, Bull found that it would not fit in the space provided because a valve protruded an inch farther than expected. Rather than relocate, Bull simply knocked a hole in Patterson's office wall.

(In 1968, Bull designed an even larger tunnel. Once again, problems with the dimensions arose. This time, the air storage chamber would not fit through the office door, so Bull left the chamber in the passage, returning at night with ax and hacksaw in hand. He removed the door frame and maneuvered the chamber into the room, then restored the door frame in a way that ensured the door would never close properly again.)

Over the next two years, Patterson found his office gradually shrinking as the wind tunnels expanded. The final straw came when he arrived at work one morning to find his office covered in glass fragments after the wind tunnel's observation windows had shattered during one of Bull's experiments in pushing shock waves through the tunnel at three times the speed of sound.

Clearly the cramped quarters could no longer sustain a proper working environment, so Patterson persuaded the Royal Canadian Air Force to loan the institute a few buildings at Downsview Airport, outside Toronto. With the new space would come a new tunnel, slated to be one of the largest in the world at that time. At a cost of $200,000, then an enormous sum, the institute began constructing a tunnel capable of producing winds traveling at fifty-five hundred miles an hour, or seven times the speed of sound. To create the vacuum, a forty-foot sphere, made of layers of reinforced steel and having one-and-a-quarter-inch glass observation windows, was fixed to the side of one of the buildings. Bull was responsible for designing the test section of the tunnel, the point at which the tunnel narrowed to channel the wind against the airplane models fixed inside.

Construction of the tunnel took eighteen months, and a grand opening was scheduled for September 26, 1950. The Canadian government expected that the research connected with the project would lead to breakthroughs in the science of super-sonics. More important, perhaps, the defense department in-tended to use the test results to give Canada a crucial lead in the development of new missiles, rockets, and aircraft. Conse-quently, the opening of the tunnel was planned as a lavish affair, with officials from the United States, Australia, Britain, South Africa, and New Zealand attending the ceremony. Air Marshal W. A. Curtis of the Royal Canadian Air Force was chosen to press the button that would send the first blast of wind down the tunnel.

Everyone worked feverishly to finish the tunnel on schedule, especially Bull, who was also trying to complete his Ph.D. thesis.

"Jerry was working much too hard," recalled Aunt Edith. "On nights he didn't stay at the institute, he would come home, have dinner, go in his room to study, and close the door at seven o'clock. At eleven or twelve, when we were going to bed, we would knock on his door and tell him he should get some sleep. Through the crack under the door, we'd see his light go out. Then, in a little while, it would come back on. He would wait until we were in bed, then he'd get up and continue studying."

Three days before the wind tunnel was due to perform pub-licly, Bull ran an initial test at subsonic speed, which seemed to go well. The next day, the floor and walls of the building that housed the tunnel were being painted, so no tests could be run. That night, Bull tried to drive a supersonic wind through the tunnel, but no shock wave appeared. The staff suspected a leak. Four hundred bolts had to be removed to inspect the seals, which were found to have been packed incorrectly. New seals were put on and the bolts replaced.

After three more hours, the vacuum chamber had done its work and the button was pushed to start the air through the tunnel once again. This time, the staff could see the shock wave forming inside but their jubilation was short-lived. There was a massive explosion, the blast ripped through the night, and the air dissipated. Two blocks of wood, which gave the tunnel its contours, had been torn from their mountings and had crashed down the tunnel's interior. In the rush to complete the construction, Bull had used softwood instead of hardwood, and the shock wave had simply destroyed the blocks.

It was now 3:00 A.M., and the visiting dignitaries were due to arrive in twelve hours. Bull, working with two machinists, had to unscrew the four hundred bolts again in order to crawl inside the tunnel and replace the wood blocks. Dean Kenneth Tupper, head of the university's engineering department, came by as they were starting this tedious task, took off his suit jacket, and began to help. Tupper was the one who crawled inside the tunnel to fix the blocks.

This was the project's last setback. Later that day, when Air Marshal Curtis pressed the button to start the demonstration, everything worked perfectly.

The wind tunnel put Canada on the cutting edge of supersonic technology. Only Britain and the United States, among all the Western allies, were similarly advanced. Neither of them, however, were in a position to share their knowledge with the Canadian defense department. The science was so new that both countries wanted to produce their own missiles and aircraft before sharing their production techniques and raw research with anyone else. The Canadians realized that if they were to take advantage of the work done by Bull and his colleagues, they would have to go into the missile business for themselves.

Consequently, the government asked the Defence Research Board to produce designs for a Canadian air-to-air guided missile, code-named Velvet Glove. The DRB then passed the task to the Canadian Armament Research and Development Establishment (CARDE), based at Valcartier, near Quebec City. Gordon Watson, CARDE's thirty-four-year-old chief engineer, was ready to start but needed an expert in aerodynamics who also had a good understanding of the new science of supersonics. Watson turned to Gordon Patterson for advice.

Because most of Patterson's students left Canada after graduation to take advantage of American salaries, four or five times those being offered in Canada, Watson asked Patterson to persuade one of his students to stay and work for the government. In particular, Watson told Patterson, they needed help with the design of Velvet Glove.

Bull had been told that he would have to stay in Canada for another year to complete the university attendance required for his Ph.D. Patterson made him a deal: Bull could get his Ph.D. now, in 1951, before satisfying his residency requirements, provided he went to work for the government.

At first Gordon Watson was put off by Bull's youth—he had just turned twenty-three—but once again a meeting resolved all doubts, and Bull became responsible for making the missile fly. At this stage, Watson was in serious difficulty with the Velvet Glove project, which was behind schedule. Not even a basic airframe had been conceived, let alone built.

Thirty years ago, the problems facing missile engineers were enormous. Missile design had to accommodate the variable pressures of operating at subsonic speed, breaking through the sound barrier, and then operating supersonically; the mechanisms for controlling the missile had to be sensitive enough to make course adjustments, in fractions of a second, to allow for changes in the atmosphere, including cross- and headwinds; the missile had to have an accurate navigation system, which had to take into account the missile's changing weight during flight as its fuel load burned up. Finally, the missile had to be made out of materials that were light enough to be propelled through space, yet strong enough to withstand the enormous stresses and heat generated by supersonic flight.

Within a year, Bull had designed an airframe for the missile that was test-fired successfully, putting Velvet Glove back on track.

For the young Jerry Bull, these were challenges he was prepared to meet and confident he could overcome. They were happy times filled with moments of great opportunity. His contributions to Canada's defense program were being appreciated by the Ottawa establishment. He had earned the recognition of his peers, as well as the opportunity to use his talents to open new scientific territories. His personal life, too, had settled down and had become relatively stable.

In 1953, he met Noemie Gilbert, the petite and exceptionally pretty daughter of Dr. Paul Gilbert, a successful surgeon who owned his own hospital in Charny, a small town across the St. Lawrence from Quebec City. Mimi spoke English, which was unusual for a Québecois, because she had spent a year at a boarding school in New York State. Jerry, on the other hand, was not fluent in French, which may have accounted for his indifferent social life before meeting Mimi. At the time, she was living at home with her parents and taking a secretarial course in Quebec City. After three dates, Bull, as impulsive as ever, proposed, and they were married the following year, when she was just twenty-one.

The marriage was an enduring oasis of stability in a turbulent life. The couple had five sons and two daughters: Philippe (Pilpot), Michel (Bako), Stephen (Tepi), Richard (Pooh), Robert (Bobelino), Kathleen (Kapoup), and Noemie-Jane (Jane-Jane). Despite his difficult childhood, Bull largely succeeded in creating a warm and loving family environment. The children lived in one house the whole time they were growing up, and Bull remained devoted to his wife. When his sons were old enough, he tried to instill in them an enthusiasm for aeronautics. Once he bought them a model airplane and helped them put it together. But the model remained unfinished in the garage.

According to Marcel Paquette, a Montreal lawyer and one of Jerry's oldest friends, the young scientist was convinced that he had "a good star" that protected him in some way.

"Jerry had one motto that he lived by all his life," said Paquette. " 'There is no tomorrow.' "[2]

T W O

THE COCKTAIL
SCIENTISTS

WAR WILL never occur until a nation planning aggression thinks it can win," Bull said in 1953. "As long as the nations desiring peace can maintain better weapons than the nations desiring war, there will be a deterrent to aggression. Then they are not weapons of war, but weapons of peace."

Given what was to happen to him later in life, such statements may appear disingenuous now. However, there is no doubt that for the first half of his career, Jerry Bull was motivated by a purely scientific drive to discover new things, to shape history. He also sincerely believed that his work would bring about a new era of peace in the world. He thought that if he could develop new missiles and aircraft that would act as a deterrent to war, then his work would have been worthwhile. It was only later, when he felt rejected by his country and his peers, that his idealism became fatally compromised.

At first the race to space was relatively simple. Rockets were fired vertically, to gather data and test the atmosphere, so that accurate performance requirements could be obtained for future designs. In February 1949, the U.S. Army fired a two-stage rocket to a height of 250 miles, a record that remained unbroken for the next eight years.

Americans had known since World War II that unmanned rockets were potential weapons of war. The Germans, under the direction of the brilliant Wernher von Braun, designed and built the V-1 and V-2 rockets, which were used to bombard Britain in the closing stages of the conflict. While these rockets were inaccurate and ultimately proved to be of little military value, the possibilities of future development were clear.

And so, in the war's final days, the United States and the Soviet Union made strenuous efforts to retain German rocket scientists and their research. During Operation Paperclip, the United States persuaded Wernher von Braun to move to America and begin the development of long-range missiles and rockets for the U.S. military.

But no clear goals had been established for a space program, which was also being actively pursued by the Soviet Union, although there was some discussion in the U.S. about shooting a "moon" (as satellites were then called) into space. Inevitably, developing systems that could shoot the "moons" down was discussed as well. Curiously, more advocates of space research, including rocket scientists, worked in the army than in the U.S. Air Force, whose head, General Curtis Le May, showed little enthusiasm for this new branch of service.[1]

Predictably, Wernher von Braun demonstrated the vision so lacking in the U.S. military establishment. In a March 22, 1952, issue of *Collier's* magazine, he told readers of his plans for a large manned satellite that he had been trying to persuade his new countrymen to build since his arrival in America in 1945. He envisioned a space station orbiting a thousand miles above the earth, manned by technicians who would be able to observe the military actions of foreign countries through giant telescopes. He also saw the station as a possible weapon of war: "Small winged rocket missiles with atomic warheads could be launched from the station . . . and accurately guided to any spot on earth. This would offer . . . the most important tactical and strategic advance in military history."

He gave further details of this plan in a later book:

Whether in the hands of a single peace-loving nation, or in the hands of the United Nations, the space station could be a deterrent which might cause a successful outlawing of war. . . .

The space station, with all its potentialities for exploration of the universe, for all kinds of scientific progress, for the preservation of peace or for the destruction of civilization, can be built. . . . Perhaps the military reasons for establishing such a station are in the long run the least significant, but in the existing state of the world they are the most urgent. Unless a space station is established with the aim of preserving peace, it may be created as an unparalleled agent of destruction—or there may not be time to build it at all.

Under the impetus of these considerations, therefore, perhaps the space station will become a reality, not a generation hence, but in—say—1963.[2]

Von Braun may have been overly ambitious, but he was articulating a view held by governments in both East and West that the militarization of space was unavoidable. This was given added urgency with the development of the thermonuclear bomb in the mid-1950s, immediately instigated new work on missiles capable of delivering the bomb to its target. In 1954, the U.S. Air Force began studies that led to the deployment of the first reconnaissance satellites, Discoverer and SAMOS, launched in 1960 and 1961.

All along, however, the United States maintained the underlying assumption that no serious competition existed in the race to conquer space. The Soviets were considered to be several years behind the Americans. In fact, the U.S. was so confident of its leading role that in 1955 the White House announced that the U.S. would send a rocket into space in 1957, the International Geophysical Year. The honor would go to the U.S. Navy's Viking rocket, which was the cornerstone of its Vanguard program. This was not a missile but a sounding rocket, which used technology that had been developed much earlier for the vertically fired atmosphere-testing rockets.[3]

Meanwhile, the U.S. Army, having procured the services of von Braun because the air force wasn't interested, had already designed a new missile at the Redstone Arsenal in Alabama, but it was considered too technically risky for such a prestigious program as Vanguard.

On October 4, 1957, the U.S. government was caught by surprise when the Soviets launched Sputnik I from Tyuratam, making history as the first nation to send a satellite into space. The surprise was all the greater because the U.S. didn't know that the Soviets were in the game, let alone winning it. The following month, the Soviets launched Sputnik II, this time with a dog on board. Later information, made available to the CIA, revealed that Sputnik II was equipped with cameras as well, making it the first reconnaissance satellite to be put into space. The Soviet Union made history once more. Later that same year, they launched what they described as an intercontinental ballistic rocket.

In a radio broadcast, the Soviets announced, "Today, after the firing of Sputnik Two, it is perfectly clear that the Soviet Union possesses intercontinental ballistic rockets. . . . This means a real change in the method of warfare, in military strategy, and tactics."

These developments raised two immediate concerns. National pride had been hurt, since the Soviets had managed to get into space first, and there was a huge worry that the Soviets had gained a significant advantage over the West by developing a crude reconnaissance satellite that could not only spy on Washington, but could also blast it with one of the new Soviet long-range missiles, perhaps fitted with nuclear warheads.

The U.S. space program suddenly produced a flurry of activity as the Americans tried to catch up. On December 6, 1957, two months after the first Sputnik launch, the first navy Vanguard rocket was on the launch pad at Cape Canaveral, Florida. In full view of the world, the rocket exploded into flames. The navy immediately started work on another Vanguard, which would not be ready for two months.

At this point, the army, which had always argued that its project team, under the direction of von Braun, should lead the U.S. space effort, came to the rescue. Von Braun had used the basic design from his V-2 rocket to create the Jupiter system, a

larger rocket that fired in stages. This rocket then evolved into
Juno, which was ready for launching on January 31, 1958. The
rocket lifted off from Cape Canaveral with a small Explorer
probe on board. The flight went flawlessly, and the first U.S.
earth satellite was in orbit.

Unfortunately, five days later, the second Vanguard launch
did not go so well. After three and a half miles of flight, the
rocket blew up. The same month, a second Explorer mission
failed, but then the launch of a third Vanguard and a third Explorer were both successful.

As the race between the USSR and the U.S. gathered momentum, it was clear that the American space effort needed
some coherence. The Soviet program had grown from a single
clearly focused research effort. The American program, on the
other hand, was burdened by the traditional rivalries between
branches of the armed services, which meant a more costly and
unnecessarily inefficient space program. Consequently, in 1958,
the National Aeronautics and Space Administration (NASA)
was established by Congress with a mandate to develop aeronautical and space vehicles; to examine atmospheric and space
phenomena; to address the problems of developing space for
peaceful purposes; and to provide the military with any discov-
eries of significance to national defense.

While NASA acted as a clearinghouse for the mostly peaceful exploration of space, the military continued to consider the
possibilities of using satellites and space stations to spy on other
countries, and as bases from which to launch nuclear weapons
at earth. The underlying assumption was that the Soviets were
proceeding along exactly the same path. As a result, the focus of
the space program shifted to designing systems that could destroy missiles and satellites that posed a threat to the United
States.

The first U.S. Air Force study of an antisatellite system
(ASAT) began in 1956. General James Gavin, head of army re-
search and development, initiated a similar project in June 1957.
The army's project concentrated on a derivative of the Nike-
Ajax antiaircraft missile system that had been developed in the
early 1950s. The new version was the nuclear-armed antimissile

system known as Nike-Zeus. While money had been allocated to research the effectiveness of an ABM system, no cash had been set aside in the defense budget to pay for the Nike-Zeus to go into production.

Research on the system was carried out using Atlas rockets. The tests were conducted primarily on the Kwajalein atoll in the South Pacific, at the western end of the U.S. Pacific Missile Range. Laboratory research was done mainly in the United States and Canada with funding from the U.S. government. CARDE was among the institutes to receive grants for the work, since it was one of the few centers in the world with an effective aerophysics division.

At CARDE, Jerry Bull had begun work to assess the aerodynamic characteristics of missiles and aircraft in flight. In particular, he was studying the performance of objects moving through space, at very high speeds. Bull believed that if he had a better understanding of the composition of the layers of the atmosphere and space, then rockets and missiles could be designed accordingly for faster, stable flight.

Bull's pioneering work on projectile flight stability at CARDE brought him into contact with many of the scientists in Canada, Britain, and the United States who were working in the same field. The most important of these meetings occurred on October 19, 1955, at a conference of NATO weapons experts at the Picatinny Arsenal outside Dover, New Jersey. There, he met Dr. Charles Murphy, who was doing similar work at the U.S. Army's Ballistics Research Laboratory at the Aberdeen Proving Ground, north of Baltimore, Maryland.[4]

The first evening began formally enough with the scientists eating canapés and drinking cocktails, but it soon degenerated into a Manhattan-drinking contest between the Americans and Canadians, with Bull leading the Canadian team and Murphy the American. At the end of a long night, the two men were bundled into the backseat of a car by a junior Canadian army officer and driven to their hotel in Dover. During the journey, the two men had a drunken, lively discussion, debating who was the stupidest British general in history. During the drive, the two men in the front seat, whom neither Bull nor Murphy had met, remained silent.

Early the next morning, when Murphy appeared at the conference (Bull did not make an appearance that day), the Canadian staff officer told him that the two men in the front seat had been British army officers, one a major general, the other a lieutenant general. But the British officers took the criticism in the proper spirit and spoke amicably to the scientists during the conference.

Murphy and Bull shared a sense of humor, a dislike of bureaucracy, and, above all, a passion for aeronautics. They were the same age, and had read and admired each other's work. Already, Bull had developed an intense dislike of the government bureaucrats who were to play such an important part in his life. He referred to them dismissively as "cocktail scientists" and made no secret of the fact that he despised their interference in his work. He had the arrogance of the exceptionally talented with none of Murphy's tact.

Bull also made friends with another young scientist, Reed Johnston, who had been trained in mathematics, physics, and physical chemistry before becoming an engineer. Both men had a strong imagination and a professed disdain for the bureaucratic restrictions at CARDE and the Defence Research Board.

During the last two years Bull spent at CARDE, he worked closely with Johnston on a NASA contract to examine the instability of the Atlas rocket, which was then the main vehicle being used for America's exploration of space. They were designing a skirt that could be attached to the rocket to give it stability in flight. The research was conducted by building scale models of the rocket and firing them, at very high velocities, down the 250-foot CARDE space simulation chamber, whose vacuum let them approximate the weightlessness of space.[5]

In addition, Bull was working on another contract from NASA, which had been subcontracted by Arthur D. Little, the Cambridge, Massachusetts, management consulting firm. Bull was hired to research the hazards that meteoroids posed to spacecraft; his findings were later transformed by his fertile imagination into one of the first ideas for what came to be known as the Strategic Defense Initiative, or Star Wars.

During the years he worked at CARDE, Bull believed he had detected signs that the Canadian government, while publicly claiming commitment to the space race, had privately made a decision to opt out. Certainly the degree of ambivalence that existed in Ottawa was based on money, not opportunity. At the time, Canada was well placed to compete. During World War II, the British government had relocated large parts of its defense establishment to Canada, and many of its best scientists had also relocated, in case the Germans overran Britain. Consequently, after the war, Canada's reservoir of talent and its manufacturing capability were among the best in the world.

One of the most far-reaching projects that Bull was called upon to evaluate was the CF-105 Arrow supersonic fighter, capable of flying at mach 2, which was being developed by A. V. Roe. This was a prestigious and immensely expensive project that carried with it the political benefits of establishing a separate Canadian fighter manufacturing capability. In the reports he prepared for CARDE, Bull was expansive in his enthusiasm and forthright in his support for the project. By 1959, four Arrow aircraft were flying, another eighteen were in production, and the CF-105 project seemed secure. Even the Belgian air force had told the Canadians that they would buy a few of the aircraft that were in production. Then, on February 20, 1959, at 4:00 P.M., the House of Commons announced that the project was canceled, effective at 5:00 P.M. the same day. Bull's unpublished authorized biography describes the "wanton, destructive irresponsibility" that followed:

> In a completely inexplicable course of action, the Canadian government, adding to the enormous monies already spent on creating an airplane far superior to any other contemporary machine, placed an order with a scrap dealer for the total physical destruction of all assets. Within a few weeks, wreckers arrived with torches, and the aircraft,

which had established world records, were burnt into pieces no larger than what could be carried off by a small man. All tools, jigs, fixtures, along with drawings and reports, were similarly burnt.[6]

The Smithsonian Institution had requested an aircraft but had been turned down. The British and French governments, who were working on the supersonic Concorde, also asked for an aircraft, as well as design details, but were turned down as well.

At a time when the United States was investing billions of dollars in the space program and billions more in the development of conventional weapons, the cancellation of the Arrow project was a visible sign of the Canadian government's general disenchantment with defense projects. A great deal of funding for CARDE projects had come from the United States, which was followed up by routinely enthusiastic and supportive evaluation trips by U.S. officials to Canada, usually at the rate of about three a month. In contrast, Bull told friends that he was never visited by Ottawa officials; he would see them once a year at a conference of the Defence Research Board. As a loyal Canadian, Bull simply could not understand why the government was behaving this way. In his view, the arguments for expanding the Canadian defense industry made perfect sense. His country had the necessary talent and the industrial base, if only the government were prepared to exploit it. The situation was all the more galling for Bull, since he was one of only a handful of his contemporaries who had remained in Canada after graduation, the balance having emigrated to the U.S. for better-paying jobs.

During this period Bull was not short of corporate suitors, and he was consulting for a number of aerospace companies in the United States. But at this stage, he was still committed to Canada and wanted to remain there, regardless of the bureaucracy at CARDE.

At McGill University, Don Mordell, dean of the Faculty of Engineering, had watched Bull's meteoric rise with interest. An expert in gas dynamics, Mordell had ambitions for himself and the university. He wanted to expand his facilities in a field that had considerable opportunities for pioneering studies, in order to win plaudits from the scientific community. He had met Bull at conferences and was impressed with his intelligence and no-nonsense approach to work, which matched his own.

A tall, slim, bespectacled man with a bushy salt-and-pepper mustache, Mordell was a talented scientist, popular with both students and the academic community. He loved to fly and had his own pilot's license, which engendered the nickname given to him by his students, "that magnificent dean in his flying machine."

On January 13, 1958, Mordell wrote to Dr. Cyril James, the principal and vice-chancellor of McGill, arguing that the university should fund a new department to study the problems of propulsion at extreme altitudes and speeds:

> I regard my mandate as Dean as the obligation to do my utmost to lead the faculty toward a higher standing, with special emphasis on graduate and honors students. This is, of course, the challenge that makes it worthwhile spending less time on my own research.[7]
>
> You will recall that at the start of my work on Gas Dynamics the Board put up less than $50,000 in cash to prime the pump. As a direct result, we have enjoyed Research grants and contracts totalling more than $1,100,000 and, I believe, done much to spread McGill's name around the engineering world. I believe that if, in the coming year, we can put operation on a proper basis, we can look forward not only to generous support from DRB, but also from American agencies who are vitally concerned with the problem. . . .
>
> If we fail to make this start the immediate and obvious effect will be that virtually all of the research and post-graduate work of the Mechanical Department will stop. Even more serious than this, I believe, will be a great blow to morale in our faculty, many of whose members are counting on me to be able to encourage and develop research and postgraduate work.

By March, the board of governors at the university had approved Mordell's proposal, and he had written to Dr. G. S. Field, the chief scientist of the Defence Research Board, asking for $58,000 in grants to support the new department. Interestingly, he did not propose appointing Jerry Bull to the position of professor of mechanical engineering. Instead, he approached two other scientists, R. P. Probert and S. L. Bragg of Rolls-Royce, where Mordell had formerly been employed. Both men turned him down, considering the project too risky.

On July 8, 1958, Mordell wrote to Jerry Bull at CARDE:

> You may perhaps have heard that there has been quite a change in our research programs at McGill which have been financed by DRB and we are planning and embarking upon a coordinated program of research on problems that will be encountered in the application of air-breathing engines for flight at extreme speeds and altitudes. The University has established two appointments, one of which will be a full Professorship in the Department of Mechanical Engineering with the proviso that not more than three hours per week will be spent on undergraduate teaching, the rest of the time being available for research and the supervision of graduate students.
>
> I am presently looking for someone for this new Chair. The information above is probably adequate at the moment except for the salary which will be in the range initially of $11,000 to $13,000 per annum, and my purpose in writing now is to enquire whether you would be interested in making an application.

The two men talked on the telephone shortly afterward. Bull said that he was very interested in the job, explaining that he thought CARDE might be happy to let him go since his outspoken views had made him unpopular with the establishment. Mordell then wrote to Dr. G. S. Field at the DRB, who had approved the $58,000 grant that included the salary for a new professor. The letter informed Field of his progress and then approached the thorny subject of Jerry Bull.

> We have created three new appointments . . . and the senior post is a new full Professorship in the Department of

Mechanical Engineering whose incumbent will assume direction of this work. . . . During the past six months, I have been getting applications for this post from Canada, the U.K. and the U.S.A. Some of those persons who have had the most previous experience on more or less conventional propulsion have not wished to apply and I have come to the conclusion that insofar as we are looking a long way ahead, a vast amount of experience on conventional engines is perhaps not the best qualification we are interested in. We should be interested in a scientist who is thinking a long way ahead and whose fields of interest align with our work as we already have people on the staff, including myself, who are familiar with what one might term the present day technology. Accordingly, I have cast my net a bit wider and one of the individuals who rather appeals to me as a possible prospect is your own Dr. G. V. Bull.

I have not as yet had any detailed or formal conversation with him but I have gathered that he could be interested in such a post but before making any formal arrangements with him or having any serious discussions, I would like to confirm with you that DRB would not feel that we are raiding them in our search for a good man.

It is my understanding that Dr. Bull may have sometimes been criticized by the Board because of the extremely futuristic nature of his thinking which I presume may have conflicted with the day to day requirements of a service establishment. However, as our aim is to look a great distance into the future, this seems to me to be a good point in his favor.

The letter was not a true account of the facts. Mordell had not been reviewing applications from three different countries. He had solicited three applications, two of which had not materialized. The third was Bull's. He had approached Bull directly, and Bull had expressed an interest in the job. Understandably, Mordell was trying to smooth the transition so that delicate relations with Ottawa, and the all-important grant money, would not be jeopardized.

But Dr. Field clearly felt he did not owe Bull any favors and responded with a letter that also was not accurate. After getting three paragraphs of pleasantries out of the way, Field wrote:

> With respect to the question of Dr. G. B. [sic] Bull, I understand you have been in touch with him and that while he is interested in the post you mention, he feels he would prefer to stay at CARDE for the time being. As he may have told you, we have recently completed a reorganization at CARDE in order to give Dr. Bull more scope. We are also building up a number of new facilities to enable him to go further with some of the ideas he has had. Thus, we would not have been too happy to have him leave us at this time. In fact, we hope he will stay at least until his program has developed considerably further and he has trained someone else to carry on.
>
> I am sorry that at the moment Dr. Bull does not seem to be available for your appointment but I hope you are successful in getting a good man elsewhere.

This brush-off provoked a burst of activity from Mordell. He first telephoned Bull, who assured him that he did indeed want the job. He then wrote a letter to Cyril James, McGill's principal, "in case there are any repercussions at a higher level which might catch you uninformed."

> I find myself rather puzzled by Field's letter of the 12th August, as I am not quite clear whether he has completely misunderstood my letter or is obstructing deliberately. Actually, the facts which I have since found out are that Dr. Bull is not under formal contract to DRB anyway and would be perfectly free to leave them at a month's notice. In a recent conversation with him, he assured me that the arrangement I have suggested is what he would personally like and he agrees that there would be ample time to train a successor.

At the same time, Mordell wrote back to Field suggesting as a compromise that Bull be released in a year and, in the meantime, that he be allowed to work one day a week at McGill. Field's response showed that he was thoroughly unwilling to cooperate.

In reply to your letter of 18 August 1958 regarding the possibility of releasing Dr. Bull about one year from now, I would like to emphasize that the facilities which we have contracted to supply to Dr. Bull will not be in operation in less than two years and under the circumstances, we would be extremely reluctant to agree to releasing him until such time as he has had the opportunity to make use of the equipment that he is designing. Although I agree entirely with the contention that to have Dr. Bull on your staff at McGill would produce very valuable contacts between DRB and the University, we within DRB are supporting a very considerable capital investment that we are most anxious to see pay off.

Although you are quite at liberty to approach Dr. Bull and make him any offer you see fit, he is already committed to us to bring the program that he has instituted to a reasonable conclusion. I estimate this will require at least three years. After this time, if you should be interested in obtaining Dr. Bull's services, I would be glad to discuss the matter with you.

In copying this correspondence to Cyril James, Mordell added a typewritten postscript: "I enclose a copy of Dr. Field's letter. I find it incredible that any responsible outfit would engage on a large capital program which demands the continual services of one individual for three years. I hope for their sake and for mine, as a taxpayer, that Dr. Bull doesn't get killed in a traffic accident tomorrow."

After numerous telephone conversations, Bull finally closed the exchange on September 10 with a letter to Dean Mordell.

Shortly after talking to you on the telephone I received instructions from Headquarters that my assuming additional duties (i.e. as proposed with your group) would not be approved, and that a letter would be forwarded to you stating the same. I awaited a copy of this letter, which has just now arrived on my desk. . . . I regret very much indeed that the decision which the Board made will not permit my assisting you actively this year. . . . In as much as regular contacts are not approved, I note that visits of your personnel to us are encouraged. I will be most happy to receive your people at any time and to assist them whenever possible.

This whole exchange was interesting for two reasons. First, it established a bond between Mordell and Bull that would last more than thirty years. The two men had both run up against the obstructive bureaucracy in Ottawa. Bull was keen to move on, free himself from the constraints at CARDE, and take up the exciting promotion and challenge of a full professorship at a university where he would head his own department. Mordell had seen the kind of sums that could be generated from ambitious research projects and wanted to begin his new project as soon as possible. Both men were united in their frustration.

The DRB and the government scientists clearly viewed McGill's attempt at poaching as out of order and Bull's willingness to leave CARDE to be some kind of betrayal. They felt that they had encouraged Bull in his work and supported him with equipment and staff; the ungrateful Bull was prepared to leave CARDE with the research in its infancy and nobody qualified to take his place. This souring of relations between the government scientists and Bull and Mordell was to have important implications for the future.

To many in the Canadian government, Bull was simply a talented nuisance, a maverick with no understanding of political realities. Some saw him as a publicity seeker, particularly following the "Boy Rocket Scientist" article in *Maclean's*. Others saw him as an ignorant critic of the government who should be silenced. During one press interview, Bull said that Canada was planning to put a satellite into space. The next day, a reporter relayed this information to the Canadian prime minister, John Diefenbaker, who angrily denied the story. The government demanded an explanation from CARDE, and a brigadier general was ordered to drive down to Ottawa from Quebec City immediately to provide an explanation.

Even today, thirty years later, mention of Bull in some government circles in Canada is sufficient to reinvigorate old enmities. He is considered an arrogant, frequently ignorant scientist who was doing work that some saw as morally corrupt and others saw as irrelevant to Canada's needs.

·"He antagonized enough people in Ottawa," said Murphy, "that they still tell libelous stories about him. His remark about cocktail scientists, for example, hurt a lot of people because it was so true."[8]

Canada has always had an ambivalent attitude toward her more powerful southern neighbor, and there is a deep distrust of those who are too close to the Americans. Bull was accused of being in Washington's pocket, and, therefore, too pro-American, a serious crime at the time. He was encouraged to withdraw from some of his American projects, particularly his work on the first antiballistic missile system (ABM) that was the precursor of Star Wars.

Working, literally, in the pressure chamber at CARDE, Bull was studying the flight patterns of different objects in order to distinguish warhead patterns from those of decoys that could be packed into an intercontinental ballistic missile (ICBM) to deceive an ABM system. In fact, he'd come up with a novel method of carrying out the ABM research that was being done at the Kwajalein atoll. Instead of using expensive Atlas rockets as targets for the Nike-Zeus missiles, Bull proposed using a large gun buried in the ground to fire targets on a fixed trajectory. He believed that he could fire a small rocket forty-two miles into space. At the top of its flight path, a motor would cut in and launch the rocket back toward earth in exactly the profile of an incoming Atlas. A Nike-Zeus could then be launched to attack it. In papers submitted to the U.S. Army, Bull argued that each firing of his gun would cost around $100,000, compared with the several million he estimated for each launch of an Atlas rocket.

In principle, the idea was a creative, inexpensive, and work-able solution. But, for the first time in what was to be a long and bitter experience with military politics, Bull found that the army was not interested in his solution. The army was getting its Atlas rockets free, out of surplus stocks belonging to the air force. Saving the American government large sums of money made no difference to the army. Such was the lack of coordina-tion in the American space program that each vested interest cared only about its own narrow slice of the pie. Under the circumstances, it was hardly surprising that Bull's first plan to use a big gun in space was turned down.

Although the ABM testing scheme was abandoned, Bull was impressed that the Americans, at least, had taken his work se-riously. The Canadians, on the other hand, saw no real need for an ABM system and dismissed the work as an American-driven obsession of no value to Ottawa.

"The Canadians didn't give a shit what Bull did on ABM," said Murphy. "Everyone who did care worked in the U.S., and the U.S. government cared enough that Quebec City was full of U.S. engineers for five years in the late nineteen-fifties. Bull made CARDE the center of ABM research in North America."[9]

At the beginning of 1960, the Canadian government finally came off the fence and decided to get out of the military defense business altogether. A freeze on all defense spending was an-nounced. For Bull, this was the last straw. On April 1, 1960, he resigned from CARDE in a welter of publicity. He took every opportunity to criticize the Canadian government's de-fense policy.

"I didn't just leave the government, I quit," Bull said later. "I was disgusted with its [Canada's] attitude towards research. Canadians always say, 'Why should we do that, a little country like ours?' The Americans say, 'Great, let's find out what's going on out there.' They have research money at work all over the place. They offered fifty thousand dollars not long ago to Brazil just to see what researchers there could do with it. The Cana-dian government makes you feel like a small boy, hat in hand, when you go to ask for money for research. And don't get the idea the Americans haven't been tough about this program.

They've asked plenty of questions. We've got too many cocktail scientists. Our people rationalize everything. They could even rationalize themselves out of going to the bathroom"[10]

Immediately after resigning, Bull drove down to Aberdeen to stay a few days with his friend Charles Murphy. He then headed west for California, where he had lined up a series of interviews with American defense contractors. His future, he thought, lay in the United States.

T H R E E

THE SEDUCTION

OF HARP

IN 1959, one year before his resignation, Bull had met Lieutenant General Arthur Trudeau, then head of research and development in the U.S. Army, when he had come to visit CARDE. Trudeau was inspired by Bull's vision, and Bull liked the straightforward army officer who seemed to offer freedom from the bureaucratic fumbling that dogged his relations with the Canadian government.

Trudeau had been trained as an engineer and earned his place in cold war history when, as a lieutenant colonel, he was commander of the Berlin constabulary during the Berlin airlift. The Allied commandant in Berlin, General Lucius Clay, was convinced that the Russian blockade could be broken and, if confronted, the Russians would disengage. He proposed bringing an Allied convoy from western Germany through the Russian lines to Berlin. This was a highly controversial military plan that had not been politically approved. The Allied policy at the time was to wear down the Russians and not seek a direct confrontation. The commandant's plan could well have provoked another war.

Clay was concerned that the Russians would blow up the bridges between Berlin and western Germany if a convoy tried to pass through. He approached Trudeau and asked him if he would organize a task force of engineers and bridge builders to lead the relief column. Task Force Trudeau was duly formed. When it was ready to go, Clay communicated his plans to Washington, timing the dispatch to arrive in the middle of the night when he hoped everyone would be asleep. He expected that officials would not be able to react in time to countermand his orders. But an alert duty officer saw the incoming message and notified his superiors. The order was immediately countermanded, and Task Force Trudeau stood down.

Trudeau remained a fast-track officer and became a likely candidate to head the Army Corps of Engineers. During the Korean War, he asked to be transferred to a cavalry unit so that he could see some action. He became a divisional commander and, in 1953, led his men through the Battle of Pork Chop Hill, the bloodiest engagement of the war. He won a Silver Star for personally leading a batallion reconnaissance party onto Pork Chop under fire, after switching helmets with his driver. "I lost men faster than Westmoreland at any stage of the Vietnam War except Tet," he once commented.[1]

Bull also met Charles Poor, the deputy assistant secretary of the army for research, development, and acquisitions and Trudeau's civilian boss. Until 1958, Poor had been chief of the Exterior Ballistics Laboratory at the Aberdeen Proving Ground. Poor's relationship with Bull and Trudeau was marked by conflict and mutual antagonism, partly because Poor brought to his work a clear logic and a high moral standard that bordered on rectitude.

During his time at the Aberdeen Proving Ground, Poor had given a briefing on weapons of the future with which Trudeau disagreed. In front of his senior colleagues, Trudeau told Poor to go back to Aberdeen and design cannonballs, an insult that rankles Poor even now.[2]

This kind of straight talk did not sit well with the coldly analytical Poor, who made a clear distinction between his work as a scientist and his personal friendships. He saw Trudeau and Bull as enthusiasts who allowed their vision to overcome proper scientific skepticism of all new ideas.

Nonetheless, Poor has very positive memories of his first

meetings with Bull at CARDE in the late 1950s, describing him as "very personable . . . charming . . . bright . . . well thought of by his Canadian and U.S. associates." Poor even visited Bull at his home at Charny, across the St. Lawrence River from Quebec. The house, which had the unusual feature of being all electric, had been bought for Bull by Dr. Paul Gilbert, his father-in-law. Poor was clearly seduced by the surroundings and the air of prosperity that surrounded the family. Bull took the opportunity to convince Poor that he should buy some shares in an asbestos mine owned by Dr. Gilbert. The stock price collapsed; Poor later used the certificates to wallpaper his bathroom. Despite this small difficulty, Poor says that he never saw any evidence of criminality or greed in Bull's character. Rather, he accepted that Bull was a talented scientist "who could sell anything," a judgment that would color Poor's approach to all Bull projects.

Trudeau encouraged Bull to move to the States and gave him some introductions to aerospace companies, such as General Motors on the West Coast, all of whom made him offers. In addition, Bull was invited to Cambridge, Massachusetts, to have dinner with Arthur D. Little executives. They proposed that he leave Canada and join them on a program to perfect a new type of dynamite based on ammonium nitrate. Since this was not his field, Bull recommended his friend Reed Johnston for the job. ADL made Johnston an offer, which he accepted, giving Bull a friend in the heart of one of the most aggressive consulting companies in the United States. Johnston was to prove a useful ally in the years to come.

Bull also spoke with Don Mordell, with whom he had been in negotiations two years earlier. The two men had kept in touch. Mordell had been unable to fill the position at McGill; once again, he offered it to Bull.

Mordell argued that, despite the difficulties Bull had experienced at CARDE, Canada was his home and the university would be the perfect place to continue his research. Mordell sweetened the offer by giving Bull a chair in engineering science, in addition to the professorship in the Department of Mechanical Engineering. While the U.S. might pay better, he said, the two men were friends, united in their ambition to prove the Canadian establishment to be a blinkered bastion. In June 1961,

Bull accepted the appointment and, at the age of thirty-three, became the youngest full professor ever appointed at McGill University.

The appointment was all the more radical because Bull was Catholic and McGill was a center of conservative Canadian Protestantism that operated almost as an outpost of the British Empire. When news leaked of Bull's impending appointment, McGill University was warned by a government official in Ottawa that if the arrangement went ahead all federal funding for the university would be in jeopardy. Cyril James, the university vice-chancellor, was told that Bull was a security risk—perhaps even a CIA spy—who had been too critical of the Canadian government to be trusted to work on any classified projects, or to be the beneficiary of central funding. James refused to bow to outside pressure and challenged the Canadian government to act on their threat, warning that any sanctions would raise fundamental issues of academic freedom. In the end, no action was taken against McGill.[3]

Mordell wanted Bull to research the practicality of using large guns to fire objects into space, the same innovative idea Bull had put forward to the U.S. Army for their ABM project. Despite his setback with the army, Bull was convinced that large guns had a future; the U.S. military was becoming obsessed with rockets and missiles to the exclusion of all alternatives.

Two years earlier, Bull had his first discussion concerning the use of large guns in the space program with Charles Murphy and scientists at the Ballistics Research Laboratory (BRL). At the time, Murphy had been making preliminary sounding shots using a five-inch gun, while Bull had been studying the ballistic characteristics of shells to see if muzzle speeds could be increased by changing shell design. In effect, the two men had been approaching the same problem from different perspectives. In 1960, Bull sold General Trudeau on the idea that big guns had a future in the space program. Bull explained that Murphy, down at BRL, which was under Trudeau's control, was thinking along the same lines. Trudeau immediately sent Murphy to CARDE and ordered him to concentrate his work on the five-inch gun.

But the project did not really get started until Bull left

CARDE and joined Mordell at McGill. Bull was unwilling to encourage Trudeau to commit funds to CARDE, an organization in which he had lost confidence. He preferred to wait for funding until he had a new home worthy of support. But even though he was under contract to McGill, Bull prudently kept a foot firmly in the American camp by continuing as a consultant with ADL in Cambridge.

During his first year at McGill, the university funded Bull's research through money made available to the Department of Mechanical Engineering. Meanwhile, Trudeau and Murphy remained enthusiastic about carrying out more in-depth research. Their studies suggested that not only would big guns work, but that they would be much less expensive than rockets. At the time, the cost of boosting a rocket to a given altitude averaged $1.25 per payload pound per mile. Bull argued that he could do the same job for 21¢ per payload pound per mile, a significant saving. The army was beginning to see that an economical program might keep them in the space business.[4]

Mordell and Bull negotiated with Trudeau to extract some army funds for the big-gun project. Trudeau did not have much money to spare—he had no research slush fund to draw from—so he was able to commit only two thousand dollars, a tiny sum that would not even cover one shot into space. But the money was symbolic of a general commitment. It also enabled Bull to say that the project had funding from the U.S. Army and to use that fact as leverage to gather cash and support elsewhere.

Trudeau's most important contribution, however, was in using his influence to siphon off valuable equipment to Bull's project. In the strange way that the U.S. military works, it is much easier to channel a million dollars' worth of equipment to a research project than to commit one thousand dollars in cash funding. This anomaly was to be exploited by Trudeau to great effect in the years to come.

To point up the commitment from the U.S. Army, McGill established a new department, the Space Research Institute, to handle the funds and the research. To mark its new status, the project even received its own acronym: HARP, for the High Altitude Research Project.

Dean Mordell officially announced the HARP program in March 1962. McGill issued a research statement that read, in part:

> The program will have two natural stages. In the first stage, a small installation will be built around a converted naval 5-inch gun. This size of the launcher will be just barely sufficient for useful scientific work, but a most valuable tool for the training of various operating crews and for the testing of models of the larger vehicles to be fired when Stage Two is completed. [In fact, the five-inch work was to be done at BRL while McGill concentrated on sixteen-inch systems.]
>
> With the smaller unit, there will be a capability of putting some five or six pounds of instrumentation or payload up to about 150,000 feet, and [with the larger unit] 200 pounds of payload to 500,000 or 600,000 feet.
>
> Moreover, when Stage Two is reached, it will be possible to extend range still further by using, as the payload of the main vehicle, a standard solid-fuel type of rocket which, taking over at some 500,000 feet, can boost the instrumentation or payload to a much greater altitude, and in due course probably to such a velocity that it can escape the earth altogether. The vehicles will be tracked from the ground by radio and possibly radar sets which will also provide the surveillance to make sure that the area is clear of all aeroplanes or satellites before launching. Tracking information will also be gained from automatic direction finders. . . .
>
> The types of experiments fall into various classes. Because these vehicles are launched from a gun, the acceleration is very much greater than that experienced with a rocket and this to some extent limits instrumentation design.
>
> On the other hand, it has been amply proved that instruments and radio transmitters can be built to withstand many times more acceleration than that which will be imposed in these vehicles and it will be possible right from the start to provide instrumentation to measure the pressure and tem-

perature of the atmosphere and the acceleration and attitude of the vehicle, and to radio this information back to the ground. It is hoped at a later stage to develop special mass spectrometers and electronic apparatus which will make it possible to find out more about the chemical and electrical properties of the atmosphere. By measuring the pressure at certain points around the vehicle, much useful aerodynamic information can be gained.

In addition to experiments of this type where measurements are made on the vehicle and radioed back to earth, there is another class of experiment in which a seeding agent is carried on the vehicle, which either reacts with the atmosphere or is carried by the atmosphere in such a way that observations can be made from the ground.

As an example of this, one experiment to be carried out involves the discharge of suitable radar reflecting chaff. This being ejected at a certain altitude can be tracked from the ground by radar and its subsequent motion allows information to be gained about winds at high altitude. . . .

Alternatively, it is possible to arrange to eject small grenades which will explode at high altitude. By measurement of the sound on the ground, it is possible to produce information concerning the temperature of the atmosphere. As another variant of this experiment, it is possible to eject suitable chemicals which will react with the atmosphere in such a way as to permit observations from the ground.

The gun-launched probe will not be suitable for doing all the scientific work that can be done with rockets, but it can do a great deal of this work and has many advantages as compared with a rocket. . . . It is cheaper and, in the second place, it is much more predictable and reliable. It can stand in a state of instant readiness and be fired with great frequency if need be.[5]

Bull added his own endorsement.

There are many advantages to this project. In the first place, the whole business of firing the rockets opens up an interesting area of engineering. Some of our chemists at McGill want to use the projectiles to spread chemicals in the upper atmosphere for research work. A scientist at the University of Toronto wants to take aerodynamic measurements of the projectiles in flight.

If we were using standard rockets, this sort of work might cost more than $25,000 for each "shoot." Our shots will cost in the neighborhood of $1,000 each.

It's a do-it-yourself type of rocket project tailored to our resources. But it also opens up an interesting and brand new method of space research with exciting possibilities.

Understandably, Mordell's explanation of the HARP project caused quite a stir. A small, provincial university was planning to play a major role in the space race, possibly competing with the United States and the Soviet Union. It was certainly a bold stroke. As the Montreal *Gazette* stated in an editorial on March 27, 1962, Mordell, Bull, and McGill were to be congratulated on the scheme:

The high altitude research program announced by McGill University makes an immediate appeal to the imagination. For it breaks down the barrier of remoteness that has inevitably surrounded the space research programs of the United States and Russia; programs which have only been possible for the most powerful states, prepared to spend billions of dollars and able to tap almost unlimited resources.

McGill's program involves different techniques. But its high altitude projectiles should enable much useful and, in this age, vital information to be gathered. That this will be done by a private institution, with limited finances, brings a new horizon of research possibilities into view. . . .

Scientists in every university, in every country, must have looked upon the space research programs of the great powers and wondered how they, too, might one day be able to participate in this new and exciting field of research. Scientists at McGill University, under the leadership of Professor Gerald Bull, have met this challenge. If the projectiles which are to be fired this year are successful, McGill will have opened a new field to research by universities.

This local enthusiasm for the project was not matched in Ottawa. There, Bull's betrayal of CARDE was still fresh in the minds of Canada's senior scientists, who were already engaged in a more conventional experimental program using rockets. A base at Fort Churchill, Manitoba, was using Black Brant solid fuel rockets to gather meteorological information and to study the atmospheric layers. The Black Brant rockets were made by Canadian Bristol Aerojet; the solid fuel was manufactured by Bull's old employers at CARDE; and the instruments were designed by the University of Toronto's Institute for Aerospace Studies.

The Black Brant project was a Canadian endeavor with no American participation. Its competitor, HARP, on the other hand, was not even a truly Canadian project, with its funding from the U.S. Army adding salt to the wound. This nationalistic concern, coupled with Bull's reputation and his criticism of Canada's lack of support for scientific projects, meant that Ottawa had a hard time acknowledging McGill's inventiveness. From the outset, Black Brant, and not HARP, received the money and attention from the Canadian government.

In the meantime, Bull did as much as he could to further his cowboy image, and the journalists who interviewed him went along with the idea. In a long profile that appeared in *The Montreal Star* on March 28, 1962, Bull, dressed cowboy style in a check shirt, jeans, and high leather cowboy boots, blasted the "reactionary outlook" of Canadian businessmen and government officials:

When it comes to research, we're looking at things from the viewpoint of 30 years ago.

Canadian scientists are appreciated outside of Canada far more than they are in Canada. The States are full of Canadians, many of them in senior research positions. But Canadians won't gamble on research unless it's aimed at earning a dollar. The general attitude toward the research scientist in this country is that he's some sort of parasite.

All this talk about the necessity of training more scientists in Canada . . . all we're doing right now is training them to go to the United States.

Of course, I don't see Canada engaged in massive research programs, but I do see us operating in highly imaginative fringe areas, coming out with novel ideas and revolutionary-type thoughts.

At these moments of public scrutiny, Bull did not concern himself with the reaction of Ottawa or the sources of funding for HARP. He was satisfied to have won the sponsorship of someone as influential as Trudeau. This naïveté was the hallmark of his career. He didn't seem to be aware that the money he received both in 1962 and later was not new money but funding that had been siphoned off from other Aberdeen projects in atmospheric physics. This caused considerable resentment among other scientists in the ballistics community who were concentrating their research on rockets and missiles and considered Murphy and Bull to be part of the lunatic fringe.

To further aggravate the situation, Bull remembered that the army had obtained surplus Atlas rockets free from the air force for their ABM research. He asked Trudeau if he could locate any surplus guns that could be used by McGill and the Ballistics Research Laboratory for live experiments. Trudeau asked around and discovered that the U.S. Navy, which was moving away from the large battleships of World War II, had some surplus sixteen-inch guns. Bull asked for and received the guns, which were the biggest in the navy surplus stores.

HARP was in its infancy, and a shot had yet to be fired. Bull now needed a site where the big guns could be discharged without disturbing the neighbors, in a climate that made year-round experiments possible, and with an overall environment that took account of the limited budget. The one place that fit all the criteria was Barbados in the congenial Caribbean, over three thousand miles from Montreal.

F O U R

THE LIGHT OF ONE
AND A HALF MILLION
CANDLES

McGILL ALREADY had two research institutes, the Brace and the Bellairs, based in Barbados. These labs ran programs on solar energy and wind patterns, as well as oceanography. The Barbadian government was familiar with the university and they had a good working relationship.

There were also strong scientific arguments as to why the HARP site belonged on Barbados. The island was almost on the launch path from Cape Canaveral; large radar tracking and receiving stations were nearby; the government permitted firing over the sea with a virtually unlimited fallout area; and frequent hurricanes made it an area of interest to researchers studying tropical atmospheric science.

More important, perhaps, Barbados had a pleasant climate and none of the freezing-cold winters that made life so uncomfortable at McGill. The other suitable site would have been at Fort Churchill, Manitoba, on Hudson Bay, but it is accessible by sea for only six weeks of the year. In the end, the choice was not very difficult.

From the moment that Dean Mordell had approached him, Errol Barrow, the prime minister of Barbados, was enthusiastic about the idea. McGill was a significant employer of local labor and a source of much-needed foreign investment. In addition, if HARP proved to be a breakthrough, the reputation of Barbados as a sleepy Caribbean outpost could be changed overnight by its association with such a high-technology project.[1]

The support of the Barrow government was so strong that four postage stamps were issued to commemorate HARP and World Meteorological Day in 1968. The stamps showed the landing of the guns at Foul Bay, the transportation of the guns across the island, a gun on its mounting, and a gun firing.

Barbados is a pear-shaped coral limestone island about twenty-four miles long and eighteen miles wide that is part of the British Commonwealth. The landscape varies from lush tropical valleys to dry desertlike regions where cactus struggles to grow in the bleak coral. The eastern shores, where the wind blows at an average of eight to ten knots day and night, are craggy and pounded incessantly by the surf. The leeward side has calm seas with crystal-clear waters and stunning white beaches.

Bull chose a small bay in the southeast corner of the island, close to the eastern end of the Seawell International Airport, as the site for HARP. The project's headquarters, west of the actual gun site, was at Paragon House, a pink stucco sugarcane estate house set in formal gardens. This building housed the range control systems and some of the tracking equipment. From here, the firing sequence was decided and controlled and information from outlying radar sites was received and collated. To the east was the gun site itself, which was prepared by pouring several tons of concrete as a foundation for the gun platforms. Eventually three guns would be installed, two sixteen-inch and one five-inch. They would be generally stored in a horizontal position, then raised to vertical for firing.

In the beginning of HARP, the gun firings were advertised in the local paper with warnings to the locals to stay out of the way. This had the opposite effect, attracting hundreds of boats to watch the firings. Night shots provided a spectacular fireworks display, releasing a massive plume of fire hundreds of feet into the night sky, the shell leaving a clear wake of light in the darkness. Each shot also produced a huge explosion that could be heard all over the island. In the course of the HARP program, however, no complaints were made by the local people about the noise. On the contrary, they adopted HARP and its engineers as welcome guests on the island.

The first gun to be used in the project was fired not in Barbados but at the BRL site in the U.S. as part of the close cooperation between Bull and Charles Murphy. This was a surplus five-inch smoothbore, supplied by General Trudeau and installed on the Edgewood peninsula, seventeen miles from the center of Baltimore, Maryland. To achieve the velocities required, the engineers needed to extend the length of the barrel by joining another length of tubing to the original. For the first two firings, lack of support for the barrel and the pressures produced by the explosive force of a round being pushed up the tube were sufficient to blow the gun apart.

On the third attempt, Bull made the barrel's extension tube twice as long as before, but this time he fit exterior stabilizing bars that ran the length of the barrel and provided a great deal of additional support. This time, the gun fired successfully, and five shells reached a maximum altitude of 130,000 feet. It was a case of "good engineering from bad experience," as Charles Murphy described it.

But the success of the five-inch guns did not begin to satisfy HARP's goals. To do this, Bull needed much larger tubes. In late 1961, he visited the Ballistics Research Laboratory to discuss plans for installing a sixteen-inch gun on Barbados.

Within five months of HARP's start-up, Murphy had proved the success of the sixteen-inch gun at a test site outside Yuma, Arizona, firing a shell to a height of 118,000 feet. This early success demonstrated the gun's possibilities for HARP and encouraged the army to commit a further $25,000 in funding to the Space Research Institute at McGill in October 1962.

The first sixteen-inch barrel (nicknamed Bertha by the workers in Barbados) was supplied to McGill via a research contract with the University of Toronto, which paid for the rifle barrel to be made into a smoothbore at the Watervliet Arsenal in New York State. In March 1972 a second barrel was obtained from the navy and smoothbored by Bethlehem Steel.

Two sixteen-inch guns, each weighing 140 tons, were moved to Barbados in July and August 1962 aboard the U.S. Army landing craft *Lt. Col. John U. D. Page,* the army's largest, which had originally been designed to carry the army's 280-mm atomic cannon. An additional 90 tons of spare parts were transported at the same time. Officially, of course, HARP was a private research program, partly funded through BRL, so there should have been no direct government involvement.

In fact, Trudeau's commitment to the project was significant enough that he pulled every string available to ensure that HARP received a fair shake. In this instance, the transport of guns from America to Barbados was set up as an exercise for the U.S. Army Transportation Corps; Bull paid nothing and received the best service the U.S. Army could provide. The army also supplied a $750,000 radar unit and a giant traveling crane.

The guns left Hampton Roads, Virginia, and arrived at Foul Bay, Barbados, nine days later. The army had to blast through a coral reef to allow the landing craft access to the shore. Then, from the beach where the boat was anchored, the guns had to be moved over four miles to the site.

First, the army laid railroad tracks up the steep slope from the beach and winched the barrels onto the flat plateau running through the sugarcane fields. Then, the railroad tracks were leapfrogged forward so the guns could be moved a few feet at a time. During this complicated and dangerous operation, one of the workers was crushed and killed.

This massive engineering feat was commemorated by a local bard, Desmond Burke, who wrote a calypso song for the occasion.

> *They work all day from morn to night*
> *They never had a rest or stop for a bite*
> *They were trying so hard to get the guns ashore*
> *The divers were there and the scientists too*
> *The boys from McGill and the army crew*
> *They were trying so hard*[2]

When Dean Mordell arranged the details of the gun landing, he had cleared the logistics with the Barbadian government, but nobody had told the British governor-general. When he heard the sound of the U.S. Army blasting through the coral reef and saw them unloading the massive guns onto the beach, he called Eileen Donovan, the U.S. consul, to demand an explanation. Unfortunately, the army hadn't thought to tell her what was going on either. Finally, after a number of calls to the Pentagon, where even fewer people seemed to know what was happening, it was learned that the United States was not, in fact, invading Barbados. Still, for the next two weeks, a flurry of cables was sent from Bridgetown to the Foreign Office in London and from London to the U.S. State Department. To cool tempers, the army sent Norm Hall, a colonel from Washington, to explain the situation to the British governor-general.

When the guns had finally been positioned horizontally, the extensions were welded into place, the welders sliding down the gun barrel on rolling carts. The extensions were fitted onto the end of the original barrel, flush with the surface of the gun on the outside. Inside, the extensions came together in a V shape all the way around. The welders filled this space with welding material and polished it smooth. The outside stabilizing bars were then attached. In time, the engineers would find that it was possible for the interior of the gun to be repaired in much the same way that the extensions had been welded into place. When the inside of the barrel was damaged by a shell coming apart before it left the gun, for example, a welder could slide into the barrel to patch the area that had been damaged and then grind the patch down until it was even with the rest of the surface. This technique significantly increased the life of the guns, which by the time HARP received them were already fifty years old.

The HARP project was very popular in Barbados. The site employed approximately sixty of the best-educated people on the island, who were particularly pleased to be working on a project that tested their skills rather than their service to the tourist industry.

By the end of the first year, the annual report of McGill's Department of Mechanical Engineering was able to give an account of the inception of the HARP program:

> A most important contribution to the program has been the approval, encouragement, and direct help received from the government of Barbados in establishing the launching site on the island, where the geographical position, climate, economy, and close proximity to other research activities of McGill and to American long-range radar systems in the West Indies make the location most favorable. Strong support is being given to the project through direct collaboration and assistance from other organizations outside of McGill. They are the Ballistics Research Laboratory, Aberdeen Proving Ground, United States Army, in the procurement of guns and propellant, propellant design, and radar problems; Computer Designs of Canada in the aerodynamic design of vehicles, telemetry design and construction, vehicle tracking problems, and in the loan of equipment; the National Research Council in radar; and the University of Toronto in the scientific use of the facility and in procurement of equipment.
>
> Future work is likely to encompass such things as measurements of pressure, temperatures, wind velocities, background radiation and electromagnetic phenomena, gas samples, etc.; experiments on meteor simulation, high altitude explosions, high velocity reentry and near orbital, ramjet launching, etc.[3]

For the McGill scientists, Barbados had been like a frontier town of the Old West. They had come to the island armed only with ideas. With the help of several hundred local people, they had built the gun site, installed the radar, and begun a major scientific experiment. For several months, they had lived and worked together, thrashing out problems, arguing long into the night about arcane aspects of ballistics and flight patterns. Above all, HARP had become an operation filled with promise and opportunity, with the dynamic and charismatic Jerry Bull driving it forward. Now, the moment had arrived when all the theories, the joking, the tensions, and the optimism would be put to the test.

The first of the sixteen-inch guns was ready for firing in January 1963. The gun had been painted white and its cradle red to match the colors of McGill University. On the side of the gun were three plaques: one bore the crest of the university; the second held a shield marking the participation of the U.S. Army researchers, painted on by Mimi Bull and her father; and the third carried the inscription "For Peaceful Research." This last plaque had been painted by Bull and his colleagues once the gun was safely in place.

Until its arrival in Barbados, the gun had, in fact, had a peaceful history. It had been built in 1921, at a cost of $250,000, for a battleship. It had never fired a shot in anger, and the ship on which it had been installed was sunk by the aviator Billy Mitchell during his famous experiment to prove the value of air power to skeptical military chiefs.

Bull wanted the gun to shoot a projectile as far and as accurately as possible using a barrel of standard diameter. To accomplish this, he first extended the length of the gun barrel so that the explosive force behind the shell would continue to propel the shell forward for a longer time. He also designed a new shell, called a Martlet after the heraldic bird without feet that was part of the McGill insignia. The Martlet's aerodynamic shape would enable it to fly faster and farther than conventional shells.

The result was elegant and effective. Bull created a slim shell about eight inches wide and five feet six inches long, weighing 475 pounds. The shell was surrounded by a wood cocoon that ran from the base of the shell to halfway up its length. The cocoon was made of layers of laminated plywood, glued together so they would compress uniformly under high pressure. At the bottom of the shell, sitting on the explosive charge, was an aluminum-and-steel block that would act as a pusher, forcing the shell and its cocoon out of the barrel.

The cocoon was known as a sabot, after the hollowed-out pieces of wood that French peasants once wore as shoes. Immediately after the Martlet left the barrel, the sabot would fall away, leaving the shell to fly through the air at speeds well in excess of a conventional shell and to distances far greater than anything previously achieved.

The Martlet was designed to carry multiple payloads. The rear portion generally carried payloads that could be ejected in flight, such as chemicals, chaff, or meteorological balloons, while the front portion carried sensors with radios that could broadcast detailed information back to receiving stations on earth.

At 10:00 A.M. on a clear January day in 1963, all twenty-three members of the HARP staff were gathered at the test site in preparation for the first firing. Bull also had invited a few journalists to witness what he hoped would be HARP's first success. At noon the gun was loaded with 730 pounds of propellant, the bags extending nine feet inside the barrel. The Martlet shell was encased in its sabot and slid into the barrel of the gun, which was then cranked from its horizontal position to an angle of eighty degrees.

The people at the site were noticeably nervous, concerned about whether the Martlet would fly at all and, if it did not, whether the gun would blow up and destroy the site, the nearby ammunition store, and all of the hopes and dreams of Bull and his team. Just in case, local farmers had been ordered to remove their goats and donkeys from the cliff above the site, and sugarcane workers were given the day off.

In a day of terrible tension, there was an hour's delay after Lloyds of London telephoned to say that HARP's insurance policy did not adequately cover public liability. In a scene of near farce, frantic telephone calls ensued between London and Barbados until the correct wording for the relevant clause in the policy was achieved.

At exactly 5:30 P.M., Jerry Bull pressed the button on the launch panel in Paragon House and the Martlet was sent on its way. Seconds later, it exploded at eighty-five thousand feet, releasing a flare with the light of one and a half million candles.

Journalist John Clare, who witnessed the first firing, takes up the story:

> In many ways the first shots followed the almost ritualistic pattern which has become familiar to television viewers and those of us who have sat in on launchings at Cape Canaveral as observers. There were the same tight-lipped tension, the nagging doubts, the agonizing delays, and the presence of at least one German-speaking missileman who is apparently as essential to these scientific rites as the countdown itself. Then there was the moment of triumph, the release of tension as the bird flew high into the expansive blue yonder and then fell into the sea.
>
> The moment of triumph lacked some of the classic ecstasy of these affairs. A warning flare failed to fire, and a radio went dead, so that press photographers were chattily exchanging light meter readings when the missile left the nozzle of the gun with a bang at about 3,350 feet per second, close to 2,400 miles per hour. So, after the firing, at a time when they should have been exchanging firm handshakes of mutual esteem and congratulation, the embattled scientists were trying desperately to explain to the cameramen what had happened. They escaped by promising a benefit or dummy shoot for the press at a later date and comforted themselves with the knowledge that the firing itself had been a scientific success, if a photographic failure.[4]

This first successful firing from a big gun at the Barbados site was a major achievement for Bull and his small team. Without any of the enormous infrastructure that is endemic to military research, Bull had managed to establish a working base several thousand miles away from his home institution, using equipment that was mostly secondhand and supplied as a favor by his sponsor, General Trudeau. At this stage, the funding he received from the U.S. Army was scarcely sufficient to pay for costs of the team's commute between McGill and Barbados. Yet the leadership that Bull provided was so inspirational that his people worked happily and successfully under these difficult conditions.

For Bull, the firing of Bertha on Barbados was the culmination of his ambition to control his own destiny and achieve international recognition. After the frustrations of CARDE, he had found a home at McGill where he was truly appreciated. He was surrounded by colleagues and students who respected him and his work, and he had received the enthusiastic endorsement of the media, who delighted in covering this engaging personality involved in the hottest story of the decade—the exploration of space. Bull also found satisfaction in settling his old scores against the Canadian establishment.

F I V E

DUMB PEBBLES

HARP WAS the single most important project driving Bull's ambition. He believed that if HARP succeeded, as he was convinced it would, then the future of the world's space program would be in his hands. It was a breathtaking ambition, which had as its goal a network of hundreds, perhaps thousands, of big guns in countries all over the world, allowing rich and poor countries alike to have almost unlimited access to space. At this stage of his career, neither Bull's intelligence nor the breadth of his vision were doubted by anyone. Even his peers in the scientific community were impressed with his talents if not by his obsession with HARP.

McGill's 1961–62 annual report for the Department of Mechanical Engineering confirmed that Bull's arrival at the university had improved the institution's fortunes, stating, in fact, that "financial support received from various granting bodies has almost doubled . . . under the stimulus and leadership of Professor G. V. Bull."

The annual report also publicly revealed for the first time that Bull had been secretly working with NASA on the space program. However, the report, told only part of the story:

Bull's work in hypervelocity impact studies using a light gas gun had won a NASA contract to study the effectiveness of thin bumper plates in protecting space vehicles from meteoroid impact. . . . It is assumed that if the collision energy is sufficiently high that the particle and the affected portion of the bumper plate are vaporized.

The work so far has enabled the development of a fine research facility consisting of a light gas gun with multistage compression which is capable of firing a two gram pellet at velocities of 25,000 to 30,000 feet per second. The gun fired into an evacuated range, with highly sophisticated photographic equipment, including a "spark shadowgraph" and a "flash X-ray system" to record the pellet's flight and impact.

It [the contract] brings to McGill a vital problem closely linked with a priority space program. It allows support of basic research and is developing a team of experimentalists in an extremely advanced field.

The report says that McGill received $55,000 under the NASA contract from the Arthur D. Little corporation, for whom Bull was also a consultant. The key influence at ADL in linking up with Bull was Bernard Vonnegut, brother of the novelist Kurt Vonnegut, who had received a Ph.D. from the Massachusetts Institute of Technology in atmospheric studies and had joined ADL in 1952. His particular interest was lightning, tornadoes, and seeding clouds with dry ice to create snowstorms, which, at the time, was considered a possible solution to drought and a method of inducing better crops from farmland. Vonnegut was also interested in using rockets for meteorological research, but he had become intrigued by Bull's theories about using large guns to do the same job. Vonnegut expressed enthusiasm to his colleagues at ADL, and they were persuaded to invest in Bull's NASA contract.[1]

However, neither Arthur D. Little nor NASA knew the hidden agenda behind Bull's experiments at McGill. The publicly stated purpose of the program was to judge how satellites would perform when hit by meteorites or other objects floating in space. Understanding atmospheric impact forces would help improve the design of satellites and rockets.

One of the graduate students working with Bull at the time was Charles L. Murphy (no relation to Charles Murphy at BRL). He is now an associate professor of mechanical engineering at McGill—a tall, thin, almost meek man who seems to fit the stereotype of the bookish, dry engineer. He first met Bull when he took his fluid mechanics course and remembers him as "a ball of fire" who attracted students by his "enthusiasm, his outgoing character, and his willingness to involve them at the highest intellectual level of research."[2] Officially, Murphy was told that McGill's NASA contract was to "simulate the collision of meteorites and satellites with a view toward developing a form of bumper" by which satellites would be protected in orbit. The experiments involved firing projectiles at very high speeds into targets made of various materials. The goal was to fire a pellet so fast that it would vaporize upon impact with the hard surface.

While the university and students were assured that Bull was working on a peaceful system to deflect meteorites, Bull was actually working on a military system designed to destroy incoming ballistic missiles. Bull believed that large guns could be used to fire shells high into the atmosphere. Each shell would explode into many thousands of fragments totaling several tons, forming clouds of shrapnel that would devastate incoming intercontinental ballistic missiles as they passed through.

This concept was the forerunner of what became known as Brilliant Pebbles under the Strategic Defense Initiative, or Star Wars program, announced by President Reagan in 1983. While Bull had envisaged a cloud of shrapnel to destroy incoming missiles, Star Wars took the plan a step further by sending into space hundreds of small rockets that would hover, waiting for missiles to appear. Then they could be independently targeted to destroy the missile on impact. It was to be a much more sophisticated system than Bull's, but the premise of point defense was the same.

"You could call Jerry's concept 'Dumb Pebbles,'" said Charles Murphy of BRL.[3] Meanwhile, Bull's student Charles Murphy first realized what Bull had in mind when he invited him to attend a 1962 meeting in the United States. Murphy will not identify the location, the reasons for the meeting, or even who was present, claiming that such information even now could jeopardize his security clearances. All he will acknowledge is that the meeting was attended mostly by military men and that it was there the real purpose of Bull's work became clear. After that, he and Bull drifted apart, and Murphy never worked with him again.

The problem with Dumb Pebbles was that, in the end, it did not work. Charles Murphy of BRL had taken Bull's initial test results and run them through his own analysis. A team of scientists from BRL was sent to CARDE for three weeks to study the results. While Bull showed that shrapnel could indeed destroy a missile, Murphy's tests demonstrated that hundreds of rockets firing simultaneously would be needed to spread a shrapnel cloud large enough to act as an effective screen against incoming missiles. A similar criticism would be leveled at the Strategic Defense Initiative; some experts argued that it would be impossible to launch enough ABM systems to annihilate all incoming missiles. But in the 1980s, SDI had enough political momentum to force it ahead despite such reservations. In the late 1950s, however, the ABM program was chaotic. Little political leadership was provided by the White House, and the project's critics won the day.

In addition, the BRL scientists calculated that a ground team would have only a ten-minute warning of a ballistic missile attack; all the guns would have to be prepared and fired in that time. A large gun has to be loaded—first with a shell, and then with an enormous explosive charge—before it can be fired, a process that can take a highly trained crew as long as ninety minutes, by which time incoming ballistic missiles would have reached their targets. A missile, on the other hand, could be left on the launching pad, primed and ready to fire, for long periods and could be brought into action almost immediately.

As always with Bull's projects, the experiments were on the cutting edge of science. But the actual tests were carried out in the basement of the engineering building, a vast, nineteenth-century Gothic stone structure. In 1964, during one of its early firings, the light gas gun exploded after Bill Friend, one of Bull's colleagues and, later, a close associate at the Space Research Institute, put too large an explosive charge in the gun in an attempt to get the pellet to go faster. Although no one was injured in the explosion, all the windows in the engineering building were blown out, and the basement was seriously damaged. Murphy, Bull's student, still keeps a fragment from the gun on his office bookshelf as a memento.

After the explosion, Dean Mordell ordered Bull to take his experiments off campus so there would be less risk to students and university buildings. The accident could have been disastrous for the project. The university had no space to construct another laboratory and no funding available to start from scratch.

Two years earlier, Bull had spent several weeks touring the area around St.-Bruno with his friend Marcel Paquette, looking for some land to buy for his new home. Paquette, a lawyer, had good connections in the property business and was responsible for Bull's contact with a contractor that had led to the purchase of his St.-Bruno house the previous year. The two men had become firm friends after they met at a wedding in Quebec City in 1959. Paquette was still a student at McGill at the time, but he had started practicing law when Bull moved to Montreal in 1961 to take up his professorship.

During his first year at McGill, Bull's family had stayed in Charny, outside of Quebec City, so Bull was alone in Montreal most of the week and spent much of his time with Paquette. Paquette also lived in St.-Bruno, just a few blocks from Bull's house.

Then the family arrived in June 1961 and Paquette recalls how, on Saturday mornings, Bull would be awakened by his rowdy children and be driven out of the house. He would walk over to seek some peace at Paquette's, get him out of bed, and persuade his friend to cook them both breakfast. On these occasions, Bull would speak French, while Paquette would reply in English.[4]

In 1962, Bull and Paquette finally found the right parcel of land, at the top of the southern end of the Sutton mountain range on the Quebec-Vermont border, one hundred miles southeast of Montreal. On the northern side of the border, the nearest habitation was the town of Highwater; on the American side was North Troy, a small town with a population of seven hundred, including three hundred children.

The area was remote and desolate. Most of the roads were unpaved, and the only traffic was the occasional hunter walking through the forests of spruce and pine, looking for deer. The tranquil setting and breathtaking scenery would provide a refuge for his family, Bull thought, and it brought back memories of his childhood on the LaBrosse farm.

With the help of his father-in-law, Bull bought the first piece of land with the intention of building a family home. Construction began almost immediately. From the front of the hillside, the house was a triple A-frame with a vast expanse of glass that overlooked the forests below. From the side, the house was a single A-frame with another expanse of windows. Shortly after moving in, Bull decided that he wanted to have a basement constructed, but he discovered that the building was perched on solid rock. Undaunted, Bull called a dynamite expert who blew a hole in the rock underneath the house, a risky venture that was accomplished without mishap.

By 1964, the family house was finished. A swimming pool and tennis court were added to make the compound a haven for the entire family. Paquette described the place as unrelentingly active. Weekends were taken up with swimming and tennis. Particularly when Bull was at home, the place was lively.

Highwater exuded a seductive, exclusive atmosphere. The senior staff of scientists on HARP would gather at Bull's house for drinks or Sunday brunch, when the conversation always centered on the next exciting development in space research. The house, described by one visitor as something out of Disneyland —with acres of glass and wonderful views over spruce trees— was also a happy family home. Bull took great pride in Mimi and his growing family and would sit with them, telling stories, laughing, and joking for hours.

Mimi never showed any real interest in the technical matters that were discussed around the dinner table. Instead, she spent all her spare time painting landscapes and portraits in oils, moving to watercolors in 1980. In 1988, she was elected to the Quebec Watercolour Society, and several of her works are now in private collections in Canada. But some of Bull's children were bitten by the space bug, especially Michel, who would later help Bull run SRC in Brussels. Michel was thrilled by the launch of the Apollo space mission, which the family watched together on television in 1968. Michel was only eleven years old at the time.[5]

While Bull had originally planned to make Highwater a family estate, the explosion at the McGill laboratory changed his priorities. He now urgently needed somewhere to continue his experiments, and Highwater seemed the natural solution. It was isolated, so firing the guns would be no problem, and it was possible to commute from the house to McGill.

Bull went to Dean Mordell and suggested that McGill buy some extra land next to his own property as a new site for the experiments. Under the terms of its charter, McGill was prohibited from such direct financial involvement with the work of its professors, so Mordell asked Bull if he could buy the land himself and let McGill pay an annual fee for use of the property and facilities.

Once again, Bull spoke to his father-in-law about money, asking if he would be prepared to fund the deal. Gilbert agreed, and the two men formed a new company called Giltaur, after the first syllable of Gilbert's name and the first syllable of *taurus*, the Latin word for "bull." Over the next few years, Giltaur bought a further thirty-six lots; eventually, the site encompassed approximately 10,000 acres straddling the border between the U.S. and Canada. Bull's original parcel of 148 acres, designed entirely for private use, had been expanded beyond all recognition.

A laboratory was constructed on the property, and Bull continued his high-velocity impact studies using the most advanced photographic techniques available. Funded by the HARP project with cash funneled from McGill, building the laboratory was a perfectly legitimate use of the money and the site, since neither

Barbados nor McGill had the facilities that were now available at Highwater.

The Canadian site provided the laboratory, but Barbados was still the primary focus of attention. The firings continued to go well. The first successful firing in January was followed by a second series in June, utilizing a new version of the Martlet. The Martlet 2 came in three slightly different styles to allow for the varied missions assigned to the program. The rocket, weighing 185 pounds, was surrounded by a 230-pound sabot and could reach a maximum height of 111 miles. The missions for this projectile were basically the same as those for Martlet 1, with one critical difference: the newer version could reach higher layers of the atmosphere.

Initially, each of the firings was given a woman's code name. The conversation among the men at the Barbados site (there were very few women) often seemed as if a bachelor party, rather than a scientific experiment, were in progress. Babs, Alice, Carol, Daphne, Gail, Hilda, Irma, Janet, Kate, Ursula, and Rhoda all flew around this time. By the end of the project, Bull and his colleagues were struggling to find other names for the rockets, and they eventually started naming them after counties in Quebec, such as Brome and Chicoutimi.

Martlet 2 was designed to carry a number of payloads. In the center and rear of the missile were the chemicals, chaff, or meteorological balloons that could be ejected out of the missile base on a time-delay release. The nose carried a spike antenna, with a small data-processing unit behind it, to record telemetry details for relaying messages back to earth.

The first sixty miles of the flight could be tracked by ground radar. Above that height, the missile got lost in the atmospheric clutter, and the operators had to wait until it fell back toward earth before picking it up on the airwaves. Throughout the flight, however, the missile would continue sending and recording data on both wind speeds and the composition of the atmosphere. Each flight produced valuable intelligence at a surprisingly low cost.

The January firings had shown that using a missile of

smaller dimension than the gun barrel would produce a significant improvement in range. Yet Bull believed that the range
could be extended still farther by simply increasing the length
of the gun barrel. He argued that the longer the barrel, the
greater the muzzle velocity and the farther a missile could be
fired into space. Between January and June 1963, he lengthened
the barrel of the sixteen-inch gun from 78 to 118 feet, making
the HARP gun the longest operational gun system in the world.

The June series set a world record for a gun-fired space shot
when the Martlet 2 reached a height of 340,000 feet. The firing
beat the previous record held by Bull's friend Dr. Charles Murphy, who generously described Bull's effort as an "exceptional
performance."[6]

One of the first publicized reports assessing the HARP program appeared in the journal *Missiles and Rockets* one month
after the last firing. The article, which had been prepared with
the cooperation the HARP team, began by declaring that "gun-
launched missiles have been fired successfully to altitudes of
nearly 65 miles in the early stages of Project HARP, a just-
disclosed joint U.S.-Canadian project with possible antisatellite
and anti-ICBM applications.

"The tests also indicate the possibility that small nations
may be able to put satellites in orbit very inexpensively."

The article pointed out that in the June test firings, missiles
regularly landed less than one hundred feet from their target in
the Atlantic Ocean after the flight into the atmosphere. (In fact,
accuracy to within four thousand feet of the target was more
common.) The final paragraph of the article concluded, "For use
in an anti-satellite or terminal A-ICBM role, the guns employed
could be swivel-mounted and linked to tracking radars. Development of a solid state guidance system would be necessary but
the fact that McGill already has developed successful solid state
telemetry for the project puts [the university] a good way along
on guidance development."

This was the first suggestion that Bull had revised his thinking on Dumb Pebbles and was moving toward a more conventional gun system that could shoot down incoming ballistic
missiles. The fact was picked up immediately by *Newsweek*
magazine, in its July 15, 1963, issue.

Project HARP has already launched upper-atmosphere and electron-counting rockets. But it has even greater promise as an anti-satellite and anti-ICBM weapon—particularly when fitted with tracking radar and jam-proof guidance. With hundreds of unused 16-inch guns lying idle at army and navy centers, U.S. cities could be protected by batteries of such anti-missile missile cannon at far less cost than the weapons now in use. Because of its high velocity (5,400 feet per second), says Bull, the missile could be shot through the worst weather with virtually pinpoint accuracy.[7]

The U.S. Army had been aware of the program's potential for some time, ever since the success of the early Martlet firings. The army's tiny initial investment, designed to maintain its toehold in the space race, looked as though it was paying off. At the end of June, after the second series of tests, HARP's funding was increased to $250,000. The total funding from October 1962 to June 1963 was $449,000. The army once again channeled funds through BRL and Charles Murphy.

To Bull, Murphy, and their colleagues, the increased American investment was welcome but insufficient. At every stage of the project, the team leaders had been forced to scrimp and save. Cash was short, and they were frustrated by their inability to exploit all the opportunities they thought had been revealed by the first probing shots from the big gun. Nonetheless, the additional money allowed them to step up the pace of research.

Over the next year, experiments progressed in Barbados as well as at NASA's Wallops Flight Center on Wallops Island, Virginia, where five-inch guns were shooting scaled-down Martlets under a program directed by Murphy from BRL. In September 1963, the first gun-boosted rocket, the Marlet 3, was launched from Barbados, marking a major development in the HARP program. Bull was hoping to push the Marlet twenty-five hundred nautical miles into space, where the payload in the missile's nose cone could achieve an orbit around the earth.

Although these new rocket-assisted missiles were fired successfully and the rocket motors kicked in after a few seconds of free flight, the missiles had problems reaching the heights required. Nose cones blew apart; barrels of the elongated guns bent under the stress of firing bigger missiles; and some of the missiles themselves fell apart.

As Bull and Murphy wrote in their own account, *Paris Kanonen—The Paris Guns and Project HARP*, published in 1988:

> From the inception of the HARP project until mid-1964, the program funding limited both the objectives and the rates at which these objectives could be achieved. Starting from virtually a zero base, the launching facilities had to be developed; pioneering engineering research and development on all aspects related to the unorthodox use of guns, along with payloading and scientific experiment techniques, had to be undertaken.
>
> Aside from the funding limitation, the HARP project had to work within the assigned range limit of the U.S. Army, specifically, systems with ranges not in excess of 60 miles. Thus, aside from proving itself as a viable, low cost system, the project had to concentrate on the early successful gathering of atmospheric scientific data.[8]

Bull had emerged as one of the world's leading experts on ballistics.

Within the scientific community, Bull was ahead of his time. Even though HARP may have begun to prove itself, Bull was impatient. HARP worked in theory and in practice, he believed. Now he wanted more from NASA than just research contracts. He wanted HARP to go far into space. He had sketched out plans for an enormous gun four times the size of those installed in Barbados and was ready to fulfill his dream of designing a corresponding missile that could launch a satellite into space.

He was constrained, however, by the lack of funds. But in June 1964, help arrived from a most unexpected source—the Canadian government.

S I X

THE TORCHERS

BULL AND his colleagues had believed from the beginning that the Canadian government had set out to sabotage HARP in every way possible.

According to Bull's unpublished authorized biography,

The Canadian government orchestrated a program of derision of the project from the very start. They labelled it a publicity stunt, invoking their previously established label on Bull. It was inconceivable, they stated, that a university group could cope with the enormous logistic and organization problems associated with the establishment of the largest gun facility ever built, and that installation to be on a remote island thousands of miles from Montreal. Appealing to a superficial sophistication, they stated that the technical objectives were impossible, suggesting the extreme problems of World War II gunnery in reaching high flying aircraft. They doubted that guns could obtain over 70,000 feet altitude. As far as sophisticated payloads and the boosting of multi-rocket assisted systems, this was within their highly qualified technical abilities . . . a patently obvious absurdity.[1]

Both Charles Murphy at BRL and General Trudeau in Washington had heard the same criticisms from the Canadians. A faction in Ottawa seemed to have decided the Bull was bad news for Canada and, according to the prevailing political views at the time, he was bad news for the world as well, given the military applications of his research.

Invariably, Bull did not ignore these attacks. On the contrary, he acted as though he welcomed the confrontation. In repeated interviews with the press, he suggested to journalists that they examine the qualifications of those who were criticizing him.

Despite obvious reservations, however, the Canadian government did eventually become involved in the HARP program. The test firings received extensive publicity, particularly in the Canadian press, and the articles were often accompanied by critical comments from Bull, which may have stung the government into action. Without any direct contact with the McGill team whatsoever, officials from the Department of Defense Production approached Bull, in May 1964, telling him that Canada now wanted to participate.

As Bull's official unpublished biography explains it, "The officials claimed that the misunderstandings and feuds of the past must not be allowed to continue to harm the national interest of the country. . . . Their position was stated as wanting specifically to sponsor the long range and orbit missions as a Canadian national effort." This great contradiction of his past experience amazed and impressed Bull.[2] In fact, the Canadians appeared to be interested not because of any great enthusiasm for the project—Bull was still intensely disliked by much of the Canadian establishment—but because they had been shamed into action.

Bull flew to Washington in May 1964 and met with a number of U.S. officials, including General Trudeau, Charles Murphy from BRL, and Dr. Hoyt Lemons from the Army Research Office at its headquarters on Columbia Pike in Arlington, Virginia. The U.S. Army team was skeptical about the Canadian government's involvement. They argued that the project was running smoothly and that a good working relationship had been established between McGill and the army. They were not anxious to share the success or bring in a third party who might produce new tensions. They also did not accept the Canadian government's protestations about having a new understanding with Bull, and they believed that the old enmities would continue.

But other considerations had surfaced that, in the end, swayed the army toward the Canadian offer. The army had been considering HARP as a possible launch vehicle for orbiting satellites. However, the army had never been given a mandate to send orbiting satellites into space either by the Pentagon or by Congress. That mandate had originally been placed with the navy, then transferred to the air force after the first Sputnik launch in an attempt to cut down on the interservice rivalry that had been dogging the American space program and allowing the Russians to move ahead faster than the U.S. To further this end, the army had been limited by Congress to the development of short-range tactical missions involving rockets and shells with a maximum range of sixty miles, the very limitation that was preventing Bull from expanding his project any further.

Inevitably, neither the navy nor the army took kindly to the air force being free to carve out such a large slice of the space program for its own fiefdom, and each tried to stay in the game. They wanted to be prepared in the event that the shifting political winds put them in a better position to regain the initiative. For the army, HARP represented exactly the type of project that would allow them to continue in the space business. However, because the press had referred on a number of occasions to HARP's potential in the development of space and orbiting systems, the air force was beginning to see the program as a possible rival. If the early reports about HARP's success and its relatively inexpensive cost compared with rockets were true, then the project could pose a serious threat to those in the air force who saw rockets as the way to space and wanted nothing to threaten their program. The air force had already raised questions in the Pentagon and with Congress about the issue of the army's mission amid suggestions that Trudeau might have exceeded his remit by funding HARP.

To counter these accusations, the U.S. Army representatives

and Murphy had emphasized to the air force that HARP's research had applications for gun technology and the results would affect the development of future battlefield artillery systems. This was true but, again, only part of the story. The army realized that the more successful HARP became, the more likely it was that the air force would move to shut it down. The army was interested in combining forces with the Canadians to support the project so that the space aspects of HARP could be relegated to Ottawa on paper, enabling the U.S. Army to argue legitimately that they were supporting only those segments of HARP that related to their prescribed mission.

One month after Bull's meeting with the army, three members of the Canadian Department of Defence Production arrived in Arlington, Virginia, to discuss, in detail, their plans for HARP. To the surprise of Trudeau and his colleagues, the Canadians came with a clear brief from their government. They told the Americans that the decision had been made to develop a gun-launched rocket system designed to launch small orbiting satellites. Although not specifically stated, the implication was that Canada planned to go ahead with this development—with or without HARP. Even if the army had not been driven by political considerations, the Army Research Office could not allow the Canadians to compete directly with their own project. They had little choice but to accept the Canadians into HARP.[3]

In a clever manipulation of the rules, the army allowed the Canadian Department of Defence Production to pledge $2.5 million to HARP over three years, beginning in 1964. The Canadian money would be earmarked to pay for all the HARP experiments relating to orbiting. This was obviously a fiction, since a division of money inside HARP could not plausibly be done. But at least the army could stand back and remain poised to exploit the opportunities that research might reveal—without breaching the rules of interservice competition.

From the Canadians' perspective, the U.S. Army's interpretation of their involvement was of little concern. Ottawa had signed on to the project only to still the political voices at home. They actually had little interest in the research and played no part in HARP, rarely attending any of the many gun launches in Barbados or querying any of the test results.

Canada's participation was of some significance to HARP, if only because it made it an international collaborative project, which gave HARP a measure of protection from the budget cutters in Congress for as long as the Canadian funding lasted.

The joint agreement was signed in November 1964 but made retroactive to July 1, 1964. Dean Mordell agreed that McGill would finance the program for a short time until the funds arrived from Ottawa. The U.S. Army's contribution would be sent from Washington to Ottawa, where the monies would be combined with the Canadian funding from the Canadian Commercial Corporation. By August 1964 a contract would be sent to McGill, which would be used by the university for billing purposes.

A joint U.S.-Canadian steering committee was formed to oversee the new deal. Under instructions from Ottawa, Bull moved the Space Research Institute to 892 Sherbrooke Street West in Montreal, a building owned by McGill. Managers were hired to oversee the contract.

By the end of 1963, HARP had begun attracting serious money and had become the most significant source of funding for McGill University. The 1963–64 annual report of the Department of Mechanical Engineering listed ten full-time technical staff working on the project, in addition to the faculty and graduate students. During the year, the department received $690,000 in HARP grants—$490,000 from the U.S. Army and $200,000 from the Canadian Department of Defence Production. Bull's hypervelocity impact study had received $125,000 from NASA. The $815,000 raised by Bull far exceeded the sum total of all other grants to the department, including funds from the university for its operating budget, which totaled only $550,000.

This upbeat report concealed a growing financial crisis inside the project, however. By late September 1964, the promised contract had not arrived from Ottawa, and without a contract, McGill had no way of billing the Canadian Commercial Corporation and actually receiving the money. Dean Mordell approached government officials and was told that even though the cash had been received from the U.S. Army, the Canadian government had changed its mind and no cash would be forthcoming. Mordell contacted the Americans who, in turn, spoke to the Canadians, pointing out that an international legally binding agreement had been signed and no changes would be accepted. The Canadians then contacted McGill to say the deal was on again.

Meanwhile, McGill continued to finance the HARP project in Barbados and at Highwater. Together, the two sites were employing over two hundred people, and the project had gained a momentum that McGill could not sustain without outside financing.

Despite all the promises, neither the contract nor the money appeared from Ottawa. By the spring of 1965, something close to panic was beginning to infect McGill and the HARP team. McGill had a total annual budget of approximately $15 million, and the HARP project was soaking up about 10 percent of that sum. Finally, some ten months after they were due, the contract and the money arrived, and HARP was saved. But the relief was short-lived. As the following year's budget neared completion, reports began to appear in the Canadian press suggesting that, once again, the government was planning to cancel the project.

A steady stream of leaks from Ottawa rumored that either the project was in trouble or that funding was about to be stopped. These reports made any coherent planning for the project virtually impossible. Dean Mordell made several visits to Ottawa to track down the source of the leaks and to get reassurance from the government. He failed on both counts.

Bull became convinced that the bad press was coming from a clique inside the prime minister's office that was opposed to the possible military applications of the HARP program. His conviction that the opposition to HARP was based on leftist ideology would shape his political views in the future. An essentially apolitical scientist, Bull seemed to have been scarred by his early HARP experiences. He remained suspicious of liberals and distrustful of the Soviet Union and its supporters. This did not turn him into a right-wing ideologue or a tool of the conservatives, but he was certainly more inclined to support and count as friends those people who encouraged his project.

Despite the political infighting, HARP was achieving some

impressive results. By the end of 1965, the project had sent over one hundred missiles more than fifty miles into space, making it the most productive space program in the world. The sixteen-inch Betsy comfortably held the world altitude record for a gun-fired projectile, having pushed a 185-pound projectile eighty-four miles into space.

In September 1965, SRI had started installation of a second double-length gun at the army's Yuma Proving Ground. In November 1966, Murphy and a BRL launch crew used this gun to fire a Martlet 2 one hundred twelve miles above the Arizona desert. This altitude remains a record and is listed in the *Guinness Book of World Records*.

Each of Bull's missiles carried a scientific payload, which proved the validity of the HARP concept. The first of thirty-seven academic articles had appeared in the specialist press, under such arcane titles as "Profiles of Winds in the Lower Thermosphere by the Gun-Launched Probe Technique and Their Relation to Ionospheric Sporadic E" and "Comparison of Ionospheric Drift Velocities by Space Receiver Technique with Neutral Winds from Luminous Rocket Trails." While the papers meant little to the average reader, they formed a considerable body of work that was exciting the interest of the scientific community. This steady flow of literature was opening doors that had been shut tight until HARP started firing its big gun.[4] Finally, Bull was able to talk about the future of HARP with total confidence to the McGill University newspaper:

> We must have goals and they must be big goals. A space program in a university atmosphere is a good thing, because we have freedom to think here. Even though government and business interests are supplying the money, McGill has made the project by sticking with it through good times and bad. HARP has proven itself, and I'm very hopeful that we'll continue and grow with it, here at McGill.

At the same time, Dean Mordell developed this theme of bringing HARP away from its strictly military application and making the research accessible to a wider audience. In any country that is developing industrially, the pace of development is intimately related to an engineering school or an institute of technology. We should develop work at the University which would feed industry directly—not pure scientific research, but new ideas, from which new products can be made. This is happening with HARP.

The first sixteen-inch gun at Highwater, nicknamed Betsy Jr., was installed in November 1965. Unlike the Barbados gun, which could be elevated to ninety degrees, Betsy Jr. could only fire horizontally and was used for ballistics testing. A horizontal position made the rig much simpler to erect and operate. One of the most difficult problems associated with firing such a big gun was absorbing the enormous recoil. A gun in the horizontal position could be mounted on railway lines; the recoil would drive the gun backward down the track. It was a cheap and effective solution.

The firing of the gun could be heard by local residents for many miles around the Highwater site, but rather than complaining about the project disturbing their rural tranquillity, the locals seemed to take pride in the big gun. Loudspeakers were set up in the two hotels in Highwater, Quebec, and North Troy, Vermont, so that residents and visitors could listen to the countdowns, which might last as long as two hours, followed by the actual explosions.

The firings at Highwater were designed to produce data for a projected firing in 1967 of a rocket that would establish an orbit above the earth—the first stage in a planned launch of a satellite into space.

At the time of the Highwater firings, Bull was also working in Barbados on a highly secret U.S. Defense Department contract relating to the survival of fuses in nuclear weapons upon impact with their targets. U.S. nuclear targeting policy required that ICBMs be able to penetrate hard silos in order to destroy the Soviet Union's nuclear weapons as well as the country's command and control centers. These silos were built underground and protected by several feet of reinforced concrete.

The concern was that the fuses in the warhead that sparked the nuclear explosion might not survive the impact with the concrete and the missiles would thus fail to detonate. Bull's contract required him to fire scaled-down versions of the warhead into blocks of reinforced concrete. The fuses in the nose were supplied with sensors that could relay their performance under stress to monitors in the laboratory.

Bull had a good working knowledge of nuclear weapons and an excellent understanding of the technology needed to design conventional weapons carrying nuclear payloads. However, he was never involved in the design of nuclear warheads and indeed never received the top-secret Q clearance which would have allowed him access to official designs.

In may 1965, cracks started to appear along the barrel of the sixteen-inch gun in Barbados. The HARP team figured that the stresses of firing the longer-barreled gun with larger propellant charges had finally destroyed the gun and, with it, the project. "We thought it was all over," recalled Murphy.[5]

But a close examination of the original 1921 drawings of the gun's design showed Bull and Murphy that the gun was made up of eight metal layers sandwiched together; as luck would have it, only the outside layer was damaged. Even so, they were unwilling to risk any further damage to the Barbados gun, which was the most impressive piece of equipment to show to people interested in HARP.

Consequently, in October 1965, a 180-foot horizontal gun was erected at Highwater. Two months later, it blew up during a ballistics test. This was a major setback to the project at a time when the whole future of HARP was being questioned by Ottawa and its funding was in doubt.

The guns at Highwater remained a constant problem as Bull and his team repeatedly pushed the technology beyond its limits. On one occasion, a cannon blew up just a few weeks before the U.S.-Canadian steering committee meeting. Bull did not want to wait that long for the formal approval to order a new gun. Instead, he ordered a gun barrel from the U.S. Navy storage facility in Pocatello, Idaho (150 miles north of Salt Lake City and 600 miles from the sea). Bob Stacey, Bull's administrative assistant, who handled the logistics for HARP, arranged transport for the gun from the storage facility to Vermont.

Stacey, a Briton, was one of the few acolytes surrounding

Bull who gave him unswerving loyalty. He had served as a Guardsman, part of the most traditional branch of the British army, in World War II and retained many of a Guardsman's attributes. He had a trimmed military mustache, a ramrod-straight bearing, and, in a world of disorganized scientists, a demanding personality that insisted on timely efficiency. Stacey was known to Bull and one or two very close friends as Major Blimp, which was not a criticism but a term of affection. He died of alcoholism in the early 1970s and was buried in the SRC compound in Highwater.

The new gun was scheduled to be brought from Idaho on specially articulated railway cars that had been designed to allow the navy to transport extra-large artillery. The gun was held at two points near the middle of one car, while the other cars would swing with the curvature of the track. This arrangement imposed a limit on how fast the train could travel, so it took three weeks for the barrel to arrive in Vermont. But, with typical Stacey efficiency, it came just in time for the committee meeting.

In the interim, the Highwater site had been visited by Premier Jean Lesage of Quebec, who was ushered to Betsy Jr. to observe a ceremonial firing of a Martlet into the hillside five hundred feet away.[6]

This kind of high-level political support may have put a positive public face on the government's attitude toward HARP, but privately, doubts remained. By March 1966, the Canadian government had told General Trudeau that their funding would not be extended beyond the final year of the contract's commitment. If McGill chose to use the last *tranche* of $1.5 million for purposes other than HARP, the government would have no objection.

When Bull heard the news, he was furious. He told both Trudeau and Murphy that he would refuse to accept any money from the Canadian government whatsoever; HARP would survive with the support of the U.S. Army and other sponsors. The university was horrified at this cavalier attitude, and several university officials from the principal on down spent a week persuading Bull to change his mind.

Writing in McGill's annual report of 1965–66, Dean Mordell criticized the Canadian government's decision: "This means that the first satellite conceived and designed in Canada, will rise up with the insignia of McGill, Barbados and the United States, but no Maple Leaf. It is the more tragic since the launch will be closely watched by NASA, who see in the system the possibility of a major breakthrough in space technology, and the great industrial potential which might have been Canada's."[7]

Bull and Mordell still hoped they might be able to rescue the project by getting Ottawa to change its mind. But any chance of this happening was removed with the publication in March 1967 of a Canadian government report concerning the country's space program.

The report argued that Canada needed to invest more men, equipment, and money in an independent space program. It recommended that funding should be increased from $17 million to $60 million within five years.

The report stated that "the field of space activities should in Canada include all activities directly associated with rockets and other launch vehicles, with spacecraft, and with those ground-based activities which relate directly to upper-atmosphere and space phenomena."

While this appeared to be an endorsement of HARP, in fact, the report examined the project in some detail and attacked Bull's failure to provide accurate information about the project. "It cannot be overemphasized that both the advantages and limitations of the gun-launching technique need to be disseminated and understood in an undistorted fashion through the Canadian scientific community before any appreciable Canadian interest can be expected."

The study listed three significant advantages to gun-launched projectiles:

1. Efficiency: The projectile muzzle velocity is achieved more efficiently than with conventional rockets because very little energy is used to accelerate a propellant which is later on burned to achieve the necessary altitude.

2. Fuel Economy: Due to the fact that the gun barrel contains the propellant, the powder or explosives used are far cheaper per unit of impulse than conventional rocket motors.

3. Accuracy: The vector direction of the projectile as it leaves the muzzle can be established with considerable precision because of the fixed geometry of the gun barrel and equivalent accuracy can be achieved with rockets only through relatively complex guidance systems.

Two major disadvantages were listed:

1. Acceleration: The accelerations from a gun barrel are so great—up to 10,000 G [10,000 times the force of gravity] or much more—that the vehicle being lifted and all of its components must be capable of withstanding such a force. The components also may experience high stresses in the opposite direction on leaving the barrel due to the relaxation of compressive strains in the vehicle itself.

2. Payload dimensions: The ability of the vehicle fired from a gun barrel to reach extreme altitudes depends upon factors which make it desirable to use sub-calibers—that is, vehicles smaller than the diameter of the barrel—and this places severe limitations on their size. Vehicles that are gun-launched but rocket-propelled as well are not subject to this but still are limited by the caliber of the barrel.

The report concluded that there appeared to be "no immediate Canadian scientific requirement for HARP-type vehicles, apart from meteorology. The study group could also find no Canadian companies who showed any interest in using the HARP system for scientific research."[8]

Two months later, in May 1967, the Associate Committee on Space Research of the Canadian National Research Council submitted a report to the United Nations on Canada's space effort. The report made only passing reference to McGill and almost no reference whatsoever to HARP, which provoked a sarcastic letter from Dean Mordell to the chairman of the committee, Dr. D. C. Rose.

"I have received with some interest the report," Mordell wrote.

This report, of course, is largely taken from the minutes of the proceedings of the 10th meeting of the Associate Committee on Space Research that were issued on 15th May. I was interested to find that whereas for the most part the description of the Canadian Space Program published in the report is taken verbatim from the published minutes of the earlier meeting, when it comes to considering the activities of McGill University, there seems to be a departure from the rule. In Appendix 25 of the minutes, a report which I had prepared giving the briefest possible summary of our work here . . . occupied 16 pages of the minutes. In the report, however, I find that the only reference to the project is some 6 lines in Appendix 25 of the report which gives no indication of the technical or scientific progress whatsoever.

I suppose it could be argued that although all this work is done using vehicles invented, designed and manufactured in Canada and launched by a Canadian technique, the actual vehicles are not launched into that particular part of space which happens to be overhead of Canada at the precise time of launching, and I thought that perhaps this was the reason for the exclusion until I found other references to Canadian work done from such places as Wallops Island, where we also have worked.

The answer received by Mordell from Dr. Rose provided no real explanation for the omission. This merely helped to convince Bull and Mordell that HARP had no future at McGill or in Canada.

Over the next few months, Bull and Mordell tried to persuade the Canadian government to change its mind, but to no avail. They began to explore alternative sources of funding. Both the U.S. Army and the navy suggested that the whole HARP program be moved to the United States, where it would be likely to receive funding if it became a wholly American program. This plan obviously had some merit, so Bull started searching for an

American university that would be willing to provide HARP with a home.

Certainly, Bull and his team assumed that the U.S. Army, which had stood by them faithfully through all their difficulties with the Canadian government, would continue to provide financial support. However, while some army people remained very committed to HARP, others in the army, who had seen the project as either a waste of time or as a backdoor way of keeping the army in the space business, were less enthusiastic. Bull seemed to have been unaware of criticism. When the Canadian side of the contract ran out in June 1967, the U.S. Army was no longer obligated by an international agreement to resume a new round of funding. Considerable pressure was exerted on the Army Research Office to cut the project altogether.

While operating under the Canadian umbrella, HARP was able to explore the outer reaches of space, well beyond the sixty-mile limit that was imposed on the army's own experiments. And, as HARP progressed, the focus had been on firing payloads farther and farther into space. If the army continued its funding, the entire HARP operation would have to be scaled back, so that Bull would be, once again, operating inside the limit. The army's version of space research could hide behind the Canadians no longer.

Also, the army was chronically short of funds as the cost of America's growing commitment in Vietnam began to eat away at the defense budget. Spending in every area had to be curtailed, and HARP was one of the projects targeted for the ax.

In addition to opposition from atmospheric physicists who were engaged in other projects but were competing with HARP for research funds, the Army Missile Command (MiCom) in Huntsville, Alabama, had developed serious reservations about the program. These doubts were not based on scientific arguments; they arose because HARP had been held up by Congress as an example of a cost-effective space program. Congress had argued that if HARP could run its projects so well and for so little money, MiCom might not need their extravagant funding. Naturally, these arguments were not appreciated by MiCom, which generated a significant lobbying effort within the army to have the competition eliminated by ensuring the preeminence of rockets in space.

The withdrawal of U.S. Army funding spelled the end of the HARP program. On July 1, 1967, termination notices were sent by McGill to approximately one hundred employees involved with HARP. Bull, of course, was excluded because he had tenure at the university. However, he felt a strong sense of responsibility to all those who had given so much to HARP, and he was determined to find another source of money.

At this point, Dean Mordell was forced to issue a prepared statement:

> It is more than a year since the Canadian government gave McGill notice that it did not propose to continue its support beyond June 30, 1967. Until very recently it was believed that it would be possible to maintain the Institute without Canadian support, and to continue to develop the benefits to McGill and Canada. However, in the last two months it has become clear that American support of the magnitude required to maintain the Institute at its present level would not be available.
>
> The Canadian Government was made aware of the situation, but no action was forthcoming. McGill University, conscious of what has been accomplished, and of the distinguished team of engineers, scientists and technicians that would otherwise have to be disbanded, is happy that the work of the Space Research Institute may be continued at the University of Vermont.[9]

In fact, negotiations with the University of Vermont broke down and Bull had to look elsewhere. General Trudeau approached General Barksdale Hamlett, the president of Norwich University. Before he retired from the army, Hamlett was a career artillery officer who commanded a unit in World War II as well as the artillery of the Twenty-fourth Infantry Division in Korea from 1951 to 1952. The SRI team found a ready listener in the retired general, who was enthusiastic about HARP.

Norwich is the oldest military college in the United States.

It is located in Northfield, Vermont, close to the Highwater site at North Troy. With only 1,250 students, Norwich has a small campus that is dedicated to training students in business or the professions through accredited academic programs, and to training in the military field "to meet any challenge of danger to our country."

While Norwich had a faculty of engineering at the time, the school had no record of involvement in any kind of space program, and the university had no facilities to exploit such an involvement. Despite these apparent difficulties, the university agreed to a new arrangement (living up to its motto of I Will Try) whereby the Space Research Institute would transfer its research to Norwich, supported by grants from the state of Vermont.

The announcement that HARP was leaving Canada resulted in considerable criticism by the Canadian press, and the Canadian government was forced to defend itself. Industry Minister C. M. Drury issued a statement saying that the HARP program was an adjunct to the much larger high-altitude research program sponsored by the U.S. Army. He argued that the Canadian withdrawal had been precipitated by the U.S. Army withdrawing its funding, which was untrue. The Canadians had withdrawn first, forcing the army to reconsider its position. Drury's statement went on to say that "HARP provided an alternative to already developed rocket launch systems for certain purposes, but the scientific tasks presently being undertaken have little relevance to Canadian national interests or environment."

He added that "in the case of HARP it has not proved possible to justify a continuing expenditure for duplicating our existing probe launching systems in preference to support of other aspects of space research, or the competing demands of other equally important scientific fields of more direct economic or social significance to Canada."

As Bull was to explain in a letter to his lawyers in July 1979, "The total strength of the [Canadian] Department of National Defence (Army, Navy, Air Force and Brass) was reduced below that of the New York City police force. In the early 1970s,

[Prime Minister] Trudeau came under bitter attack by NATO and the U.S. [because] the Canadian defense expenditures per capita were the second lowest [next to Luxembourg] in the world."

Bull had been unable to conceive of or accept the idea that his personality might have contributed to HARP's opposition in Ottawa and, therefore, to the project's downfall. He also seemed to have been entirely unaware that, at the same time he was making enemies of the scientific establishment, a rift had been growing between General Trudeau and his deputy, Charles Poor, over HARP's significance.

Trudeau had always been an enthusiastic sponsor, while Poor had maintained his distance. While Trudeau saw HARP as a way of financing the army's continued participation in the space program, as well as a backdoor method of extracting some interesting research on shells, Poor saw it as a low-priority program. Nevertheless, Trudeau would argue, big guns might be a cheaper alternative to rockets for earth-based applications, such as the delivery of chemical shells.

"Personally, I'd prefer a rocket," said Poor, "because rockets have a low acceleration and are easier to control than shells. HARP made difficult what was easier to do with rockets and, additionally, wasn't as cheap as its proponents often claimed it would be."[10]

Although the project was scientifically interesting, Poor saw HARP as a simple notion that Bull had oversold to get attention for himself.

In hindsight, this seems an unduly harsh judgment. As the HARP program developed, Bull produced test results that showed that his theories concerning guns as a cheap alternative to rockets had some validity. He also had done some remarkable work on shell design that revolutionized artillery shells and battlefield guided weapons. These results alone provided complete justification for the HARP program. But Bull and Poor had been set on a collision course, and their political and scientific rivalries contributed significantly to the program's collapse.

. . .

Immediately after HARP was canceled, the sites at Highwater and Barbados were visited by a group of men whom Bull and his colleagues had nicknamed the Torchers.

This peculiar group from the Canadian Department of National Defence is dedicated to the destruction of technical projects. When a cancellation order takes effect, the group rushes into action, torching and burning all technical hardware (machinery, software, documentation) connected to the program so that there is no chance of resurrection of or memorial to any of its accomplishments.

In this case, to the astonishment of everyone involved, the Torchers wanted to demolish the guns, dismantle the laboratory equipment, and incinerate all the records of the HARP program. This is exactly what had happened to A. V. Roe's Arrow fighter aircraft nearly ten years earlier.

There was no logical reason for this action, which appeared to be motivated entirely by spite. It seemed a final chance for those whom Bull had crossed to pay off old scores by obliterating all that remained of his work.

However, Giltaur, and not McGill, was the owner of the Highwater equipment. Consequently, Bull instructed the guards at the site to allow the government team to inspect but not to touch anything. Naturally, this restraint provoked an immediate response from Ottawa, and a meeting was called at McGill in September 1967, when the university's lease for the use of the land would expire.

Clearly, the Canadians were going to push for the complete destruction of all the facilities. Indeed, Charles Murphy at BRL and General Trudeau had warned Mordell that the meeting would be a showdown between Bull and the Canadian government. The U.S. Army was not prepared to risk an international confrontation over the issue, Murphy added, and they would go along with whatever the Canadians decided to do.

Bull sought the advice of his friend Marcel Paquette, who had drawn up the original agreement between Giltaur and McGill. Under the terms of the lease, Paquette told him, the

Joint International Steering Committee, which was responsible for the HARP project, had a legal obligation to restore the property to the condition in which it was found when the college took over the land and all its facilities. The work had to be completed within thirty days of the lease's expiration.

Such a clause is standard in many leases and is designed to ensure that buildings, roads, and other facilities are properly maintained during a tenancy. But a repairing clause was hardly appropriate to the Highwater lease. The land had been virtually virgin territory at the start of the lease, and the Canadian government's lawyers had played into Bull's hands by allowing the repairing clause to remain. Since the deal had been done, the Highwater site had been fully developed with new buildings, roads, communications systems, and underground bunkers, and this work had required the logging and grading of hundreds of acres. The repairing clause meant that all the construction carried out since the start of the contract would have to be dismantled and the land restored to its previous natural state. Obviously, this was impossible.

Bull, Mordell, and Paquette agreed that they would attempt to enforce the terms of the lease.[11]

At the meeting of government officials, the Canadians restated their intention to destroy all the records and equipment relating to HARP. This was followed by a moment of high drama, in which a bailiff, retained by Paquette, entered the room and served a court order on Mordell as the Joint International Steering Committee's representative, instructing him to restore all lands pertaining to the lease to their original condition. Bull pointed out that not only would the forests have to be restored, but the underground bunkers at Highwater would have to be blown up and the holes would have to be filled in with earth and the surface replanted. All buildings would have to be knocked down and the hundreds of acres they rested on would have to be recultivated.

Alternatively, Bull explained, the Americans could sell all their equipment at Highwater and Barbados to the Canadians for one dollar. The Canadians could lease all *their* equipment to the university for ninety-nine years, and, in turn, sell the American equipment to McGill for a dollar. McGill would then assign the lease and resell the U.S. equipment to Bull for the same dollar. If all sides agreed, the legal action would be forgotten.

The shrewd move caused consternation in the enemy camp. The meeting was adjourned. When the two sides returned later that day, Bull had a deal that allowed him to retain the sites, as well as the hundreds of thousands of dollars' worth of government equipment that had been loaned to him over the years, particularly by the U.S. Army, including the sixteen-inch guns and a number of five-inch guns.

They also agreed that all the facilities would be sold intact to a nonprofit organization in Quebec, then resold for a nominal sum to a parallel nonprofit organization in Vermont associated with Norwich University. Giltaur would waive the restoration clause and assume all financial obligations for maintenance and protection as of the date of transfer. The facilities would remain staffed, operable, and available to any U.S. government agency at no cost.

This proposal proved acceptable to the Canadians and was the perfect answer for the U.S. Army. HARP would be transferred to the United States and come under the control of Norwich University. Space Research Institute would take control of Highwater and the Barbados site and, if additional funding could be found, the U.S. Army would be free to maintain interest in HARP without violating its space research restrictions.

This agreement meant that for the first time Bull himself would have a large measure of control over his own destiny. Initially, HARP had been controlled by McGill and the conservative university administration, which had acted to restrain Bull's more extravagant ideas. But with the ending of the HARP program, SRI became Bull's operation. Once new funding was found, SRI would become the Space Research Corporation (SRC), the company that would run Bull's enterprises until his death.

HARP left a considerable legacy that establishes, without question, the pioneering aspects of Bull's work. He conducted the first serious studies on transmitting data from gun-fired projectiles, using horizon and infrared sensors; he developed the technique of firing rocket-assisted projectiles from guns, a technique that was also being evaluated by the U.S. Army; he designed fins that would pop up on a missile before it left the barrel; he refined saboting techniques; and he created the technology for constructing longer gun barrels.

Today many artillery and tank rounds use sabots, and sensors are commonly used on terminally guided munitions. The Copperhead guided missile, which is currently in service with the U.S. Army, was designed by engineers who were trained at the HARP site in Barbados. The Copperhead has pop-up fins, is rocket assisted, and has sensors in its nose cone.

From the beginning, HARP appeared full of promise for Bull, McGill, and Canada. In the more than five hundred firings that had been achieved, the practicality of using guns to launch projectiles into space had been fully demonstrated. Bull's Yuma gun held a world record for the highest shot into space (112 miles), and a wealth of new atmospheric data had been gathered.

The reason most frequently cited for the Canadians' withdrawal from the project is that they were uncomfortable with HARP's military applications. In addition, Ottawa was seeing little return on its investment in terms of jobs or exports. Instead, officials had watched a number of American companies, such as Lockheed, begin to utilize HARP's research to develop new types of missiles and guns. Canada's defense industry was not large enough to exploit the research, and the Canadian military had neither the cash nor the enthusiasm for a national space program. Whatever happened with HARP, the results would be of little interest to Canada—or so it seemed to the people running the Canadian government.

This may have been true, but Charles Murphy believes that the decision was based on hardheaded economics. "They got out because they were more interested in promoting economic development and making wheelbarrows than in doing anything to further defense science," said Murphy.[12]

The government report on Canada's space program, drawn up in May 1967, was critical of HARP, but it provided the perfect public platform against the private government decision to cancel HARP's funding. It stated that Canada needed a major commitment to a space program if the country was to have any influence at all on the progress of technical space research.

Today, Canada has no space program whatsoever and does no work of any significance in missiles or rocketry. Instead, Canada is entirely dependent on the United States and other NATO allies for defense equipment. Canada has never even put a satellite into space.

Bull's dependence on the United States was one of Ottawa's main objections to HARP. Yet it was the only program that might have produced a worthwhile contribution to the space race, which Ottawa itself had acknowledged would need a major commitment in order to make any difference. There seems little doubt that HARP could have had an impact on Canada and possibly the world by making space accessible to countries that otherwise would have been excluded by high costs. During the first years of the HARP experiment, Bull's guns were restricted by the small amount of weight they could carry. But as Martlet 1 evolved into Martlet 2 and 3, followed by plans for Martlet 4, the missiles were flying farther and carrying larger payloads. The rapid progress of chip technology would have eventually made it possible to launch small satellites into space. Instead of an exclusive club limited to rich nations, space could have been available to poor countries as well.

From the outset, however, Bull had been limited by the size of the guns available from the U.S. Navy. No gun larger than the sixteen-inch existed, and barrels were limited as to how far they could be extended in the search for greater velocities. But, at the time of the project's cancellation, Bull and Murphy had designed an even bigger gun, twice the size of the sixteen-inch. Bull estimated that the gun would have a five-hundred-foot-long barrel and weigh three thousand tons. Using seven thousand pounds of powder, the gun would be able to fire a sixteen-thousand-pound projectile hundreds of miles. Alternatively, the gun could fire a thousand-pound payload into a hundred-nautical-mile orbit, or a hundred-pound payload could be fired into a five-hundred-mile orbit at a cost of approximately $50,000. Bull estimated that the cost of manufacturing such a gun would be around $1.5 million.

This gun, Bull believed, would justify all his work on HARP. Building a new, larger gun from scratch would be the ultimate vindication of his faith in gun-launched space exploration. Early drawings of this enormous gun show a long barrel, recessed into a large pit in the ground, and supported by two stupendous scaffolds through which the barrel thrusts toward the sky.

The cancellation of HARP affected Bull deeply. He was unable to understand how the Canadians could have behaved so stupidly. As far as Bull was concerned, HARP had been a triumph. He had delivered everything he had promised, and yet his own government had betrayed him, cutting off support just at the moment it was essential for the project's survival. Now he would have to do it on his own. Driven by loyalty to his staff who had lost their jobs and by a firm belief in HARP, he had no compunction about making the move he had considered seven years earlier and heading south of the border. The seeds of his future had been sown.

S E V E N

ARTHUR D. LITTLE
AND THE COMPOUND
PRINCIPLE

THE HARP program never really recovered from the move south. The old boy network may have persuaded Norwich University to sponsor Bull, but this deeply conservative college showed considerable nervousness at accepting such a high-profile and controversial project. Neither side was particularly comfortable with the other, and the relationship proved to be a short-lived and unhappy affair. Before the relationship began, however, the administrators contacted the consulting firm of Arthur D. Little for advice.

Arthur D. Little founded his company in 1886, when he was a young member of the faculty at the Massachusetts Institute of Technology. After setting up MIT's chemical engineering department, Little decided to create his own research and consulting firm. ADL had a difficult beginning because the need for a service to address the problems of corporate technology had not been recognized. Nevertheless, the company gained a reputation for resolving apparently intractable situations, a reputation that was enhanced during World War II when ADL assisted in a variety of projects, including effective management for the D-day landings.[1]

In 1935, Arthur D. Little died, leaving his majority stake in the company to MIT. Little had no children, but a nephew, Royal Little, a successful businessman in his own right, had been raised almost as a son and had taken a keen interest in the company, serving as a member of the board. Royal borrowed ten thousand dollars in 1923 and launched the Special Yarns Corporation, drawing on experience he had gained working at ADL in the development of artificial silk. The company evolved first into the Atlantic Rayon Corporation and then into Textron, generally considered to be the first conglomerate. By the early 1970s Textron had fifty thousand employees at 150 plants and annual sales—of machine tools, flatware, golf carts, chain saws —of more than $3 billion. While Textron had no formal connection with ADL, Royal remained on the board of both companies, and he would occasionally seek the advice of ADL's experts when planning an acquisition.

Meanwhile, the Arthur D. Little company was promoting an atmosphere of creative fervor, where all employees were encouraged to think of brilliant new ideas, such as an antitheft device for automobiles and an automatic toilet bowl cleaner. The scientists at ADL failed to produce the perfectly shaped golf ball, however, despite considerable investment in test machinery and management time on the golf course.

In 1953, Royal Little devised a clever scheme to establish a profit-sharing trust for ADL employees that would reduce the company's tax liability and provide a pension plan for the staff. He set up a new vehicle for this called the Memorial Drive Trust (MDT). As representative of the new trust, Royal arranged with MIT, which owned 55 percent of ADL, to sell its shares to MDT for an initial payment of $1.3 million. He also arranged for MDT's acquisition of MIT's remaining ADL stock over the following nine years through a loan from the First National Bank of Boston. This scheme, which MIT later regretted, was made possible because Royal was on the board of MDT and the MIT trust that held the ADL shares and so had some influence over the outcome. The deal was financed by the First National Bank of Boston, using the stock that was being purchased as collateral. Every year, MDT would take about 15 percent of each employee's earnings and invest it in a number of projects that produced sufficient return to make many of them millionaires upon retirement.

Royal had no interest in running MDT and started looking for someone to take the job. At the time, he kept an apartment at the Boston Tennis and Racquet Club—one of the few real tennis (an "unusual variation on tennis" imported from England) clubs in the country—where he played regularly. He eventually played against Jean de Valpine, a young man with a master's degree in engineering and a degree from Harvard Law School. The two men got along well, and Royal decided that de Valpine was the man to head up MDT. He appointed him chief executive officer shortly thereafter.

The Memorial Drive Trust was worth about $10 million when de Valpine took over in 1960. Instead of acting like most trustees and investing in U.S. Treasury bonds and conservative stocks, de Valpine, with Royal's support, put MDT money into more risky ventures, such as cable television, semiconductors, computer technology, robotics, and artificial intelligence. Most people had never heard of these inventions, but de Valpine was able to spot the trends. As a result, MDT became a leading venture capital investor in the post–World War II technological revolution.

De Valpine's aggressive investing and his preoccupation with backing individuals on the cutting edge of scientific thinking made MDT a huge financial success.

When the funding for HARP was about to be withdrawn, ADL suggested to de Valpine that Bull might be an appropriate investment for the Memorial Drive Trust. While at Harvard, de Valpine had spent four years in ROTC working with field artillery, and he had been commissioned into an artillery unit during World War II.

"Taking three class hours per week in the history and theory of field artillery, the science and tactics, must have enhanced the enjoyment of my association with Jerry Bull and the SRC," said de Valpine, "not to mention the many more hours of drill and my regular courses in engineering, mathematics, physics, probability, and statistics. Ultimately, however, I declined the opportunity to invest in SRC. I thought it was an inappropriate venture for the MDT."

Obviously, de Valpine was not convinced that SRC could be a success, so he discussed Bull's ideas with General James M. Gavin. In 1958, Gavin, the youngest divisional commander in World War II, and the commanding general of the airborne division at Arnhem in the Netherlands, resigned as chief of the army's research and development branch to become executive vice-president of ADL. He would eventually become president, chief executive officer, and finally chairman. Gavin, through his Pentagon connections, had helped General Trudeau expedite the delivery of surplus equipment, including sixteen-inch guns, to Bull's sites at Barbados and Highwater.

When ADL was asked by Norwich University to evaluate Bull's operation, Gavin brought his considerable consulting skills to the table. At the time, high-risk and innovative ventures on the frontiers of science triggered fervent institutional enthusiasm. ADL had none of the hesitancy about pursuing such projects that had plagued the U.S. Army or the Canadian government. On the contrary, ADL's philosophy was based on a heady mixture of hardheaded business sense and seat-of-the-pants entrepreneurship.

Clearly, Space Research Corporation was in parlous financial condition, having no resources and no visible management team. Bull was surviving only by soliciting donations from his ever-supportive father-in-law. His staff of talented scientists had been accustomed to working in the cloistered environment of academia, where government grants and facilities were the sole means of support. They, especially, felt threatened.

Just as Norwich was speaking to ADL about HARP and SRC, the Great West Saddlery Company (GWS), a Canadian investment firm, had been in touch with Bull to discuss his need for financial assistance. Great West Saddlery was owned by EDPER Corporation, named for its founders, Edward and Peter Bronfman. The Bronfman family owned Seagram's and founded the Distillery Corporation of America. Although the family had divided, Edgar and Peter's share of the fortune was substantial,

accounting for approximately 12 percent of the total capitaliza-
tion of the Toronto Stock Exchange in 1990.[2]

The Bronfmans, who were based in Montreal, had read about
the trials of SRC, and Peter had seen an opportunity for investment. He contacted Bull, who was, naturally, enthusiastic. The
men agreed to meet. Bull called his old friend Reed Johnston,
who was now established at ADL, and asked him to attend as a
friendly adviser. The meeting was conducted largely in French,
which Johnston had trouble understanding, since much of the
discussion related to accountancy and technical matters. In a
break between talks, however, Johnston found himself standing
next to Peter Bronfman.

"It must be nice to have the kind of funding to facilitate a
promising situation like this," Johnston told him. "But to walk
into something about which you know very little is almost ir-
responsible. You need help from someone with research capability and who understands the technology."[3]

The meeting broke up; nothing had been decided. Bull drove
home to Montreal and Johnston stayed overnight at Jerry's
Highwater house. The next morning, the telephone rang. One of
the Bronfmans' accountants was on the line.

"What you said [last night] had us talking all the way home,"
Johnston was told. "We want to make an offer. We will put up
the first one million dollars and split the company fifty-fifty
with ADL, if ADL will match our investment, dollar for dollar,
after the first one million has been spent."

Johnston relayed the proposition to Gavin at ADL, who had
by now done some work on behalf of Norwich. In a discussion
with Jack Cockwell, the South African accountant who ran the
Bronfman financial empire, Gavin proposed that ADL form a
new corporation to be called the Space Research Corporation.
ADL would own 51 percent of the shares, while Great West
Saddlery would own 49 percent. GWS agreed to this arrangement with the proviso that ADL would provide the management if GWS delivered the funds. This effectively froze out
Norwich University, which was perfectly happy to get rid of an
operation that was totally unsuitable for the college. All debts
would be paid by GWS, and Giltaur would receive shares in

GWS worth between $1.5 and $2 million. Giltaur would then distribute these shares to its shareholders and go into liquidation. Bull was named technical director of the new company. Concurrently, Bull would form a second company called SRC-Q (for Quebec) that would handle some of the administrative matters for the Canadian side of the operation.

De Valpine originally planned to hire a retiring air force or army general to oversee SRC and had interviewed several candidates. But he soon realized that Bull would have firm ideas about how SRC should develop and would not be receptive to a retired general coming into the company and trying to order him around. So de Valpine took the line of least resistance and collaborated with Jack Cockwell from Great West Saddlery to put some qualified accountants and the proper financial controls into place.

One of the men whom ADL hired to manage SRC was Jere Lundholm, then in his mid-thirties. Lundholm was charged with administering the SRC contracts office in North Troy. He had come from ADC, a company that had been involved in a fair number of apparently crazy schemes and he had met more than his share of dedicated scientists who understood almost nothing of the real world, particularly business. From the outset of his one-year stay at SRC, Lundholm found that Bull had little or no interest in the financial side of the enterprise. New work was undertaken not because it was necessarily profitable, but because it was interesting. Despite his lack of business savvy, Bull insisted on having control over every aspect of the operation.

"He would talk about his projects and have people in the palm of his hand," recalled Lundholm. "But then nothing would come of them. He was so convinced that what he was doing made sense and that he could get from A to C without going though B that it was difficult to persuade him otherwise."[4]

As accountants arrived from ADL and SRC began businesslike operations for the first time, someone (nobody can remember just who) suggested that SRC had a useful asset in the U.S.-Canadian border. Out of these discussions emerged the

Compound Principle, an exceptional deal whereby U.S. and Canadian officials administered both sides of the border owned by Bull within the SRC compound. Gus Bleyle, an ADL man who had been appointed acting president of SRC, negotiated the agreement.

A road was built from the Canadian side to the American side with the permission of the International Boundary Commission. An administrative building was constructed on the American side with grants provided by the Vermont Development Board. The facility was considered to be under the control of the United States, even though the vast majority of the complex, including the production center, the explosives store, the launch control center, the maintenance facility, the forge, and the radar equipment, was in Canada. Only the electronics laboratory and the administration offices were in the United States. All U.S. and Canadian customs and employment approvals were granted with the understanding that SRC was a U.S. corporation and operated under U.S. laws.

The entire staff was on the U.S. corporation's payroll. Canadian citizens were required to enter and exit through the north gate, which was under the control of SRC security and watched over by officials from Canadian customs and immigration. U.S. citizens came to work at the other end of the site, under the supervision of American customs and immigration services.

The intention of this arrangement was to let SRC exploit any legal differences that may have existed between Canada and the United States. While this was not illegal by itself and may have been smart business, the concept certainly drove a large truck through the legislation in both countries specifically designed to control the export of technology and arms.

"I did not work it so that both the U.S. and Canada had an interest in every project," says de Valpine, "but rather that each project, except those performed under U.S. military auspices, could plausibly be claimed as either U.S. or Canadian in origin.

"What I tried to accomplish from the beginning was the structure of corporate subsidiaries, together with the requisite evidentiary substantiation to establish that the technology was of Canadian origin, so that when desirable or appropriate sale or transmission of the technology to other countries could be positioned as being from the Montreal office and thus not requiring any sort of U.S. export license or other authorization, thus obviating the potential of charges of violations of U.S. statutes relating to the export of arms or related technology. The reverse position, namely that the technology was U.S. based, could easily be claimed where U.S. licenses were obtainable and Canadian were not. As I recall it, however, the concern was, as a practical matter, almost exclusively with respect to possible difficulties on the U.S. side."

Although SRC was a high-profile company that received considerable attention from regulatory officials in a number of government agencies, it is inconceivable that no one was aware of exactly what was happening at the compound. On the contrary, officials on both sides of the border must have known and accepted SRC's bizarre way of operating, which allowed Bull and his colleagues to deal arms through loopholes in the laws of two countries that interpreted the rules for arms exports very differently.

Bull formally resigned from his position at McGill in May 1969. Clearly reluctant to sever all connections with his former academic home, he proposed that a graduate studies program be established at the Space Research Corporation directly affiliated with the university. But the world had moved on and the bloom had gone from Bull's projects. The university wrote back, saying that the faculty was hesitant to enter into such an agreement and that the university had commitments and higher priorities elsewhere. This calculated slight effectively ended Bull's relationship with McGill, although he remained very good friends with Don Mordell until Mordell died in 1988.

As soon as SRC was under ADL's control, the Cambridge company ran into some problems of its own. In 1969 ADL heard rumors that outsiders were interested in buying the company from the Memorial Drive Trust. Royal Little did not mind selling if the right offer came along, but he had no idea how much ADL was worth. To test the market, he decided to offer 30 percent of the shares to the public.

Prior to the offering, a complete audit of ADL's investments

was carried out and SRC came into the picture. It was losing
money (as it always did), and while it wasn't a major investment, some argued that it might adversely influence the sale of
ADL shares. A pragmatic decision was made to remove a losing
operation from the books and transfer it to de Valpine at MDT
by way of a dividend in kind, the dividend being valued for
transfer purposes at one dollar.

Almost two years had passed since de Valpine had turned
down SRC as an investment for MDT, claiming that it would
be inappropriate. "But Jerry's considerable charisma," de Valpine recalls, "had persuaded ADL to become directly involved.
Then, in November 1969, the SRC opportunity, which I had
specifically declined, arrived in my lap as a company dividend."

As far as ADL was concerned, this was nothing more than
an internal accounting matter, but the Bronfmans did not see it
that way. Just before Christmas 1969, Peter Bronfman called
Jean de Valpine at his Cambridge home. He was extremely upset
that the shares had been transferred. "I am dismayed," Bronfman said, "that the stock has been declared a dividend to MDT.
We made our investment on the basis that the company would
be managed by ADL. We believe that MDT has inherited a
moral obligation to ensure a proper business management is in
place. I insist that you become chairman."

And so Jean de Valpine became head of SRC, a position he
never sought. He actually enjoyed it at first. He and Jerry Bull
were visionaries, men who believed they could cross the bound-
aries set in place by lesser mortals. Even now, when de Valpine
talks about Bull, he becomes animated, his conversation punc-
tuated by a short, barking laugh as he remembers the happy
times he spent with a man he once respected and admired. Interestingly, de Valpine described Bull as warm, outgoing, and
responsive, but so truculent that he was self-defeating. Family
and friends all talk about Jerry's sense of humor, but de Valpine
sees it slightly differently. "He laughed at people, but he was
really laughing at the bureaucracy. He had a considerable caus-
tic wit and was an excellent mimic. He always referred to those
who got in his way as clowns."

Today, de Valpine is in his late sixties and remains as imaginative and enthusiastic as he was when he joined MDT over thirty-one years ago. In his office in the ADL complex at Acorn Park in Cambridge, he speaks with a boyish excitement about beam-riding shells, Star Wars, and artificial intelligence, bouncing up from his desk to illustrate a point on the green chalkboard that lines one wall below a picture of a HARP gun. An immensely likable man, he intended to make MDT and ADL two of the most innovative companies of the century—and he succeeded. MDT is now worth between $500 and $750 million, excluding the pension benefits paid to former ADL employees, which totaled between $300 and $400 million.

But there is an air of regret in de Valpine's conversation, as of a dream soured. Back when his relationship with Bull was in its infancy, de Valpine believed he could sort him out, help him overcome his financial irresponsibility and translate his scientific talents into the hard cash that would make everyone rich. When de Valpine became head of SRC, however, the man with the apparently infallible touch lost his good judgment.

Bull and his colleagues had not given up their dream of putting a satellite into space, but there was simply no money to do it— either for the ground tests or the manufacture of the Martlet 4, the multistage rocket that would loft the satellite into orbit— so the idea had been postponed indefinitely. Bull was being forced to diversify away from pure space research.

At the time, one of SRC's main sources of income was a number of contracts with NASA to explore the effects of meteorites on satellites by test-firing small projectiles at very high velocities in the lab. These contracts had dried up rather quickly, and by the end of the 1960s, this source of income had virtually vanished.

Then ADL sent Reed Johnston to work at Highwater for six months. While Bull remained obsessed with the big gun, Johnston was convinced that SRC's economic future depended on artillery, arguing that however effective a gun-launched satellite system might be, rockets would always be able to carry larger payloads. Bull and Johnston debated the issue long and hard.

"I took a very strong view that the only real money in SRC would come from artillery," recalls Johnston. "Rocket development was moving ahead so fast that it would never be possible to push enough payload into space from a gun. As fast as a new gun design could be produced, rockets would be one step ahead. I think Jerry finally understood this."

On the other hand, Bull's Martlet shell was revolutionary. Its aerodynamic design gave it 40 to 50 percent greater range than that of a conventional shell. Johnston was certain that all branches of the military in the U.S. and abroad would be very interested in a shell that could fire farther and with greater accuracy than anything else available. He went to Washington to discuss a possible contract with the U.S. Navy. At a meeting in the Pentagon, however, the navy officials said that all they were interested in was owning the design rights to the shell, not merely the royalty-free use of the technology. At that, Johnston picked up his briefcase and started to walk out of the room. The result of this brinkmanship was a contract for some design work on the five-inch shell, worth about $56,000.

Suddenly Bull was moving out of the strictly scientific arena and into the world of Washington politics. During the summer of 1970, for example, a dinner was held in Bull's honor at the Chevy Chase Country Club in Bethesda, Maryland. Although the dinner was in fact for him, Bull had insisted that the invitations designate Mr. and Mrs. Peter Bronfman and Dr. and Mrs. Jean de Valpine as the nominal honorees.

The club is perhaps the most exclusive country club in the Washington area, with a two- or three-year waiting list for memberships. The main building is designed to resemble a grand southern plantation house, with enormous white pillars flanking the entrance. The main dining room, which serves indifferent food, overlooks the private golf course.

Attended by forty-three people (Jack Cockwell from GWS came without a partner), the guest list included some of the most prominent Washington figures of the time: Senator Winston Prouty, a longtime supporter of the HARP project; Senator Barry Goldwater; General William C. Westmoreland; and Rear Admiral Stansfield Turner, the executive officer to the chief of naval operations, Admiral Elmo Zumwalt.

At the dinner, de Valpine was seated next to Dr. John S. Foster, Jr., the assistant secretary of defense for research and development, the civilian official overseeing all U.S. military research and development for all three services. Foster, who had clearly been well briefed about SRC, told de Valpine that he was very impressed with Bull and his work.

After dinner, de Valpine and Bull had a nightcap with another guest, General Henry A. Miley, the head of the Army Materiel Command. The three men gossiped about officers de Valpine recalled serving with during his time with the Twenty-fifth Infantry Division. Bull and de Valpine spent the next day with Stansfield Turner, who was later to become director of the CIA, in the Pentagon. Turner was a keen supporter of Bull's work, and the subject of their discussion was the 130-mm M-46 Russian-made artillery that was being used by the North Vietnamese army to hold back U.S. Navy destroyers off the coast of Vietnam. The Russian gun had a much greater range than any gun on the American vessels. Turner wanted Bull to upgrade the navy's five-inch guns. He was also interested in the possibility of using Bull's big guns to bombard the Ho Chi Minh Trail from South Vietnam. At the time, attacks on the trail, which was the Vietcong's main supply route, were being carried out entirely by air. Some officials in the Pentagon believed that Bull's sixteen-inch guns could provide accurate and almost continuous bombardment of the trail, in the same way that the Germans had shelled Paris with their giant gun in World War I. Nothing came of this idea, however.

The result of the meeting was a contract to develop a new shell that would extend the range of the five-inch guns from fourteen to twenty-five miles, sufficient range to attack and destroy the Vietnamese shore batteries. SRC manufactured approximately three thousand of these shells and delivered them to the navy, hoping that the contract would lead to others. But, as in all military organizations, there was a reluctance in the navy to accept that an outsider had come up with a good idea. As a result, Bull's new design never received a large-scale contract.

Ironically, the army, which had been Bull's original source of support, showed no interest in the new shell. The army had been doing research on a rocket-assisted projectile of its own. While this projectile had an improved range, it was inaccurate. For some reason, the army was not prepared to have Bull come in and show them how to do their job.

The contract for the five-inch shells was executed at the same time the navy was reorganizing its research laboratories. After World War II, the navy had virtually given up on all gun research and development, believing that the future lay in missiles and other systems such as aircraft carriers and submarines. Belatedly, the navy realized that it had prematurely written off the gun. Now the navy was concerned that the army seemed to be getting ahead of them in gun technology. Even worse, the army was using navy equipment to do so.

At this point, the new extended-range round that Bull had refined to fit several artillery systems was receiving a great deal of international interest. Between October and November 1970, a number of demonstration firings were held at Barbados and Unterlüss, West Germany, with officials from Britain, Portugal, France, Australia, Belgium, Italy, and the U.S. in attendance. As a result of these tests, Bull produced a detailed eighty-page document entitled "New Dimensions in Ballistics," which explained how his new ammunition worked and described the increased performance it made possible. SRC officials used this document for many years as part of their sales pitch.

In the paper's summary, Bull produced five reasons why the extended-range ammunition was so effective:

1. The principle of extending the range of artillery projectiles by means of efficient aerodynamic design has been demonstrated. The result is a greater delivered weight to a greater range than is otherwise presently possible.
2. Saboted projectiles were successfully fired through muzzle attachments such as muzzle brakes. The way is thus open to the use of segmented sabots in place of "pot" or "cup" type sabots in weapons fitted with brakes or flash suppressors. Segmented sabots generally afford a more rapid and clean separation than one-piece sabots, and are therefore preferable from the point of view of accuracy.

3. Previous firings have shown that the dispersion of the Extended Range Ammunition is equal to or better than that of standard shells.

4. Extended Range Ammunition gives an added versatility to existing weapons systems. In effect, it permits a weapon firing extended range Ammunition to compete with weapons of larger caliber firing standard shells. Thus the 155mm gun matches the 175mm gun, the 155mm howitzer can compete with the 155mm gun (reduced charge), and the standard shells by both using extended-range ammunition, which has a more efficient distribution of mass and the selection of materials with better fragmentation characteristics.

5. The low drag profile of the shells results in a smaller velocity loss than that of conventional projectiles. This provides a shorter time-to-altitude for an anti-aircraft role or a flatter trajectory and greater effective range for anti-armor applications.

Bull had invented and successfully tested a whole new generation of artillery shells that fired farther and were more accurate and more lethal than anything available on the world market. His work, a natural evolution of the HARP program, was years ahead of its time and became the foundation of many fledgling arms industries in developing countries. At this stage, however, Bull was concentrating on the United States, a market he knew and thought he understood.

As one decade moved into another, the American commitment in Vietnam was drawing to a close, and so was the impetus behind U.S. weapons programs. Creative thinking, which had been a hallmark of some officials in the Pentagon, no longer sparked the search for new systems. Bull, along with other contractors, who were dependent on the largess of the Department of Defense, began the fast slide toward bankruptcy. Once again, however, the Canadians, whom Bull had continued to vilify, appeared to offer a helping hand.

E I G H T

SWIMMING WITH THE
SHARKS

AFTER THE Canadian government cut off funding and attempted to destroy all the equipment and documents related to HARP, Jerry Bull had banned any government officials from coming to Highwater. But in September 1971, he invited Ed Bobyn, an old friend from CARDE, to stay for the weekend. Bobyn was now chief of research and development in the Canadian Department of National Defence.

During what was intended to be a purely social weekend, the conversation eventually got around to the raw deal Bull believed he had received from the Canadians. Bobyn acknowledged the criticism but argued that the mood in Ottawa had changed.

SRC was really a Canadian company, Bobyn told Bull; it was ill-equipped to compete on Capitol Hill against the ferocious lobbying power of the huge U.S. defense contractors. Bobyn was familiar with the state of SRC's finances, and he dangled a large carrot in front of Bull in the shape of a contract to develop a new 105-mm training round that had been perfected in Canadian laboratories. A number of other such projects needed the expertise of a Canadian defense manufacturer, Bobyn told Bull, and SRC was the perfect company to provide it. Bull would simply have to move SRC's U.S. operations to SRC-Q, the largely dormant Canadian division.

If Bull moved his operation to Canada, Bobyn said, shifting 85 percent of the company's employees to the Canadian payroll and transferring all its Canadian assets onto the books of SRC-Q, then he was sure that Ottawa would adopt a much more supportive attitude. To reinforce his argument, Bobyn argued that the circumstances at the Canadian defense department had changed in the three years since HARP had ended. At the time, HARP had been competing with the Black Brant project, the Canadian-generated rocket program. The Canadian defense establishment had been reluctant to offer any support to Bull that might have resulted in the cancellation of one of its homegrown projects. At the same time, Bobyn understood that the Canadian relationship with HARP had never been easy, damaged on the one hand by Bull's critical and arrogant treatment of most government officials and on the other by a consistent unwillingness on the part of the Canadians to invest the sums required.

The scrapping of the HARP program had removed it as a threat to the system, and the severing of the financial arrangement with McGill had allowed new opportunities to emerge, Bobyn said. Also, he was aware of Bull's final attempt to revive HARP, which had recently failed. Bull had approached GTE-Sylvania of Waltham, Massachusetts, and Continental Telephone of Clayton, Missouri, to try to obtain $10 to $20 million for HARP. He proposed that the big gun in Barbados could be used to launch a satellite that would tie all of their communications systems together, an innovative suggestion for a system that is in general use today. Both GTE and ConTel were initially attracted to the idea, but they eventually decided that it was too risky and too expensive. Their rejection of Bull's idea was the end of any persistent notion concerning the use of big guns for satellite launches.

In the meantime, Bull had been concentrating on the development of extended-range ammunition. Canada had no facilities for manufacturing the shells, so Bull's plan to put together a modern production facility found a healthy symbiosis with the government's need to work on new types of ammunition. The

Canadians knew that Bull, despite the support of MDT and the Bronfmans, was almost bankrupt, and they saw an opportunity for all sides to make money. The Bobyn offer appeared at a time when Peter Bronfman was reconsidering his investment and de Valpine was becoming discouraged. That weekend, Bull agreed in principle to move his operation from SRC to SRC-Q, but he said the changeover could not be completed right away.

Bob Stacey, the faithful Major Blimp, introduced Bull to a lawyer who, in turn, referred him to the First Pennsylvania Bank (PENCO) in Philadelphia. The bank believed Bull's confident predictions. Not only would he secure significant contracts with the Canadian government, but he was also on the verge of making some major deals in the United States. PENCO had no real knowledge of Bull or the arms business, so bank officials took his optimistic projections at face value. As a result, in December 1972, the bank advanced SRC a $5-million loan for which it received stock options that eventually diluted MDT's company holdings to around 20 percent.

At this time there were two Space Research companies, Space Research Corporation, Inc., sometimes referred to as SRC-US, and SRC-Q, the Canadian-based subsidiary of SRC-US. Before the loan from PENCO, SRC-US owned all of SRC-Q, but over the next few years assets, facilities, and contracts were progressively transferred to SRC-Q. Eventually, SRC-US became a minority shareholder in what had once been its subsidiary.

The MDT investment, which had seemed so full possibilities, began to look less attractive. For Jean de Valpine, SRC was a small, unprofitable deal in an otherwise exceptional investment portfolio now worth tens of millions of dollars. MDT's stake was not large and he was content to let the money sit in SRC—it would have been difficult to find a buyer for the stock —in the hope rather than the expectation that Bull might yet deliver some profits. At this stage, SRC was just a small company going through difficult times; MDT saw little additional financial or political risk in sitting tight. The extra PENCO financing gave Bull the working capital he needed to survive. But as a Canadian, Bull was running into constant difficulties delivering the promised American orders for the five-inch shell.

In theory, no real barriers to contracts or to classified material should have existed, provided Bull had the proper clearances (which he did), yet a residual distrust of foreigners, including Canadians, remained within the U.S. defense establishment. In addition, since SRC was still a U.S. corporation and had been established as such, with Bull as one of its corporate officers, certain legal obligations followed. One of those was that he had to get permission from the U.S. government to deal with Canada. He also had to notify the Canadian government, as a Canadian citizen, every time he entered into a contract with the U.S. government. Predictably, all of this red tape annoyed him.

The solution was for Bull to become an American citizen. Allegations have been made that the citizenship issue arose because Bull had been given access to top-secret material that should have been off-limits to foreigners or that he needed urgent clearance to receive secret information in relation to a new contract with the U.S. military. Neither of these theories is true. While at CARDE, Bull had received the necessary clearances to work on ABM projects for NASA, ADL, and the U.S. Defense Department. Those clearances had continued while he was doing research on nuclear fusion and other contracts, although HARP itself had never been classified.

General Trudeau contacted Senator Barry Goldwater, a personal friend and a longstanding supporter of Bull's, to see if he could organize the appropriate formalities. The solution Goldwater offered was to sponsor a special act of Congress to make Bull a naturalized American citizen. This is an extremely rare accolade that has happened only twice before in America's history, for the French revolutionary the Marquis de Lafayette and for Winston Churchill. The legislation was especially extraordinary because Bull, who didn't become a U.S. resident until October 1968, which entitled him to citizenship in 1973, was able to backdate his residences by a special clause in the bill to January 1, 1955, the date on which he had first entered the United States. This clause ensured that no one could be prosecuted retrospectively for allowing Bull access to classified material barred to foreigners.

In submitting his bill for preliminary approval to the Senate

Judiciary Committee, Goldwater argued that it had been necessary for Dr. Bull to enter the United States as a temporary visitor
on numerous occasions in order to fulfill his research responsibilities. "I am informed by Dr. Bull and people who have worked
with him in the United States," Goldwater said, "that the ac-
cumulative total of these many entries into the United States
from Canada far exceeds a year and a half, which would meet
the residence and physical presence requirements of the natu-
ralization statute."

Bull's wife, Mimi, was very much opposed to his changing
his nationality. She was a staunch French Canadian, and the
couple had brought up their children speaking French first and
English second. The children had attended schools that placed a
strong emphasis on French culture, and Mimi's primary loyalty
was to Canada, particularly Quebec. Bull argued that he would
not be losing his Canadian nationality, and spoke to officials in
Ottawa to make certain he could retain two passports. He was
assured that he could, and on that basis Mimi, after keeping him
waiting for a week, signed the necessary waiver and allowed the
legislation to proceed.

Bull also spoke with the Canadian government to ascertain
whether his newfound relations with Ottawa would be placed
in jeopardy if he received U.S. citizenship. He was assured that
it would make no difference.

A number of people wrote letters supporting the bill, including Deane Davis, the Vermont state governor; Sterling Cole, a
former member of Congress; Richard Weiss, the deputy and scientific director of Army Research, Department of the Army; the
ubiquitous General Arthur Trudeau; and even Charles Poor. All
these letters, in fact, had been solicited by Trudeau himself, who
sent them in a single batch to Goldwater.

Trudeau had just retired from the army and had immediately
joined the SRC board. Even so, in his letter to Goldwater, Trudeau simply signed himself "Arthur Trudeau, management consultant," but he was referred to by Goldwater in another letter
as "Arthur Trudeau, U.S. Army retired." While revealing Trudeau's true relationship to SRC might not have materially affected the outcome of Bull's application for citizenship, Goldwater and Trudeau were dishonest in allowing the applica-

tion to go forward the way it did. It was clearly misleading and suggested that Bull had the support of a retired army general who appeared to have no connection to SRC, while in fact Trudeau was then a director of the company, not to mention a close friend of Bull's and an active solicitor of surplus equipment for HARP for many years.

In a further letter to the Senate Judiciary Committee, whose members were questioning Goldwater's unique interpretation of the residency requirements, the senator expanded his argument:

> During the 1962 to 1968 period, Dr. Bull was stationed at a defense installation whose territory crossed onto both sides of the Canadian–United States border, and as a result of this unique situation, he came into U.S. territory almost daily. There was no customs or passport office set up at the facility, and personnel would routinely cross the border, which was not isolated by barriers, in the normal course of their work.

This letter was not an accurate reflection of the facts, with its clear implication that the Highwater site was free of all customs and immigration controls. There were checkpoints on both the Canadian and U.S. entry points to the SRC compound, although the records of Bull's entrances and exits might not have been readily available, given the relaxed atmosphere at the site.

Despite the inconsistencies in Goldwater's argument, which twisted both the fact and purpose of the law, he won over the Senate, which passed the bill in August 1972. The House followed suit in October.

With American citizenship and a new deal with the Canadian government, Bull must have felt as though his setbacks were history. A new era was about to break.

The Canadians transferred the registered patent rights for the Spinning Tubular Projectile (STUP) training-round ammunition to SRC-Q, and a contract was drawn up splitting the development costs equally between Bull and the Canadian government. At the same time, the Dutch army placed a contract with SRC-Q worth $750,000 through the Canadian Commercial Corporation (the arms-dealing branch of the government) to pay for the development of the 155-mm extended-range round.

Then the Belgian firm Poudrières Réunis de Belgique (PRB) appeared with a check for $75,000 and a request that SRC-Q demonstrate a 155-mm round with a range of eighteen miles. Although the tests were successful, pressure from Rheinmetall, the German arms manufacturer, which was working on a similar round, prevented PRB from proceeding with the contract.

However, when PRB heard about the Dutch army contract, which included a clause allowing the Dutch company Eurometaal to manufacture the shells, they considered it a serious threat. It could have left them without a contract to make the shell that was expected to dominate the market for several years. Consequently, Joseph Severin, the director-general of PRB, flew to Highwater and proposed to Bull that they establish a joint venture. Though Severin became one of Bull's close friends and an apparent ally as Bull inched his way into unknown international territory, there are no innocents in the arms business. Severin was an experienced operator who knew a naive inventor when he saw one.

Bull appeared to have seen Severin simply as a likable businessman, a description Bull gave of him in a document submitted to his lawyers in 1979.

> He was not an aristocrat, but a mining engineer, born in Bastogne, Belgium, his father the station master and his mother a school teacher. However, he proved (I am told) his brilliance in Zaire, which was previously owned by the Belgians (Belgian Congo) and where Société Générale had vast holdings. He had a superhuman amount of energy, and a brain that could quickly grasp the situation and make the compromise necessary to win his point, but always ultimately turning out to be exactly as he originally desired. His deals he never revealed—even though he considered me a close friend. In fact few people (and I think it would be more

accurate to say none) in PRB knew his ultimate goal. This I was privileged to know, although vaguely. PRB would expand (after some shoulder charges) into North America, which he admired, and Brazil, which he felt he could control. He felt that the low productivity, poor workmanship, dominance of the unions and high costs limited the future of his company in Belgium to within five years.

Severin argued that a joint venture was in everybody's interests. As part of a huge group controlled by Société Générale de Belgique (SGB), PRB had access to significant markets, while SRC had the design skills that PRB lacked.

They decided to form a new company, Space Research Corporation International (SRC-I), based in Brussels, under a scheme code-named Project 8. PRB and SRC-Q would each own 38 percent of the new company. Twenty percent of the company was given to Eurometaal, at the suggestion of Severin; this was a convenient way of eliminating the threat of Dutch control over the market for the extended-range round and was never meant as a serious business proposition. A further 4 percent was held by H&FI, a Belgian marketing company. Soon after the deal was agreed upon, Eurometaal was squeezed out and PRB took over the manufacturing as well.

The extended-range round went through a number of refinements as Bull tried to find a reliable way to obtain the extra range without sacrificing payload or the safety of the gun crews. When a barrel is over one hundred feet long, sabot fragments scatter well clear of gun crews. With more conventional artillery pieces with standard barrels, however, the risk of injury is great.

After some months of work, Bull settled on a shell that had a bore of 150mm for a 155-mm barrel. He placed small knobs near the nose of the shell to stabilize the front end and a band made out of composite plastic at the base. When the shell left the barrel, the knobs fell off and the plastic band disintegrated to dust. A further refinement was then added in the shape of a base bleed system, invented in Sweden, which involved attaching a container to the bottom of the shell that ignited in flight.

But despite his connections in North America, it was neither the United States nor Canada that produced the orders for Bull's shells. In 1972, Yitzhak Rabin, Israel's ambassador in Washington, asked Henry Kissinger if the U.S. could supply a strategic shell that would give the Israelis enough range to hit the Syrian capital, Damascus, from the Golan Heights. Kissinger came up with Jerry Bull and SRC. The first order was completed in time for Israel to deploy five thousand extended-range shells during the 1973 Arab-Israeli war.

Immediately after the war, Bull was invited to Tel Aviv. The Israelis took Bull out into the desert and showed him the destruction that had been wrought on their tanks by Egypt's Russian-supplied antiarmor missiles. The simplicity and effectiveness of the technology impressed Bull; he pointed out to the Israelis that his shells were designed on exactly the same principles.[1]

During the visit, Bull was introduced to Shaul Eisenberg, Israel's most successful arms dealer at the time. Eisenberg had sold nearly every weapon Israel had produced, from grenades to fighter planes. A few weeks after Bull's visit, Eisenberg went to Highwater and was so impressed that he suggested to Bull he might make an offer for the company. But Bull was feeling optimistic. He had deals with Canada, Israel, and Holland in hand and several others in the pipeline, and he wasn't ready to sell.

The Israelis then asked Bull if he could deliver a second contract for extended-range ammunition, which could be filled via the U.S. Navy or directly by SRC, which the Israelis preferred. In an effort to get their new joint venture off the ground, Bull suggested to Severin that SRC-I should be used as the vehicle for the contract. SRC-Q would provide the designs and the metal components, Eurometaal would make the shells, and PRB would finance and administer the contract.

However, the contract, known by the code name Norway, ran into difficulties at PRB, which had a large number of Arab customers who the company feared might take exception to an Israeli contract. The problem was overcome by Bull's setting up a shell company in Barbados, SRC-B, where the contract was transferred from SRC-I. Errol Barrow, ever cooperative with Bull's projects, personally signed several import and export permits in advance so that raw materials and finished shells could transit through Barbados. But this arrangement failed to satisfy the Arab supporters inside PRB and SGB, delaying the delivery of raw materials. Finally, Bull was told that the contract with Israel had been canceled. By this time, late 1973, the changeover of operations from SRC-US to SRC-Q was complete, so Bull persuaded Eurometaal to supply the raw materials to SRC-Q, and he manufactured the shells at Highwater. By 1975, SRC had sold fifteen thousand shells directly to the Israelis.

Bull later learned that the Israelis had sold a third of the ammunition to the shah of Iran in order to raise enough cash to pay for the whole of their contract with SRC.

During 1974, SRC-Q was hard at work filling the Israeli contract and trying (without success) to win others. Then the Canadian government suggested that SRC-Q take over a company called Beaconing Optics, which had gone into receivership. The government officials suggested that a large number of orders were available for radio direction-finding equipment, but the company had failed to deliver because it lacked the technical expertise. Bull agreed to the deal after he had received assurances from the Canadians that grants to help the new company get going would be available.

Bull's purchase of Beaconing Optics was funded, in part, by Prime Minister Barrow, who had agreed to buy all the SRC equipment still in Barbados, such as air traffic control equipment, over a three-year period. The deal was done with Giltaur, which, in turn, sold its contract for the Barbados income to Paragon Holdings, a new Cayman Islands company that Bull had established to handle the deal. Bull had also formed Shefford Electronics, another new company based in Granby, Quebec, and run by technical director Klaus Urbatzka, who had been transferred from Highwater.

Among the mass of companies that were springing up around this time, two more would become extremely important. The first was Canadian Technical Industries (CTI), which acted as a central holding company for the entire group; the second was Valleyfield Chemical Products Corporation, a former division of the British company Imperial Chemical Industries that had been purchased by CTI. Valleyfield had the only plant in Canada that could manufacture propellants.

In an attempt at diversification, Bull used the newly formed Shefford Electronics to produce air traffic control simulators, drawing on his experience with radar during the HARP program and the knowledge that SRC staff had gained while running air traffic control in Barbados. At the time, air traffic controllers were almost always trained in control towers, an expensive and wasteful use of precious resources. Bull had spotted a useful market niche that he immediately exploited, with some success.

His first customer for the simulators was South Africa, a country that had been subject to a United Nations arms embargo since 1963. Simulators were not embargoed items, however, so there was no restriction on their export.

The minutes of the SRC executive committee of November 4, 1975, opened with Bull, clearly impatient with the formality of the occasion, suggesting that the meeting should be as brief as possible, owing to the multitude of subjects that required his immediate attention.

> Proposals have been sent to Ottawa for contracts with West Germany and America.
> Eight-inch contract is awaiting approval from Congress.
> We are convinced that the Army does recognize the value of our development work.
> South African simulator. This entire program is on schedule and we expect equipment to be in South Africa by 15 November, 1975. Field maintenance engineers are going to South Africa for a year.

Two months later, the executive committee minutes of January 14, 1976, reveal that Bull had reviewed the current contracts.

Much effort has been devoted to winning new contracts.

Our Israeli contracts are on schedule (for 155-mm and 175-mm shells).

We expect an early commitment from them on other projectile contracts.

The installed simulator for South Africa is working perfectly. We have been advised that the official ceremony of acceptance will take place next week. Klaus Urbatzka, the head of the electronics division, will attend. Pictures will be brought back for our use. Urbatzka expects to be given several other contracts from South Africa, mostly in connection with the simulator.

In the space of three years, since moving his operations back to Canada, Jerry Bull had graduated from designer of weapons to arms manufacturer. It was an evolution he welcomed. He had always argued that SRC should move from simple designs to the metal-bashing end of the business. It seemed to Bull a logical development to bring all aspects of the gun business under one roof. But others, such as Reed Johnston at ADL, had advised him against expansion. Even if Bull did not recognize his own weaknesses, his friends knew that he was a hopeless businessman. They believed that the bigger the business, the more likely a disaster became.

Even with the apparent support of the Canadian government and a solid product to sell in the form of the extended-range ammunition, Bull was incapable of running a profitable corporation. For reasons that were always the fault of somebody else, the company consistently traded at a loss, a situation that in the end destroyed SRC.

Bull maintained that from the time he shifted SRC's operations, government officials had promised large grants to his company. When he established Shefford Electronics and bought Valleyfield Chemical, the government told him that he would receive financial aid for creating jobs in a depressed area of Canada. No significant assistance ever materialized.

Writing in 1979, Bull claimed that the company had received

only $160,000 of the $3 million that had been promised. "The Ottawa civil servants are saying that they cannot go ahead because of Bull, an American. . . . Yet I personally can arrange Europeans and Americans to finance the company. . . . We have letters (somewhere) that state a $750,000 grant was refused because the company was too rich. Now we have letters saying the grant cannot even be considered because we are too poor. I gave copies to the Europeans who laughed."

Bull repeatedly portrayed himself as an innocent victim, as the man who had fallen foul of an evil system that had set out to destroy his life's work. There is no doubt that he had made plenty of enemies, but his naïveté was also to blame. Although the deal with PRB was agreed upon in 1973, no signed contracts were actually handed over until 1978, causing SRC's bankers some concern. It was in PRB's interest to keep SRC dangling. While the company was kept in limbo, PRB was gaining access to all of SRC's technology, something that Bull couldn't see because of his friendship with Severin.

As far as Bull was concerned, his American citizenship should have silenced his critics in the United States. But he still showed a lack of understanding of the niceties of Washington politics. The appointment of Arthur Trudeau to the board of SRC at the beginning of the 1970s upset a number of people in the Pentagon. In particular, Charles Poor, who was now deputy assistant secretary of the army for research, development and acquisition, believed that there was an obvious conflict of interest. Poor was not alone.

Bull compounded the criticism by hiring Richard Bissell, a former deputy director of plans at the CIA, as a lobbyist for SRC in Washington. Bissell was a strange choice. After training as an economist at the London School of Economics, he had joined the CIA in 1954. After a few months he had become Allen Dulles's personal assistant and then, as one of the agency's rising stars, he had been promoted to the Plans Directorate, where he was instrumental in bringing about a technological revolution in intelligence gathering.[2]

Bissell recognized that the United States had a major technological advantage in the intelligence war, and he set about ensuring that the agency made the most of it. He was the supreme intelligence operative—dispassionate, calculating, a brilliant analyst. He understood that modern intelligence required a vast array of machinery if information was to be disseminated in a timely fashion.

He funded the development of the U-2 spy plane that provided the evidence of Soviet arms shipments to Cuba in 1962. He then authorized two planned assassination attempts on Fidel Castro and designed the abortive invasion of Cuba at the Bay of Pigs. He also set up the Cosmos satellite surveillance program. In 1962, he resigned from the agency to become a lobbyist in Washington, where he still lives.

Bissell was exceptionally well connected. He knew President John Kennedy well and had worked in the White House before joining the CIA. During his years at the agency he had become friendly with all the primary players in the intelligence community, as well as senior Pentagon officials and members of Congress.

Bull saw Bissell as a man who could assist him in winning much-needed contracts. Bissell saw Bull as a man who had some good ideas to sell about space, a subject in which he maintained an abiding interest.

Poor and others in the Pentagon disliked the idea of an ex-CIA man who had specialized in clandestine operations doing spadework for SRC. Poor was irritated with SRC's sales techniques as exemplified by the company's relationships with Trudeau and Bissell, which he called trying to pull political strings instead of selling SRC products on their own merits. "I was upset with Bull for not pushing his own cart," said Poor.[3]

Bull's relationship with the Israelis was the first of several that he developed with countries outside of his normal customers. Until then, Bull had traveled to scientific conferences abroad and had held meetings with NATO countries, but he had otherwise concentrated his considerable energies in North America. After nearly twenty years of effort, he had very little to show. The HARP program had failed, and his work on more conventional systems went largely unrecognized in the United States. He was convinced that the U.S. Navy had stolen his ideas and that the army had turned against him for political reasons.

Then he was introduced to another kind of customer altogether, from whom he received a completely different welcome. Now he was not just another arms dealer, but almost a savior. He was an innovator, a creator whose work was brilliant and whose talents were worth large amounts of cash. He was courted, flattered, and seduced.

On the surface, Bull appeared to be yet another struggling defense manufacturer doing his best to survive. His business, while not profitable, was picking up. Bull's reports to his executive committee were consistently upbeat.

But the company's growth had been financed almost entirely out of debt, and its survival was dependent on the patronage of his new clients. Even though Bull was no longer swimming in a sea teeming with bureaucrats, he was now in deep among the barracudas and the sharks.

N I N E

THE DEAL

IN 1963, all Western governments endorsed the United Nations arms embargo against South Africa, the home of apartheid. Led by the United States, a policy of noncooperation discouraged companies worldwide from doing business in the country. To some, however, including Jerry Bull, South Africa also represented the last defense against the march of communism in southern Africa after Portugal dismantled its empire in 1974, leaving a chaos of civil war in Mozambique on the east coast and Angola on the west. South Africa also controlled substantial commercial resources, such as gold, diamonds, and uranium, as well as the sea around the strategically vital Cape of Good Hope.

When the arms embargo was imposed, the South African government decided that instead of buying arms abroad, the country would create its own arms-manufacturing capability with the goal of becoming largely self-sufficient. In 1964, with assistance from private industry, two state organizations were established: the Armaments Board, which administered the purchasing of arms and oversaw quality and cost control during production, and the Armaments Development and Production Corporation (Armscor), which handled the actual manufacturing. The Armaments Board later merged with Armscor to create a single entity handling all aspects of arms procurement, development, and production.

Israel might seem an unlikely ally for the oppressive apartheid regime. However, since the founding of the Israeli state in 1948, the two countries had been close. South Africa has a large number of Jews, and the two countries have always been active trading partners. Israel's diamond industry, for example, was developed with South African diamonds. In many respects, Israel has been the country of choice for the South Africans to turn to in times of need. Israel also was the country of choice for the United States when the CIA needed to maintain a covert relationship with Pretoria.[1]

After the 1967 war with the Arabs, Israel had become increasingly isolated. It began to develop an arms industry similar to South Africa's, so that by the mid-1970s, the South Africans could either manufacture under license or import directly from Israel weapons such as the Uzi submachine gun, the Galil rifle, the Reshef fast patrol boat, the Gabriel antiship missile, and several radar and surveillance systems. When Israel suffered heavy tank loses in the first few days of the 1973 war, the only other country that had operational Centurion tanks was South Africa, which shipped most of their stocks to Israel within ten days. These stocks were replaced by the U.S., which shipped spare engines and other parts to Canada, where they were combined with surplus Canadian tanks and sent to South Africa after the war ended. Both friends and members of Bull's family say the shipments were coordinated by Bull, but this claim has been impossible to verify.

The Israelis also sold to South Africa several batteries of the L-39 155-mm gun, which was a copy of the U.S. M198-towed 155-mm howitzer. This transaction broke their agreement with the Americans not to sell U.S.-supplied equipment to third countries without permission.

In addition to this mutually supportive arms relationship, Israel and South Africa regularly shared intelligence and cooperated on developing new weapons, including a ballistic missile system with nuclear capability. This was an entirely secret relationship in which both countries operated in defiance of the United Nations arms embargo in a quest to ensure their survival. In fact, in some respects Israel was actually closer to South Africa than to the United States. The Pretoria government welcomed Tel Aviv's cooperation and reciprocated by allowing Israel access to South African raw materials, including gold, coal, and uranium. Meanwhile, the Israeli government encouraged investment in South Africa so that Israeli industry could exploit the cheap labor made possible by apartheid.

As the colonial empires in the north disintegrated, the South Africans had to prepare their armed forces to defend the country against border skirmishes. The wars of liberation in Zaire, Kenya, Rhodesia, Mozambique, and Angola were not large conventional wars but low-intensity conflicts requiring new strategies and tactics.

The South Africans were extremely threatened by this southward march of liberation movements. Pretoria was convinced that left-wing governments, once established in neighboring countries, would turn their attention to South Africa and either attempt to overthrow the white majority government directly or sponsor cross-border guerrilla operations. The government therefore decided to bring the fight to the enemy, rather than wait for the enemy to come to them.

By adopting this strategy, the South Africans had taken the advice of their Israeli allies, who had trained the South African Defence Forces to fight a guerrilla war. Israeli instructors had taught them about retaliatory strikes and the value of good intelligence and superior equipment. They also had brought members of the Defence Forces to Israel in order to watch Israel's army in action against the Palestinians, and they supplied Israel with large quantities of equipment that was particularly useful in protecting borders, such as passive sound detectors and aerial surveillance systems.

The United States watched these developments with disinterest. Officially, South Africa was a pariah state disliked by Congress and a persistent target of American liberals. Unofficially, both the Nixon and Ford administrations had accepted that South Africa was an important ally and that Soviet advances in southern Africa could be checked only with the support of Pretoria.

As early as 1969, Henry Kissinger, then the U.S. national security adviser, had authored "National Security Study Memorandum 39," which suggested that the United States had five options for dealing with the instability in southern Africa:

1. Closer association with the white regimes to protect and enhance [U.S.] economic and strategic interest.
2. Broader association with both black and white states in an effort to encourage moderation in the white states, to enlist the cooperation of the black states in reducing tensions and the likelihood of increasing cross-border violence, and to encourage improved relations among states in the area.
3. Limited association with the white states and continued association with blacks in an effort to retain some economic, scientific and strategic interest in the white states while maintaining a posture on the racial issue which the blacks will accept, though opposing violent solutions to the problems of the region.
4. Disassociation from the white regimes, with closer relations with the black states, in an effort to enhance U.S. standing on the racial issue in Africa and internationally.
5. Dissociation from both black and white states in an effort to limit U.S. involvement in the problems of the area.

At the time, the third option represented American policy in the area, which was broadly in line with that of the United Nations. But Kissinger proposed that America adopt the second option, which essentially allowed a more pragmatic approach to South Africa that did not actively discourage trade and that reduced U.S. support for the antiapartheid movement in the United Nations.[2]

When Portugal departed from Africa, this essentially passive American policy took a more active turn. In late 1974, as the Portuguese were leaving Angola but before a new independent government had been sworn in, satellite surveillance revealed that the Soviet Union was backing the Popular Movement for the Liberation of Angola (MPLA), one of three guerrilla groups in the country jockeying for political power. This was an alarming development, since Angola had significant raw materials at its disposal, including diamonds and oil. In addition, Angola's road and rail network provided access to its eastern neighbors, including Zaire, Zambia, and Rhodesia. If the Soviets were able to establish a puppet government in Angola, some CIA intelligence analysts argued, then they would be in a position to influence a number of moderate African states, including the South African–controlled state of Namibia.[3]

In the summer of 1975, the Forty Committee, which was responsible for authorizing all major CIA covert operations, approved a mission in Angola, code-named Operation Feature. The agency put John Stockwell, an experienced CIA man with considerable knowledge of Africa, in charge of the project. He was an unfortunate choice. Stockwell had become disillusioned with the CIA and believed that many operations had been authorized not because they were of importance for the security of the United States, but because they were needed to keep the CIA busy. In particular, he felt that neither Henry Kissinger nor his superiors at the CIA really understood Africa, and that if they mounted a covert operation in Angola, the Soviets and their Cuban acolytes would be forced to respond. The provocation of a high-profile response, in turn, would justify the original mission.[4]

With the Soviets supporting the MPLA, Washington's options were limited to the two other groups that had been fighting the Portuguese and were now attempting to seize power in the aftermath of colonial rule. The National Front for the Liberation of Angola (FNLA) was drawn from the 700,000 members of the Bakongo tribe, more than half of whom had fled to Zaire. The FNLA was founded in 1954 by Holden Roberto, who had been fighting the Portuguese with arms from Zaire and China.

Jonas Savimbi, whose politics were a mixture of Mao and African tribalism, split from Roberto in 1966 to form the National Union for the Total Independence of Angola (UNITA). His support came mainly from the Ovimbundo tribe in southern Angola. He too had been receiving arms from the Chinese, but he had also been funded and armed by South Africa. When Kissinger wrote his national security memorandum in 1969, Savimbi was the leader given the least chance of survival.

The support of the Forty Committee for a covert operation in Angola did not meet with the approval of everyone involved. Nathaniel Davis, the assistant secretary of state for African affairs, advised against supplying arms to Savimbi and resigned in August when his advice was ignored.[5]

On July 17, 1975, President Ford approved funding of $14 million for the operation; a further $10.7 million was approved in August. By November 1975, eighty-three CIA officers were stationed in Pretoria, Luanda, Lusaka, and Kinshasa to administer Operation Feature.

Later that year, when the CIA wanted to escalate the operation still further, a discussion ensued between Ed Mulcahy, the deputy assistant secretary of state for African affairs, and Henry Kissinger, resulting in what came to be known at Langley as the "grunt decision." The most accurate description of this episode appears in John Stockwell's book, *In Search of Enemies*, and is worth repeating as a good illustration of how decisions on covert action are sometimes made.

> Potts [the CIA Africa Division chief] turned to Mulcahy and spoke pleasantly. "Well, Ed, what did Kissinger say?"
>
> Mulcahy tamped his pipe and sucked on it for a few moments, apparently having trouble framing an answer. Potts watched him quietly.
>
> Finally, Mulcahy spoke. "He didn't exactly say anything."
>
> "Did he read the paper?"
>
> "Oh, yes. I took it to him myself, just a few minutes before he left for Peking. I insisted he read it."
>
> "You mean he didn't make any comment? He just read it and took off?" Potts looked baffled and exasperated.
>
> Mulcahy nodded ruefully. "He read it. Then he grunted and walked out of his office."
>
> "Grunted?"
>
> "Yeah, like *unnph*," Mulcahy grunted.

"He's going to be gone ten days." Potts scowled. "What are we supposed to do in Angola in the meantime? We have to make decisions today."

Mulcahy shrugged helplessly. They looked at each other.

"Well, was it a positive grunt or a negative grunt?" Potts asked.

Mulcahy studied for a moment, considering. "It was just a grunt. Like *unnph*. I mean it didn't go up or down."

. . . Mulcahy grunted again, emphasizing a flat sound. Down the table someone else tried it, experimenting with the sound of a positive grunt, then a negative one, his voice rising, then falling. Others attempted it while Potts and Mulcahy watched.

On the basis of their interpretation of the grunt, they decided that inaction was the best policy. No decision was made.

Despite such arbitrary decision-making, Operation Feature was swiftly established as a major CIA program. Planeloads of weapons were sent to the FNLA via Zaire, as was an American merchant vessel loaded with armored personnel carriers, rifles, mortars, and ammunition. In theory, the weapons were for Zaire's army, but in practice President Mobutu was supposed to pass them straight through to the FNLA and UNITA. However, as the CIA expected in a country led by Mobutu, one of the most corrupt dictators in the world, very few of the arms actually reached the guerrillas.

The South Africans had been closely involved with the American operation; the U.S. plans were coordinated by the CIA station chief in Pretoria and the head of the Bureau of State Security (BOSS). Some arms for UNITA had been sent through South Africa and had reached their destination, followed by a shipment of fuel from the CIA for the local armed forces to use in their armored cars and trucks operating on the border.

Encouraged by these developments, the South Africans decided to escalate their policy of border harassment against the MPLA government, which had become established in Luanda. After the CIA received approval for Operation Feature, approximately two thousand UNITA and South African troops moved over the border in the armored cars that had been fueled by the CIA. Driving rapidly up the coast, they swept the MPLA troops before them. Within a month, UNITA and the South Africans were operating along a four-hundred-mile front and had conquered half of Angola. So successful was this operation, codenamed Zulu, that the South Africans decided to push farther north and capture Luanda, the capital.

Meanwhile, the Soviets had responded to pleas for help from the MPLA and had sent in large numbers of 122-mm rocket systems, manned by Cuban mercenaries. As the South African troops moved north of the coastal town of Benguela, they came under heavy fire from the 122-mm Katyusha rockets, which had a range of up to twelve miles, far exceeding any artillery in the lightly armed South African force. Suddenly, a triumphant advance against feeble opposition turned into a slow, costly attack against superior enemy forces. The South Africans brought forward four 88-mm artillery pieces, but these could not reach the MPLA's rockets. The South Africans had no choice but to sit it out or retreat. After two months, during which time the MPLA reinforced and caused a significant number of casualties among the invading force, the South Africans decided to retreat.

What should have been a major victory for the South Africans and a swift conclusion to Operation Feature turned out instead to have improved the MPLA's morale and resulted in a humiliating defeat for the South Africans. If the invaders had used better artillery, the MPLA would not have been able to dominate them. This lesson was not lost on the South African high command. Having seen the Israelis demonstrate Jerry Bull's new extended-range 155-mm artillery shell, which could have brought the MPLA's 122-mm rockets comfortably within range, the South Africans decided it was time to conduct a high-level arms purchase. The Israelis, they knew, had sold their surplus SRC ammunition to the shah of Iran for a handsome profit and had no more to spare. The South African intelligence service, BOSS, approached their friends in the CIA and asked for their help. In October, a formal request was made to the CIA for a supply of extended-range 155-mm ammunition.

In the summer of 1975, Israeli Military Industries approached SRC with a request to market the rights for the 155-

mm shell in South Africa. While this idea was being considered by Bull, the South Africans approached an arms dealer named John (Jack) Frost, a resident of Belgium, to see if he could arrange a purchase. Frost had worked for the CIA as one of many freelance informers and arms dealers after his retirement as a colonel in the U.S. Air Force at the end of the 1960s. He had been present at the October 1970 demonstrations in Barbados of the new extended-range shell. He had been invited as an employee of H&FI, the Belgian arms-dealing company that was associated with PRB and that, under the agreement between Severin and Bull, received 4 percent of SRC-I, the Belgian marketing arm of the SRC. The deal had never been formally signed, however, so Frost was free to act independently. He had his own company, FFE International, and was completely familiar with all aspects of SRC's operations, which enabled him to provide the South Africans with all the details concerning which shells might be available.

Frost has talked openly about his participation in the developing smuggling operation. But, like many arms dealers, he relishes the spotlight and has an unsavory reputation, so his evidence should be treated with skepticism. And yet, the documents that are available appear to confirm large parts of his story.

By Frost's account, he was originally approached by an old friend, Major John Clancey III, a U.S. Marine officer who was on loan to the Joint Operations Branch of the Joint Chiefs of Staff, from where he had in turn been seconded to the CIA. He handled the covert purchase of arms for Operation Feature. Clancey has confirmed that he was on loan to a paramilitary group within the CIA from 1973 to 1976 and that he was part of the Angola task force. Clancy was later to deny to congressional investigators that he had any relationship with Frost during the Angolan war.

According to John Stockwell, Clancey "was thoroughly professional and had no moral or philosophical inclinations. If you wanted to deliver arms to South Africa, he would find a way to do that. He was like a pistol; if you pointed him and pulled the trigger, he fired."[6]

Frost claims that he first met Clancey when Frost was working for the CIA. The two men kept in touch after Frost left the agency at the end of the 1960s to form his own business. Ironically, in a letter that he had written to Clancey on February 4, 1975, Frost had complained of Israeli interference with his SRC deals, and he had also crossed swords with the Israeli arms dealer Shaul Eisenberg.

Subject: Israeli External Sales

There is a group identified as the Eisenberg group which is selling materiel purchased ostensibly for Israel to Iran and other nations. They are closely associated with IMI [Israeli Military Industries] and in particular, Dov Peleg [IMI salesman].

Recently they got info, backdoor, of my offer for 155mm and 175mm extended range to Iran and may have pulled off a deal to manufacture in Israel inasmuch as Israel has the rights after a purchase of 10,000 from SRC.

They appeared also to be selling a wide range of Russian stuff captured; however, I'm of the opinion PRB has acquired the Russian stuff from Egypt and is selling through the Israelis.

Clancey told Frost that the arms were for Zambia and included ten thousand 7.62-mm assault rifles, 50 million rounds of NATO 7.62-mm ammunition, ten 81-mm mortars, five thousand rounds of 81-mm ammunition, ten 106-mm recoilless rifles, and one thousand rounds of standard ammunition. Frost placed a preliminary order with three companies—Heckler and Koch, Tampella, and SIDEM—confident that, with official U.S. government backing, approval would be a mere formality.

However, on September 30, 1975, Frost traveled to Madrid to meet with Clancey and his Zambian customer, who turned out to be Denys Zeederberg, the head of development at Armscor. Frost realized then that the arms were destined for South Africa. Rather than shipping from Europe, he decided it would be sensible to seek another route. Zeederberg gave him a letter of credit for $13 million drawn on the Credite Bank of Brussels.

With cash in hand, Frost placed the order with Commerce International, a Brussels-based arms dealership run by an American, who told Frost that the arms were available in Thailand. He would ship them to Taiwan, where they could be collected. The paperwork would show that the matériel had been moved out of Taiwan under an order signed by the Supreme Command authorizing the dumping of the arms at sea; in fact, they would be shipped to South Africa.

Frost also met with Zeederberg in November 1975 at the Erawan Hotel in Bangkok, where Frost reviewed the weapons that might be available. He explained, "I was describing different technologies. I had described the extended-range capability of Space Research. [He] became very interested in the program, because this then gave [South Africa] a capability to counteract the Soviet threat, or the possible Soviet threat, of the 122-mm and 130-mm guns being supplied to the forces in southern Africa. [He] certainly took a lot of notice."

While Frost and Clancey continued to follow one deal, Denys Zeederberg set off to pursue Jerry Bull. He flew to Highwater for a meeting with Bull; soon afterward, Bull flew with his wife to South Africa as a guest of the government, stopping in Israel on the way. Mimi had two uncles who were missionaries in South Africa, so the trip was part holiday as well.

According to Bull's official biography,

> The South Africans were in a considerable state of change, as apparently they had embarked on a policy of building their own defense industries, since they felt that in time of emergency they could easily be isolated physically. The organizational details had not been clarified, and were to evolve rapidly in the near future.
>
> This visit was spent in visiting plants and [having] general discussions. The South Africans were trying to assess Bull, and many discussions centered [on] how certain he felt of the ultimate successful development of the [extended-range] round. From subsequent actions, it is clear that they were satisfied that SRC-Q had good technological capability.

Bull himself later wrote in the letter he left with his lawyer, "I visited South Africa to discuss the contract and contract potential as outlined to me for our Air Traffic Control work. They are more than willing to show off everything, from armored cars to aircraft, to tour you until you are dead. They definitely want you to be friendly, they even want to recruit you if you appear interested. My visit was certainly enlightening."

According to both family and friends, Bull had no particular affection for the South African regime, but he did support their anticommunist stand in southern Africa. Bull's view of South Africa illustrated his very naive view of politics in general. Fiercely anticommunist, Bull could support South Africa without expressing any views about apartheid, other than a general feeling that South Africa was getting a raw deal from Western governments. He felt a certain sympathy because South Africa was the underdog being unfairly treated by the United States and the United Nations, an image with which he could identify.

While Bull was being courted by Armscor, Frost and Clancey were still trying to put their deal together. A number of telexes during November reveal that Clancey was playing a central role in orchestrating events.

Frost's operations in the United States were being run by his daughter, Barbara Frost, who was based in Washington. On November 4, she sent him two telexes in Bangkok. In the messages, Clancey was referred to by a code word based on his initials (here his real name appears in brackets). The messages read:

> [Clancey] desires urgent speech with you on delay of order discussed during your last trip . . . await your telex and he will contact me here.
>
> Mr. [Clancey] feels that it might be more expedient and less expensive if his representative in Thailand, who is aware of the program, contacted you personally. . . . It is hoped that the project can be completed within the time frame of the next week or two. The commitment is positive.

This was followed by a November 10 telex, which reported that "Mr. [Clancey] has had a query from his overseas friends regarding the order placed with you. They are trying to contact you. Would it be possible to telex the Brussels office with a limited progress report?"

The next day, Frost replied. "Progress so far and subject to last minute schedule revisions twenty-six hundred tons will sail between November 12 and 15, arriving between November 16 and December first. Priority items by aircraft departing November 15/16. Require [Clancey's] approval for export. Will contact him November 12/13 direct."

Frost felt that the deal was not as secure as it might be, so he arranged with Clancey and Armscor representatives to meet Major General Lay Ying, the chief of staff of the Taiwanese armed forces, to discuss the project. General Lay said that the proposed deal could be expedited provided that the U.S. government agreed. Both Frost and Clancey told Lay that this would be possible, and it appeared that the deal would proceed. Then everything began to go wrong.

Reflecting the Taiwanese concern, on November 17, Frost telexed Barbara: "Contact [Clancey's] office. Seller here in Taipei must have approval of U.S. to sell co-production items. I can coordinate with the MAAG [U.S. Military Assistance Advisory Group] to expedite."

All covert arms deals are marked by betrayal and paranoia, and this one was no exception. Frost discovered that Armscor had been negotiating with Commerce International as well as with the Taiwanese, and he feared that he was about to be cut out of the deal. He then realized that he might be taking part in an illegal sanctions-busting operation and he worried that his future relations with the U.S. government might be in jeopardy. No legal deals with South Africa were possible at this time, since a United Nations arms embargo was still in force.

In any event, Frost got nervous and put off a December trip to South Africa that had been scheduled to finalize the deal, pleading high blood pressure. On December 3, Frost wrote to Drago saying that "a meeting was arranged by and between [two other officials of Commerce International], Mr. Smith [Piet Smith, chief of procurement at Armscor], Mr. Zeederberg and myself to discuss the status of our purchase program. . . . I was certainly misled as to who if anybody controlled the materiel [causing] me to expend time and funds on a will-o'-the-wisp. So therefore I have no alternative but to terminate."

The arms deal apparently never went through, but Frost then wrote to Rodgers Gregory, the vice-president of SRC, on January 13, 1976, asking for an SRC proposal to develop a long-range 155-mm shell and an estimate for the cost of producing 10,300 units. The letter refers to "our prior discussions" and mentions Frost having had contact "that day [with] the buyer" for the 10–12 155-mm Long Tom cannons. "One of the requested provisions in the proposal is for complete transfer of technology and know-how for in country continued use." Both Frost and Gregory later confirmed that this proposal was for a shipment to South Africa.

By March, discussions between the South Africans and SRC had progressed, and a deal was in its final stages of negotiation. On March 20, 1976, the main participants flew to Rio de Janeiro and checked into the Meridien Hotel. Among those present at the meeting were Jerry Bull, Luis Palacio, the manager of SRC-I, and Joseph Severin of PRB. They agreed that sixty-five thousand of the extended-range 155-mm rounds would be delivered to South Africa and, under a second stage of the contract, several howitzer conversion kits would also be delivered. The first contract was code-named Elena I, after one of the attractive nightclub hostesses; the second was called Elena II.

On March 28, Denys Zeederberg of Armscor checked into the Hotel Jay in Jay Peak, Vermont, five miles from SRC headquarters. Later that day he was joined by Piet Smith, another Armscor official, and Colonel P. M. Lombard, who had headed South Africa's artillery effort during the invasion of Angola in 1975. They later met with SRC officials at the Highwater compound, and the final details of the $50-million deal were agreed to.

The deal represented salvation for SRC, which was virtually bankrupt. Despite repeated promptings, no contract had been forthcoming from PRB, which was also in financial trouble. Severin had insisted that all meetings with Bull take place without any advisers being present, so no record existed of their verbal agreements. Bull thought this was because Severin was a nice guy who wanted decisions made by the principals without any interference. A more reasonable explanation may be that Severin knew a sucker when he saw one and hoped that, on his own, Bull could be talked into virtually anything. Certainly, Bull passed over a great deal of technical data to SRC-I, which was then used for free by PRB.

In fact, Bull never seemed to understand how the arms business worked, and his "deal" with PRB was a good illustration of this. Bull and SRC offered the blueprints for some well-designed —even revolutionary—artillery and shells. PRB brought manufacturing capability and a competent sales staff. The deal Bull should have struck would have had Bull and SRC receiving a royalty on every gun and shell sold. If he had driven a hard bargain, Bull might have received money in advance as working capital. What actually happened was that Bull handed over all his drawings to Severin without any contract, and he accepted at face value PRB's promises that both a contract and cash would be forthcoming. Even after the relationship had gone sour, Bull refused to believe that Severin had done anything wrong—one salesman seduced by the charm of another.

To pay for the raw materials to fulfill the South African contract, Bull needed to obtain additional financing from First Pennsylvania Bank. They were nervous about committing any more capital to a company whose debt had done nothing but increase ever since they had become involved. In exchange for rolling over a $5-million debt in 1972, the bank had put a lien on all SRC assets, including the buildings and land at Highwater and Bull's various life insurance policies. In the intervening three years, the situation had become steadily worse, and by the end of 1975, SRC owed the bank approximately $11 million and was failing to pay even the interest charges. To finance the South African deal, the bank would have to advance a further $2.2 million in letters of credit, although some of this would be covered by staged payments from the buyer. Even given SRC's dismal financial history, the deal was very tempting. SRC hoped to make enough profit from this single contract to pay off all its debts and have money left over.

To ensure that SRC was not breaking the arms embargo to South Africa, however, First Pennsylvania insisted that Jerry Bull write to James Hataway, the deputy director of the Office

Munitions Control (OMC), which he did on April 21, 1976, to find out if he required an export license for any of the matériel that would originate in the United States. The previous January, Bull, Trudeau, and Luis Palacio had traveled to Washington to meet with Hataway to discuss the proposed export of 175-mm shells to Israel. The meeting was necessary because the forgings for the shells were produced in the United States. In that case, the contract was with SRC-US because America allowed arms exports to Israel. Work was subcontracted to SRC-Q because Canada had a ban on arms exports to Israel, but could export to the U.S.

The same month, SRC had signed a memorandum of understanding with the South Africans for the supply of sixty M114 155-mm howitzers. Bull was confident that these could be obtained outside the U.S. or without having to go through the OMC.

In addition, the January meeting with the OMC had made clear by implication that unfilled shells, known as hollow forgings, were not subject to export control and, therefore, did not need a license. At First Pennsylvania's request, Bull wrote to Hataway to confirm that ruling.

Dear Mr. Hataway,

First may I thank you for the courtesy and patience extended to us during our meeting. In a short time I gained some insight into the sophisticated machinery associated with the licensing process, and appreciate the necessity of direct communication and proper explanations at the onset.

I would like to review and confirm our understandings of the discussions.

First, as background, the present SRC-US Corporation grew out of a non-profit Canadian organization, the Space Research Institute of McGill University. In late 1967, this organization, which had been developing advanced ordnance systems, broke away from the University (under pressure from anti-military lobbying). A Canadian Corporation, Space Research Corporation Quebec, was formed to gather up and continue on the work. At that time, it appeared that the NATO market offered the greatest potential, and a Canadian technology export permit was obtained to transfer the technology data package to a joint venture Company, SRC-International, located in Brussels.

In 1972, the US Corporation obtained a major financing through the First Pennsylvania Banking and Trust Company, and the Canadian interests were bought out. Thus, SRC-US is a fully owned US corporation with laboratories, manufacturing facilities, corporate and engineering offices at North Troy, Vermont. During the last eighteen months, SRC-Q has been split off to be fully Canadian owned, as requested by Canadian defense authorities. While at the moment I am Chief Executive Officer of both Corporations, this will be changed in the near future, since as an American citizen, I really do not meet Canadian management requirements.

Our international company, acting mainly as a marketing agency, enters into contracts with those countries permitted under Belgian law. Naturally, we try to bring to the U.S. as much of the manufacturing associated with these contracts as possible. Often, our bankers have to supply guarantees for this international work. Their lawyers have raised the question whether this implies any US approvals. You told us that this was definitely not the case, as the legal circuit through Canadian export license to Belgium is the concern of Belgian law only.

The second item you clarified to us was the requirement for OMC approval. As we understand your explanation, items recognizable as weapons require export permits from your office. Items such as rough, non-machined nosed forgings do not require munitions export permits, only the normal Department of Commerce export permits.

This classification aids us greatly, and will prevent us filing unnecessary applications, creating a burden on your office. I do believe however, that all applications submitted to date were necessary, since they involved finished weapon sub-systems. We will continue to file applications to your office, or request your advice on whether we should file if in doubt.

Enclosed you will find a perspective drawing of the SRC-

US, SRC-Q compound straddling the US-Canadian border. This compound concept was agreed to by Customs and Immigration of both the US and Canada to permit the gun ranges and heavy installations to be conserved and utilized, and to allow utilization of the local Vermont and Quebec staffs, where possible. The compound is guarded on a twenty-four hour basis, and follows both U.S. and Canadian security laws. One U.S. Customs officer is on duty at the South (US) gate. All persons must enter and exit by the same gate and are subject at all hours to security checks, etc.

I would appreciate in writing your confirmation of the main points raised here. Specifically, the non–U.S. interest in SRC-Q operations in technology exported to Belgium under Canadian export license, and secondly that export of rough nosed forging blanks are exempt from OMC licensing under ITAR [International Traffic in Arms Regulations].

A reply at your earliest convenience would be appreciated.

Thanks once again for your help.

Yours truly,

G. V. Bull
President

Two days later, on April 23, William Robinson, the director of OMC, replied:

I am pleased to respond to your letter of April 21, 1976 concerning our discussion of the activities of the Space Research Corporations as they relate to the requirements of the Department's International Traffic in Arms Regulations.

This is to confirm that your interpretation is correct that U.S. Government approvals are not required with regard to contracts of your international company acting as a marketing agent under Canadian export license to Belgium. Similarly, exports of rough non-machined nosed forgings from the United States are not considered as falling under the purview of the U.S. Munitions List so long as they are not clearly identifiable as parts or components of weapons or sub-systems covered by that list. Hence, no license is required from this office for exports of such raw materials from the United States.

I shall be pleased to be of further assistance in this matter should the need arise.

Taken at face value, this exchange of letters apparently gave SRC-US the right to export the rough forgings to South Africa. However, there was an obvious subtext to the correspondence.

Bull's letter did not talk about specifics. It did not mention South Africa and it did not mention that the forgings were to be used for 155-mm howitzer shells. The reply from OMC appeared to assume that the forgings had a nonmilitary purpose, which is bizarre, given that the only use for such forgings would have been in the manufacture of complete shells. So, by carefully constructing a request that received an equally crafty reply, Bull was satisfied that he'd received an official letter from the U.S. government that in effect granted him export approval, a letter he could produce in his defense if the deal was ever uncovered.

The contract with the South Africans was signed on April 7, 1976, between Paragon Holdings, the Cayman Islands shell company that had been set up by Bull to handle the sale of assets in Barbados, and the Colet Trading Establishment, a front company for Armscor in Canada. The contract called for SRC-US to produce and supply thirty-five thousand extended-range 155-mm artillery rounds complete with fuses, primers, and propellant charges. The contract listed each component part by its SRC-US drawing number.

On April 30, 1976, SRC wrote to the Army Materiel Command in Washington asking for fifty thousand forgings, which it said were destined for Israel. Unlike the previous deal with Israel, when the army had asked for documentary evidence of the product's ultimate destination, this time the army took SRC at its word, in a breach of its own rules. In its request, SRC asked for the army to give approval within seven days; otherwise, the order would be placed overseas.

Three days later, on May 3, the Chamberlain Manufacturing

Company, which operates the army's manufacturing plant at Scranton, Pennsylvania, asked the U.S. Army Armament Command (ARMCOM) to approve the production of the shells for SRC, which was "acting as an agent of Israel and other NATO countries." An ARMCOM memorandum the following day referred to Chamberlain's warning that SRC would place the order overseas unless its offer was accepted by May 7. The memo stated that if Chamberlain lost the order, the company would face a loss "of $182,000 in potential charges for equipment rental, overheads, and 65 skilled personnel could be laid off in an economically depressed area." The request was approved by ARMCOM the same day, and the AMC verbally approved the SRC order on May 7. Then, on June 25, the First Pennsylvania Bank supplied a $2.2-million letter of credit to the Chamberlain Manufacturing Company, which was underwritten by the patent rights to the extended-range artillery shell.

On October 9, 1976, SRC agreed to supply South Africa with two radar tracking systems and two vans to be used to test the 155-mm system. Two months later, on December 10, the South Africans exercised an option in the contract and ordered another fifteen thousand shells, together with the extras specified in the first deal. Finally, the first of the complicated financial arrangements had been put into effect.

Jack Frost then learned through PRB that the deal was going ahead without him. He wrote to Armscor's Piet Smith, whose signature was on the contract with SRC.

Dear Peet [sic],
It is indeed amusing and disheartening to discover the amateurish security practices and the lack of ethics as practiced by members of both [the Armaments] Board and Corps [Armscor]. I have now plotted the complete itinerary of my "good friends" based on my previous conversations and correspondence. You, collectively, are treading on very thin ice and, at the same time, placing some naive people in a very precarious position.
It is evident that I have exposed some companies to seri-

ous consequences if knowledge of their proposed cooperation becomes public. As you know, there was an approved and proper manner for accomplishing your requirements. Since I have been pre-empted and, at the same time, am responsible for opening the door, I feel I have only one valid option.

Before I'll allow these companies to get into trouble, I must force them out of any direct or indirect cooperation. I will be calling each and every one to advise them of the general nature of the consequences. After this, and to prevent further contact, I shall have those known to me from the Board and Corps placed on a watch list.

You know there are elements in the North American government who would make capital of the violation of the law to the detriment of some very nice people. The stupidity by which this program has been prosecuted is only exceeded by my personal affection for the people of your country. If it were any other country, I would have blown the whistle long ago, I would suggest that Denys, Gibbon, David, Malan et al. [South African government employees] cease coming this way and that you cease to invite Allen, Bill N., Gerry, Dave and Ed et al. [SRC employees] to experience the wonders of the south.

I trust you will use good judgment and discontinue the US program before it becomes a national issue.

Superficially, this was Jack Frost, concerned citizen, doing his best to persuade his friends at Armscor to back away from an illegal deal. But nothing is ever straightforward in the arms business. Frost was putting on paper enough to make sure that if anything went wrong, he would be able to avoid going down with the SRC ship.

When the South Africans ignored his first letter and the deal continued to proceed, Frost wrote again in more threatening terms.

Dear Denys,
How stupid can you people get? You know well enough

that there is a security leak in your own organization, apropos the leaks to the Far East on your and Pete's [sic] travels; but now you try to exploit the leads I have given you and Pete [sic] without regard for whom you talk to or the consequences.

Well, get this through your head, I won't allow you or anybody else to exploit these people. . . . You and your associates are placing them in a precarious position which could result in them being barred from future U.S. business and a probability of criminal prosecution. Your big mistake was contacting one group which is under continuous surveillance for violations and unfortunately has some very mouthy individuals. You could not have done a better job of exposing your activity if you had published it in the newspapers.

Right now, anti-RSA [Republic of South Africa] groups would give their right arms to have this type of incident to exploit.

At this point, I don't know the appropriate course of action. I am considering the establishment of a watch list. It is evident that you have done your job well and my people are willing, nay anxious, to take more than calculated risk for money. That's really a dirty trick. It now looks like I'll have to lose friends at both ends of the circuit, but be assured the sacrifice won't be too great.

I still view the actions of your group with incomprehension. You are unreal. Is the threat that great that you flush your ethics down the drain?

As far as the South Africans were concerned, Frost's threats were of little concern. Armscor believed, correctly, that the deal was taking place with the approval of the CIA and, therefore, that it was untouchable.

Frustrated, Frost then turned his attention to SRC and Bull. Since he was the one who introduced Bull to the South Africans, he believed that he was entitled to a fee, as is customary in the arms business. He approached Bull directly and demanded money, but Bull turned him down, partly because he had no money and partly because he disliked Frost. According to Charles Murphy, Bull thought Frost was a "real flake."

In any case, Bull's outright rejection of this idea made him an enemy in an industry where enemies can prove to be very expensive liabilities. The result was that Frost turned on Bull. He first visited the U.S. Office of Munitions Control in the State Department and told them how he had been approached by John Clancey, ostensibly to buy arms for Zambia, and how the deal had turned out to be for South Africa. Frost also named Zeederberg and others at Armscor and described the nature of their discussions with SRC. To his frustration, all his revelations were ignored.

Later, when the arms shipments were investigated by Congress and the U.S. Customs Service, Frost would have his revenge by revealing all the details of the plot. His evidence proved critical in stopping the shipment and stopping SRC.

T E N

THE SHIPMENTS

BY FEBRUARY 1977, the first batch of 740 shells was ready for shipment to Israel. Unfortunately, in the nine months since the contract had been signed, the political situation in Israel had changed drastically. Prime Minister Rabin's government was beset by scandal: Avraham Ofer, his housing minister, had been accused of corruption and had then committed suicide; Asher Yodlin, his nominee for governor of the Bank of Israel, had been accused of taking bribes; and the country found out that Rabin and his wife had maintained an illegal bank account in the United States. In addition, President Jimmy Carter, only a month in office, wanted to implement one of his campaign pledges and make some mark in the area of human rights. While Ford and Nixon had been prepared to turn a blind eye toward Israel's relationship with South Africa, Carter felt that the Israelis should do all they could to withdraw their support from Pretoria. The president let it be known that he expected Israel to take a strong position against South Africa if Israel wanted U.S. aid and economic assistance to continue at the same level.[1]

Meanwhile, in a memorandum to his Belgian partners at PRB, Jerry Bull reported that "Israel is without an effective government . . . political chaos and turmoil have spread from Washington. While the Israelis hesitate, the shells continue to await shipment." Finally, on February 17, Bull told PRB that he had received a bombshell. "The Israeli Cabinet has denied permission to IMI to enter into the [contract to fill the shells with explosives] unless (1) no Zim the Israeli national shipping company ships are used (we are loaded on Zim containers), (2) no SRC subsidiary, affiliate, etc. is involved." As far as SRC was concerned, this ended plans to ship shells first to Israel and from there to South Africa.

Some inkling of the Israeli about-face must have already reached the ears of the South Africans and SRC, because only three days later, on February 20, the vessel *Lady Scotia* left New Brunswick for Antigua with at least 740 shells, followed by two other vessels on March 7 and May 10 carrying, respectively, 7,468 and 2,688 shells.

In 1975, when Israel had bought artillery shells direct from SRC, they had been shipped via SRC's Caribbean testing station at Paragon House, Barbados. Now, the initial plan called for the South African shells to be off-loaded in Barbados, then transferred to an Israeli vessel and carried to Haifa. But the plan would not work this time; there had been a change of government in Barbados.

Prime Minister Barrow, who had been such a good friend to SRC, had called Bull for a favor at the beginning of 1976. He had ambitions to build a cement plant on the island and wanted to ship the raw materials from Guyana. To accomplish this, he needed a shallow-draft ship that could navigate the Amazon. Barrow approached Bull to see if he could get some surplus stock from the U.S. Navy, which had been so helpful with gun barrels in the past. The navy obliged, and an SRC team went to California to oversee the repairs that were needed to make the ship seaworthy. Upon its arrival in Barbados, the vessel caused a fight between the government and local opposition. Accusations were made that by bribing government officials from Barrow on down, SRC had managed to make the Barbadian government pay $24 million for the ship. In fact, the government had been given the ship by the U.S. Navy; the repairs had cost only $600,000.

A general election was called for September. Barrow lost to

Tom Adams, who had promised to appoint a royal commission to investigate the bribery allegations. While the commission exonerated Bull, enough mud had stuck to SRC's reputation to make their position in Barbados untenable.

Following the dispute, Errol Barrow approached his friend Prime Minister Vere Bird in Antigua, which lay 250 miles north of Barbados, and offered him a deal: in return for allowing SRC to operate a test site on Antigua free from local interference, SRC would establish Antigua's first army. Bird readily agreed, especially when his son Lester, the deputy prime minister and a lawyer, was retained at an undisclosed fee as SRC's legal representative on the island. It was a cozy relationship; the Antiguan army became a private security force operating independently of local controls to keep the SRC operation secure from prying eyes.

The compound, situated on a remote peninsula called Crab's Point, was the ideal secure testing ground. It was here that the extended-range ammunition was tested for the South Africans. Here, too, Bull tested a new gun, the GC-45, which he had designed to use his new ammunition. The gun had a longer barrel, a different breech, and was made specifically to handle the range of the new shells. This was the first completely new gun system designed by Bull, and it proved to be a stunning success. Bull was so confident of his new system that he told the South Africans—and anyone else who would listen—that the new gun could produce $500 million in sales. The South Africans were impressed, so impressed, in fact, that they changed their plans from simply buying equipment from Bull to secretly buying his whole company.

On May 27, the motor vessel *Tugelaland* sailed from New York for Cape Town. Although apparently registered to a German company, Globus Reedesey, and flying the German flag, the vessel was, in fact, owned by South African Marine, a New York–based company controlled by the South African government. After leaving New York, the *Tugelaland* made an unscheduled stop in Antigua and loaded on board thirty-six SRC containers and two radar vans, telling the curious dockers who helped with the loading that they were destined for Canada, where, of course, they had originated earlier in the month. The vessel then sailed for South Africa, arriving on June 7, 1977. The first load of SRC's extended-range artillery shells had been delivered on schedule.

Just nine days before, on May 18, Chamberlain had asked ARMCOM to approve another order for fifteen thousand forgings for Israel. ARMCOM officials told the company that their previous authorization was a "one time deviation" and that Chamberlain would have to go through "international logistics channels" for the necessary authority. According to an ARMCOM memorandum, Chamberlain expressed great concern over this decision because it meant the immediate dismissal of ninety staff members: "It may well be that Chamberlain could either contact their Congressman or higher authority or that Space Research will do so."

After consultations with the Army Materiel Command, however, ARMCOM approved the order on May 24. Between September 1977 and May 1978, 16,027 additional forgings were shipped to SRC-US; most were sent to SRC-Q in Canada and then shipped to South Africa through Antigua.

In the meantime, SRC had embarked on another smuggling operation that was to have far more serious long-term consequences than even U.N. sanctions busting.

In October 1976, the first of several planeloads of highly sophisticated technical equipment and testing gear relevant to artillery performance and manufacture, as well as the converted howitzers, was flown out of Canada to South Africa. On October 21, the initial shipment on Sabena World Airline from Mirabel Airport, Montreal, to Johannesburg contained the cardboard spacers and cavity liners used to separate propellant components inside the shells. Later that month, Visco Transgear Industries Ltd. of Johannesburg received several shipments by air, one of which included seven 155-mm inert filling models used to demonstrate shell loading.

SRC continued to send shipments, the most significant one occurring on February 4, 1977, when SRC apparently delivered a complete ballistics instrumentation testing system. The shipment was carried by South African Airways flight 210 out of New York City's Kennedy Airport. Included in the shipment were such items as a "Kistler Piezzotonic Gauge" and a "textronic scope." A Kistler gauge can be used to measure the interior ballistics of a gun or general explosive chemical reactions; the textronic scope records a picture of the pressure inside the barrel. South Africa had nothing comparable in its arms inventory, and such equipment was setting Armscor well along the path to developing its own artillery system. At no time did SRC make application in any official capacity to the U.S. government for permission to export such matériel, which quite clearly had only a military application.

South Africa so far had managed to obtain shells and testing equipment illegally. Now SRC was trying to fill the second half of the South African contract by supplying gun barrels. Once again the U.S. Army was happy to help. Gun barrel number 3147, a 155-mm Long Tom cannon, was ostensibly lent to SRC for six months by the Picatinny Arsenal in connection with an SRC contract to design, manufacture, and test experimental artillery shells for the army. On February 15, 1977, SRC trucks picked up the cannon at the Aberdeen Proving Ground in Maryland; the following day it was exported from the U.S. to the Canadian side of the SRC compound. A February 17 SRC receiving report bears the notation "to be shipped to Antigua." On February 20, SRC sent a shipload of arms to Antigua, and gun barrel 3147 was listed on the bill of lading. The gun was then shipped to South Africa in May 1977 and followed by several SRC representatives, who secretly based themselves at a small town known as Schmidtsdrif on the edge of the Vaal River, some sixty miles west of Kimberley. This was the site of the main artillery testing range for the South African army. Here, SRC personnel were able to give the South Africans vital insights into the working of the new howitzer.

The man in charge of the SRC contingent was Steve Adams, who had been project manager for the company's development of the 155-mm extended-range howitzer. (He would resign from SRC in early 1978, though the U.S. Customs Service believes

that his resignation was a sham and that he continued to represent the company. Later, Adams would resurface with Bull's
operation in Belgium, and he played a key role in negotiating
contracts with China and Iraq. He now lives in Brussels.)

Two years after the original gun barrel 3147 was loaned from
the Picatinny Arsenal, customs investigators examined their
files and found no paperwork beyond the initial authorization.
In February 1979, a Picatinny official told a customs agent that
he had checked with SRC and learned that the cannon was presently in Antigua, West Indies, and would be shipped back to
Vermont in "the next six to seven weeks." In August 1979, an
official of the Aberdeen Proving Ground told customs that he
had checked with SRC and learned that the barrel would be
returned in "approximately six weeks." After several further
stalling statements, the Defense Department eventually admitted in 1981 that "the property in Antigua is obviously not available for disposal at this time. Therefore, above Clearance case
has been closed."

By the end of 1977, South Africa had in its possession everything required to develop its own artillery system, but setting
up the manufacturing capacity would take time, and SRC was
anxious to fulfill the complete contract and deliver the remaining 54,104 shells. Although production of the shells appeared to
be proceeding smoothly, SRC's financial problems continued to
cause difficulty with the First Pennsylvania Bank. Even though
South Africa had paid approximately $7 million upon receiving
its first shipment of shells, SRC had used the money to pay its
suppliers, and the debt to First Pennsylvania showed no signs of
being cleared. However, since the estimated value of the contract was $30 million, excluding the technology and additional
equipment, the cash-flow problem was only temporary. Nevertheless, Bull was forced to turn to his willing South African
friends for help in resolving the difficulty.

The South Africans dreamed up a perfect solution that answered First Pennsylvania's money worries, SRC's cash-flow
problems, and their own need for continuing access to SRC research. J. S. Coetzee, the chief commercial salesman for Armscor, arrived in Highwater during the spring of 1977 with a

proposal. He served as a director of an Amsterdam company, Space Capital International NV, which wanted to make an investment in SRC-Q. Coetzee had been introduced to Bull by Frank Nel, the former president of the South African Atlas Aircraft Company and a director of Armscor. (Nel would later move to Canada to become president of Shefford Electronics, another part of the Bull empire.)

On Bull's recommendation, Coetzee went to see Bull's old friend, the lawyer Marcel Paquette, for legal advice on the deal he was proposing. Bull contacted First Pennsylvania, which immediately saw an opportunity to recoup some of its rotten investment in SRC. At no time over the next few months did the officials from the bank question the source of the money that had mysteriously appeared to bail them out. However, since most of the Space Capital participants had strong South African accents, the bankers must have known very well who was providing the cash.

"The bank didn't give a shit where the money came from," says Paquette.

On June 6, 1977, Bull, Coetzee, Paquette, officials from First Pennsylvania, and sundry lawyers met in London to sign the contracts. According to Paquette, the terms had been agreed upon in advance, so there was little for the lawyers to do. Even so, a huge volume of paperwork was generated by the meetings, which started on Monday and did not finish until Thursday evening.

By the end of the trip, the South Africans, using Space Capital as a channel, had bought 19.9 percent (investing a total of $10 million) of Canadian Technical Industries, a holding company set up prior to the agreement to control SRC after the deal went through. Of this, $3 million was converted into 545,970 preferred shares in Canadian Technical Industries, while the rest was secured by a $7-million debenture. Canadian Technical then made four transfers, totalling $6.3 million, to the First Pennsylvania Bank. It also released the bank from the initial $3.7-million letter of credit, which had been issued to support the purchase of the shell forgings from Chamberlain. In return, the bank agreed to transfer all SRC mortgages, collateral agreements, patents, and company shares they held to Canadian Technical. The bank also returned the assignment of the original shell contract with South Africa as agreed on April 7, 1976.

"Bull's motivation for the deal was entirely financial," says Paquette. "SRC needed cash so badly, it really didn't matter who took a stake in the company."[2]

For the South Africans, the deal was a dream. They now controlled all the technology relating to their new weapons systems, which gave them access to designs that would allow them to produce a gun and ammunition light-years ahead of anything else in the world. They controlled the patents and therefore could manufacture and sell the artillery and thus reap substantial profits. They also had access to all of SRC's research for the U.S government.

The deal marked the beginning of the end for Jerry Bull and SRC. Running a smuggling operation with the support of the CIA was one thing, but selling out such a high-profile company to the South Africans was quite another. Bull had embarked on the short journey from legitimate arms dealer to rogue merchant of death.

The first casualty of the arms deal was Jean de Valpine and Memorial Drive Trust. He had watched the fortunes of SRC with interest and done his best to straighten out its finances. He remained good friends with Jerry Bull but had become convinced that the company would never make money and that even if it did, the Memorial Drive Trust would never see any of it.

"The original controlling shareholder in SRC-Q [the part of SRC-US in which MDT had shares] saw its equity interest in SRC-Q diluted to virtually nothing, leaving the parent with its own operating assets consisting mainly of the electronics facilities on the U.S. side of the border," says de Valpine.

Jean de Valpine had been content to see his investment remain in SRC and even to see its limited value diluted over the years, provided there was some chance of seeing a return on his investment. But now, it was clear to de Valpine that Bull had not only undermined the MDT investment but had also become involved in shady business deals that could reflect badly on MDT's reputation as a highly principled investor. In 1977, Jean dc Valpine finally resigned from the board of SRC.

On August 5, 1977, Bull wrote back to his old friend.

It is with regret that your resignation was received. On the other hand, it is true that the company has not been operating in a manner which would allow the Board to function properly.

Without trying to offer excuses, I would like to state the reason for the virtual non-function of SRC in a conventional sense. As is clear to anyone reading the financial statements, SRC is hopelessly insolvent, and has been virtually since the First Penn loan was made. The loan was made at a time when our optimism on the future of industry and technology in the U.S. was high. We received extremely encouraging pushes from the Army, Navy and FAA. With the severe depression both economically and in morale that occurred shortly after PENCO entered the scene, the U.S. was eliminated as a market. We were unaware of this fact at the time, and continued heavy investment in trying to develop the U.S. markets. Since in all cases we knew from the international scene, the technical merits of our products and their ultimate necessity, it appeared obvious that temporary setbacks should be disregarded. However, as our expenditures reached unmanageable limits, and we felt the full weight of government purchasing practices tied to lobbying etc. it became apparent that continued expenditure on U.S. ventures, beyond that of a token presence was unwarranted.

Fortunately, the international market placed a value judgment on our products in terms of rather grim necessities. Consequently it became appropriate to concentrate on those markets where sales were likely. Canada, as the country of origin of a great deal of the technology, also came to life, reversing its twenty year freeze.

Our international business has furnished the basis for the continued existence of the operation. It is difficult by the many complicated restrictions, changing policies, and demands of each country for protection of the rights. I have indicated to you the Canadian position, which is somewhat typical.

The major problem in the international market is the commuting around the world. Couple this with the personal manner in which the company has had to operate because of its hand to mouth financial operations, and I am sure you will understand why SRC had to fade into a background operation.

We have made major advances by securing recently for SRC-Q some international financing. Perhaps foolishly, we still feel SRC will recover, and that U.S. operations will become viable. The current debt is $9.2 million, and that obviously will take some time to recoup even under the best of conditions.

A year later, MDT sold its stock in SRC for ten dollars, exactly ten times the booked cost of its original investment. By then, ADL, according to the official corporate history, considered SRC to be one venture that, "in retrospect, it would just as soon never have heard of."

With the financing finally in place, and the delivery of a gun, radar monitoring equipment, the first batch of shells, and personnel already accomplished, it must have seemed to the South Africans that the SRC deal could not go wrong. But it all began to unravel when—as with most complicated arrangements—a simple error exposed the entire affair.

On August 22, 1977, the trusty vessel *Tugelaland* picked up 10,560 shells at New Brunswick and headed for the SRC base in Antigua. While taking on some additional cargo there, a crane dropped its load into the hold, splitting open one of the containers of shells. This might not have been too alarming, particularly since the vessel was cleared to go to Barbados, but then one of the dockers, in a casual conversation with the skipper, discovered that he was actually headed for South Africa. Although the dockers allowed the ship to leave, the trade unions on Antigua refused to handle any further SRC shipments and started publicizing the case. The revelations coincided with a visit to the island by Joshua Nkomo, the leader of ZAPU, a Rhodesian guerrilla movement based in Zambia. He was told about the arms shipments, and in a speech he gave in Ottawa on October 17, Nkomo charged that nine hundred tons of arms, including mortars, machine guns, field cannons, and two mobile field communications units, had arrived in Antigua aboard the *Tugelaland* and been shipped to South Africa and then sent on to Rhodesia. This statement, while an exaggeration (there were no mortars or machine guns and nothing went to Rhodesia), was extreme enough to focus attention on the issue.

In November 1977, the Antigua Workers Union pointed a finger at SRC as the company responsible for shipping the weapons to South Africa. SRC denied the charge, admitting only that some 155-mm shells had been sent to Antigua for testing.

Alarmed at the growing attention being paid to the SRC–South Africa link, plans to ship a further 21,000 shells to Antigua from New Brunswick were abandoned. Instead, SRC applied for a Canadian export license to ship 35,000 shells to the government of Spain. The license was granted. On March 2, 1978, a Dutch ship, the *Nordfarer,* picked up 21,624 shells in New Brunswick and transported them to Barcelona, under the official Canadian export license. They were stored there for three months. Then, on June 26, 1978, they were transferred to the South African–owned *Breezand,* which brought them into Durban on July 19. On July 27, SRC shipped a further 12,648 shells from Canada to South Africa via Spain, under another Canadian export license. The ship stopped in the Bay of Cádiz on August 10 and anchored at Las Palmas, in the Canary Islands, on August 14 before arriving in South Africa on September 10.

Astonishingly, even after Nkomo had brought the SRC violation of the arms embargo to the attention of U.S. law-enforcement agencies, the Antigua route for smuggling the shells was kept open with the support of the U.S. Navy. Nkomo's statement provoked a brief investigation by the Royal Canadian Mounted Police, which found no evidence of any wrongdoing.

The U.S. government was unaware of Canada's investigation and had not been alerted to the Nkomo statement.

For two months, from December 1977 to January 1978, a convoy of trucks shipped more than seventeen hundred shells from SRC to the port at Cape Canaveral, Florida. Citing its contract with the army's Pictatinny Arsenal, SRC persuaded the U.S. Navy, by arguing it would be helping the army and the government, to charter the vessels for shipping the shells to Antigua, where they were collected by the South Africans and shipped direct to Durban. Because the shells were being shipped by U.S. government vessels, they did not need an export permit. Although dockworkers in Antigua refused to unload the shells, the local army (paid and trained by SRC) unloaded the containers and then stowed them aboard the South African vessel that arrived immediately after the U.S. government ships had departed.

Inevitably, South Africa did not waste its investment in SRC. Some sixteen artillery experts from South Africa made regular trips to SRC's Vermont headquarters in order to clarify details that were unclear on the patent drawings; meanwhile, SRC continued to supply personnel to help South Africa develop an independent artillery system. Among those who visited South Africa from SRC were Robert Mortensen, an expert in propellants who developed the charge for South Africa's 155-mm gun; John Ward, a computer scientist; John Alsop, a computer consultant; Sam Bailey, a phototechnician; Denis Lyster, a ballistics analyst; Bruce Smith, a range officer; George Tangen, a radar specialist; Luis Palacio, joint inventor of the shell and manager of SRC's international operations; George Bronson, a machine-tool expert; and Jean Vezina, a propellants specialist. Also, in January 1978, Cementation Engineering Ltd., a legitimate international construction company, bought P&E Eustice Ltd., a drop-hammer and die-forging firm near Johannesburg, which was involved in making parts for the artillery system.

On April 28, South Africa announced that it had developed its own 155-mm shell and artillery system. Prime Minister Botha denied suggestions that the technology had been smuggled from the United States. "Armscor developed and is manufacturing it and its ammunition," he said. But in a subsequent interview in the Johannesburg *Times*, Commandant P. G. Marais, head of Armscor, confirmed that its own artillery system had been developed with some help from SRC. Marais argued, however, that Armscor had simply used the SRC computer to check its own estimates of the artillery's performance and had made use of the testing range in Antigua. "No one could supply us with the weapon we required, so it was decided to produce the 155-mm locally. We were told by a defense consultant in Belgium, Mr. John Frost, that the best man to assist us would be Mr. Gerald Bull of the Space Research Corporation of Canada," said Marais.

In evidence provided to U.S. government investigators, Frost contradicted Marais's statement. "If the South Africans said the artillery system had been developed in their own country, they were full of crap," claimed Frost. "There's no question where the package came from."

Marais said he was concerned that Armscor's involvement with SRC could be interpreted as breaking the embargo and feared international outcry if the arrangement became public. "I became even more concerned when a prototype gun system was developed from the tests at SRC and it was time to try the system out. Mr. Bull refused to come to South Africa to assist with the tests because of the arms embargo, so it was agreed they would be conducted in Antigua," Marais said.

There has been speculation that South Africa used Bull's technology for more than simple conventional weapons. At 3:00 A.M. on September 22, 1979, an American Vela satellite detected a double pulse of light near Prince Edward Island in the southern part of the Indian Ocean. A pulse of this nature is characteristic of a nuclear explosion, which the Vela was designed to detect. Since its launch in 1970, the Vela had detected forty-one such explosions. But no nuclear tests had been planned by any known nuclear power for that September, and certainly no explosions were scheduled for that part of the world.

The Defense Intelligence Agency and the Department of the Navy concluded that an explosion had occurred, but a special White House committee set up by President Carter was more ambivalent, suggesting instead that the satellite could have been struck by a tiny particle that caused the two pulses of light. The consensus of the investigators, however, was that there had been a nuclear explosion and that the likely culprit was South Africa, which must have developed a nuclear weapon, perhaps with the assistance of Israel.[3]

If it was a South African device, what method had they used to launch it? Attention focused on the artillery delivered by Bull. The 155-mm howitzer is capable of delivering both chemical and nuclear weapons. However, Jerry Bull had done no work on developing a nuclear shell for South Africa, and the intelligence community and nuclear and ballistics experts were certain that a Bull gun had not launched the nuclear device.

The reason for their certainty is that a gun-launched nuclear weapon requires a high degree of sophistication. Any country wishing to join the nuclear club first tries out the simplest weapon possible, which is one that is detonated in a totally static position. The next stage is to develop a container so that the weapon can be dropped from an aircraft. The next stage is to fit a device to a missile. The final and most difficult stage is to fit a device inside a shell and fire it from a gun. At each of these stages, the weapon gets smaller and is propelled to its target at faster speeds. The smaller the bomb, the faster it goes and the more difficult it is to make. Only the most advanced nuclear countries have nuclear devices that fit into shells; in 1979, South Africa could have only just joined the nuclear club and would have been several years away from developing such a device.

But even if Bull had not contributed to South Africa's nuclear capability, the assistance supplied by SRC had given Armscor a firm grounding in the arms business. By 1982, Armscor had evolved the G-5, which had to be towed to the battlefield, into the G-6, the world's most effective self-propelled gun. With a crew of five, the G-6 can travel at sixty-five miles per hour on good roads and at more than twenty miles per hour over rough terrain. It can fire shells more than thirty miles. The G-5 and G-6 form the backbone of the South African arms export industry, which now produces more than $1 billion a year in valuable foreign exchange for the Pretoria government. Variations of the Bull gun have been sold to Iraq and the United Arab Emirates, and Chile produces it under license.

The statement by Joshua Nkomo and the amplification by the Antiguan dockworkers drew the media's attention to the issue. Both the BBC's "Panorama" and "Fifth Estate," the CBC current affairs program, broadcast shows about the case, alleging that SRC had been smuggling arms to South Africa. The investigations coincided with the beginnings of something approaching a moral crusade in the U.S. government led by President Jimmy Carter. In the new regime, there would be no favors to South Africa, a country that had finally become almost the epitome of evil. Anybody caught breaking the rules would be punished. Jean de Valpine at MDT watched the change.

"I think it's fair to generalize that the CIA, the State Department, and the Department of Defense (DOD) were strongly behind a policy of utilizing South Africa to counter Soviet efforts in Angola via Cuban proxies during the Nixon and Ford administrations. This remained true of the CIA and DOD, but during the Carter administration, antiapartheid, anti–South African objectives and policies became dominant in the State Department and at least muted the support at State for the usage of South Africa to counter the Soviets [Cubans] in Angola."

When he was questioned about the SRC case, President Carter was quite clear: "If it [the allegations] should prove true . . . I would use my full influence to comply with the UN resolutions."

The hounds were on the trail, and Jerry Bull found he had nowhere to hide.

Unless otherwise stated, all photos are courtesy of Dr. Charles Murphy.

Right: Jerry Bull in Barbados in 1963, where the HARP (High Altitude Research Project) was located.

Below: The sponsor and the scientist: Dean Donald Mordell (left) of McGill University was an early believer and helped get the HARP project off the ground. Here, in March 1962, at one of the first of many press conferences, the two men explain how the Martlet rocket could be fired from the HARP gun. Photo courtesy of Reuters/Bettmann Archive.

Below: In 1961, the first 16-inch gun had been installed at the HARP site, having been donated by the U. S. Navy and shipped by the U. S. Army. This gun was the basic version which Bull later extended.

Left: About to conquer space: Dr. Charles Murphy, Bull's lifelong friend and an expert with the U. S. Army's Ballistic Research Laboratories, Professor Bernie Yeager of McGill University, and Bull, photographed in Barbados in 1962.

Opposite: The extended HARP 16-inch gun elevated in the firing position at the Barbados site in 1963. The gun was often fired at night, as the shells left luminous trails in the sky which could be seen from up to a hundred miles away.

Center: A 1963 meeting to plan a firing at the HARP site. Bull is in the center. On the extreme right is Dean Don Mordell of McGill University, and on his right is Wing Commander John Jepson, a British Royal Air Force officer on secondment to the USAF.

Below: Conditions at the HARP site were primitive. Here Jerry Bull communicates from the site of the launch control building by telephone.

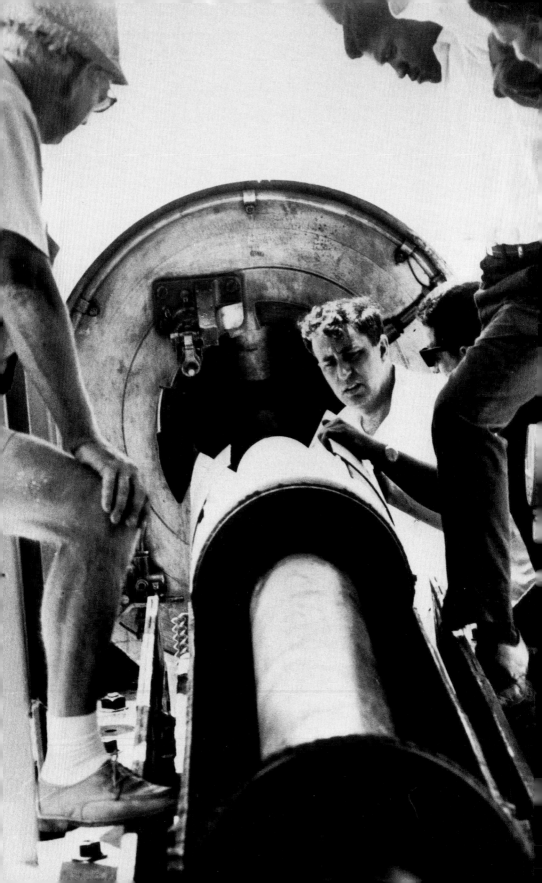

Opposite: Jerry Bull (*center*) and ex-U. S. Navy gun captain Ray Kennington with the gun's hydraulic ram in the foreground.

Left: One of a series of stamps produced by the government of Barbados to celebrate their involvement with the HARP project, which brought both prestige and money to the Caribbean island.

Below: The HARP project made Jerry Bull and his friends celebrities in Barbados. Here Charles Murphy joins Bull at the Independence Day celebrations on the island in 1966.

In 1966, Bull had joined two 16-inch guns together to form one of the first superguns, which was installed at the Highwater site on the U. S.-Canadian border.

Highwater, once the center of Bull's optimism and where he achieved many scientific breakthroughs, is now a wasteland and sad monument to Bull's broken dreams. Here (*top*) the loading mechanism and breech of the 16-inch gun and the 8-inch gun barrel donated to the HARP project by the U. S. Navy (*bottom*) lie rusting among the weeds.

Above: A GHNF artillery piece designed by Bull, built in Austria, and illegally sold to the Iraqis during their war with Iran. ©*Wobrazek/Gamma Liaison.*

Right: The South African G5 howitzer designed from plans supplied by Bull and made from barrels smuggled by SRC from the U. S. to South Africa via Canada. Bull was later tried and jailed for illegally supplying the equipment. *Photo courtesy of TRH Photos.*

Opposite: Mimi Bull hugs a portrait of her husband as she follows his coffin out of the church of St. Bruno de Montarville on March 31, 1990. The church was filled to capacity with family and friends, some of whom had traveled thousands of miles for the funeral. *Photo by Gordon Beck/Montreal Gazette.*

Inset opposite: One of the last people to see Jerry Bull alive, Christopher N. Gumbley, is the chief executive of British arm manufacturer Astra. Gumbley believes that what they discussed caused Bull's death only hours later. He fears he could be next. *Photo courtesy of Astra Holdings, PLC.*

Below: On April 10, 1990, three weeks after Bull was assassinated, British customs seized eight crates destined for Iraq. The crates were officially described as part of a petrochemical project, but were in fact the barrels of the superguns. *Photo courtesy of Press Association, London.*

Upper left: Shortly after the British Customs discovery, trucks destined for Iraq carrying more steel pipes identified only as "tubing" were stopped in Greece and Turkey. Here a plainclothesman covers a 32-ton steel tube found by Greek port police. *Photo courtesy of Reuters/Bettmann Archive.*

View of the muzzle (top) end of a 350mm supergun installed by the Iraqis, photographed in August 1991 by UN inspection teams at Jabal Hamrayn, two hundred kilometers north of Baghdad. *Photo by H. Arvidsson, courtesy of the United Nations.*

Far right: Tube sections of a 1000mm supergun Iraq was building at Iskandariyah, seventy kilometers south of Baghdad, photographed in August 1991 by UN inspectors. *Photo by H. Arvidsson, courtesy of the United Nations.*

Dr. Jerry Bull.

E L E V E N

THE CHASE

THE CALL came on Friday, April 28, 1978, to Larry Curtis at the U.S. Customs Service office in Derby Line, Vermont, fifteen miles east of North Troy. Someone from customs regional headquarters in Miami was on the line and the message was simple: investigate Space Research Corporation and its officials, who are suspected of smuggling arms to South Africa.

At the time, Curtis was a high-ranking GS-13 resident agent for the Customs Service. A local boy, born and brought up in the area, he had chosen to establish his career in Vermont rather than head south for better career opportunities. A well-built, chain-smoking, tough-looking man with piercing brown eyes and short-cropped steely hair, Curtis looks more like a retired marine than a customs officer.[1]

Curtis already knew a great deal about SRC. He had watched the compound grow at Highwater and had seen how SRC had used its position straddling the border to take goods in one side and send them out the other. Also, many of the people working in the compound were his folks; he had grown up with some of them. In many ways, he was the perfect investigator, but his job was made tougher simply because SRC was the main source of income in the area and a generous employer. Anyone who threatened the status quo was not going to be popular.

Curtis called another customs investigator, George Klinefelter, who was based in western Vermont, and asked him to help with the case. The two men had worked together before and were friends. They made something of an odd pair: Curtis, the tall, tough guy; Klinefelter, short, round, bespectacled, with an unfailingly optimistic outlook (an unusual attribute in a veteran law-enforcement agent). The two men were good foils for each other.

The following Wednesday, Curtis flew to Barbados, where he was taken to see Frank Ortiz, the U.S. ambassador, who gave him a full briefing on the allegations against SRC. Curtis then flew to Antigua to meet with the dockers who had revealed SRC's apparent involvement in the smuggling and to collect the documents that had been filed by the *Tugelaland* during her calls to the island. Curtis knew he was on to something when, instead of being met at the airport by the port collector, he was greeted by a sixteen-year-old local girl who took him to his hotel and told him to wait to be contacted by the local customs service. He didn't meet the port collector until the next day and was told that the ship's papers would not be available for a week. In fact, the papers always remained one step ahead of Curtis, and he returned to Vermont empty-handed.

During his trip to the island, he met Rodgers Gregory, who was running SRC's operations there. He showed Curtis documents that he said were logs of the SRC firing range. They indicated that the cargo of shell forgings had been off-loaded in Antigua and fired during research into the performance of Bull-designed artillery. Gregory also took Curtis on a tour of the site at Crab's Point. Curtis made careful notes, including jotting down the serial numbers of the gun barrels. This information later indicated that one gun barrel, which was supposed to be on the site, had actually been shipped to South Africa. Curtis returned to the U.S. with little more than suspicions. Within days of his return to America, U.S. Customs Service officials in West Germany located members of the *Tugelaland*'s crew who confirmed that the containers of shell forgings had been unloaded in South Africa, not Antigua.

Curtis remained unconvinced by the ship's log, which was

too clean to have been in use for several months. He was sure that the whole document had been faked especially for his visit. During his visit, he had examined fifteen metal containers on the site and found only around five hundred projectiles inside, the total inventory for the island. There was no evidence that the enormous quantity of shells that had been shipped to the island had been needed there. Yet Gregory claimed that the containers on the *Tugelaland* had been empty when they left Antigua. It seemed to Curtis that Gregory was lying. If so, the crew of the *Tugelaland* would have an interesting story to tell.

"From then on, I knew we had Bull and SRC cornered," says Curtis.

Curtis made his first appointment to meet Bull in the early summer of 1978, taking Klinefelter with him. They drove to the U.S. side of the SRC compound. Curtis had expected a small, informal meeting, but Bull had invited Gregory and two other SRC colleagues to sit in. Curtis suspected this was meant to ensure that nobody said anything that might later prove incriminating.

A major part of Bull's defense was that the work on the shells had been done in Canada and that all exports had been made with Canadian government approval. At the same time, Bull argued that he held joint U.S.-Canadian citizenship, and he had complied with all Canadian laws. Curtis checked and informed Bull that since he had accepted American citizenship, his Canadian citizenship had been withdrawn. Bull was astonished; he had been traveling abroad, often with Canadian government officials, for seven years on a Canadian passport. He refused to believe Curtis, who suggested that he try to get his passport renewed and see what happened. Bull did so, sending in his check, which was cashed. His passport was not returned for three years.

Bull was outraged at this repudiation by the Canadian government and considered it completely unjustified. There is little doubt that Bull had checked with Ottawa beforehand and had been assured that his Canadian citizenship would not be jeopardized by his becoming an American citizen. Otherwise, he would not have been able to travel on his Canadian passport for so many years without any difficulty. Bull must have thought that the bureaucrats in Ottawa were getting their revenge at last, while at the same time disposing of a potential political embarrassment.

Over the next eight months, Curtis would meet Bull and Gregory several times. Bull was gregarious and outgoing, and Curtis rather liked him, but he never believed a word Bull said to him. Rodgers Gregory, on the other hand, was a real gentleman and a better liar than Bull. "He could stand outside with you in the worst rainstorm you'd ever seen and look you right in the eye and tell you what a beautiful day it was."

At the start of the investigation, Bull refused to take the threat seriously. According to family and friends, he believed with total conviction that he had done nothing wrong and that everything had gone forth with official government approval.

To the customs agents, Bull's certainty of his innocence came across only as arrogance. Klinefelter believed that Bull dismissed the problem "because he was above us." This arrogance naturally made the investigators all the more determined to nail their man.

Once Bull realized that the case was serious, he took a strong dislike to Curtis, who he felt was unfairly persecuting him. Bull began to consider Curtis as his nemesis, describing him in his own writings as "a psychopath."[2]

"Curtis always had a personal vendetta against my father," says Michel Bull. "When he was named to the investigation, he thought he had it made, that he would be promoted to director in Washington. But it never happened."[3]

Shortly after his first meeting with Curtis, Bull heard that Joseph Severin, the head of PRB in Belgium, had been killed in a tragic fall down the stairs at his home. Severin died on June 6, and SRC's relationship with PRB was immediately in doubt. While the contract between the two companies had finally been signed a few months earlier, the whole arrangement depended on the personal relationship between Bull and Severin.

Bull must have felt that his whole world was falling apart: first the customs investigation, and now the death of a man he considered a good friend and business partner. He was unable to accept that Severin's death was an accident, and soon after his death Bull began to talk mysteriously about a plot to kill Severin, how he had been killed by hired assassins to break the relationship he had built with SRC. Bull never produced any evidence for this allegation, which evolved over the years in his mind from supposition to certainty. Severin's death would be one of the many events in the chain that Bull believed was being created to destroy him and his reputation.

After that first interview with the customs investigators, Bull and Gregory realized that the matter was serious and that they had better take some steps to defend themselves. They were recommended to Kirk Karaszkiewicz, a Philadelphia lawyer who had considerable experience as both a defense and prosecuting attorney in customs cases. He agreed to represent SRC.

On his first trip to meet Bull in the SRC compound, Karaszkiewicz was escorted to one of the company's briefing rooms. There, instead of talking about the details of the case, Bull insisted on giving the lawyer a thorough grounding in ballistics that included the HARP program and SRC's work on artillery. The lawyer followed the first five minutes and then became lost in the bewildering array of arcs, vectors, and equations that Bull scribbled helpfully on a blackboard.[4]

Bull's next step was to hire a lawyer for himself. At the outset, Gregory and Bull agreed that they would be represented jointly by Bob Bennett, a former federal prosecutor who was a partner in the Washington law firm of Dunnells, Duvall, Bennett and Porter. It was an unusual arrangement, but one that they felt would simplify the case and reduce the costs. Bennett was one of America's leading white-collar-criminal defense lawyers and a realist when it came to defending his clients. He was very experienced and a well-known figure on the Washington legal circuit. He would later serve as chief counsel to the Senate Ethics Committee during their hearings on the savings and loan scandal involving the senators known as the Keating Five. His brother, William Bennett, became director of the National Office for Drug Policy in the Reagan and Bush administrations.

The U.S. attorney for Vermont was William Gray, former

associate deputy attorney general in the Justice Department and director of the executive office for U.S. attorneys, responsible for supervising the execution of budgets of all U.S. attorneys across the country.

What might have been a small trial in a small country town was now being orchestrated by three powerful and very experienced lawyers who fully understood all the political ramifications. This produced a professional air of realism about the case; the parties soon recognized that some compromises were going to be required.

Once SRC and Bull had their lawyers in place, the district attorney moved swiftly to formalize the case. On December 7, 1978, a grand jury was convened in Rutland, Vermont, to hear evidence. While the jury's deliberations were supposed to be held in secret, they met in the federal courthouse, which was actually the second floor of the town's post office. The "courthouse" consisted of a central corridor, flanked on one side by the U.S. attorney's office and on the other by the judge's chambers and courtroom. The courthouse was an old building, with no back doors, secret passageways, or freight elevators by which witnesses could be smuggled in and out. Instead, each witness could be observed being escorted into the grand jury by the federal marshals; many of them were interviewed by reporters while the proceedings were in progress.

Some of the leaks appeared to be officially orchestrated—the jury would hear testimony one day and the details would appear in the newspaper the next. However, all the attorneys involved deny there were any official leaks. The single exception was one occasion in 1979 when Curtis was called down to Boston by Bob DiLorenzo, the regional director of investigations, who instructed Curtis to give an interview to Ben Bradlee, Jr., of the *Boston Globe.* At the time, customs had been criticized for losing a number of arms-smuggling cases, so the Curtis interview was supposed to show the public that they were finally going to win one.

Bull's frustration with the whole process is clear from his written personal defense. Throughout the document he wrote of himself in the third person:

Politically, Carter wanted an example to show his support of human rights and his desire to destroy dirty U.S. industry, particularly defense industries. That any intelligent assessment of the corporate facts would have shown no U.S. jurisdiction, seemed clear to Bull and SRC-Q. The Grand Jury system was unknown to Bull. The fact that it is hearsay, one-sided (no defense allowed, or even the allegation allowed to be known), orchestrated by evangelical driven government attorneys seeking advancement and to run for political office by pleasing political bosses, was unappreciated. The SRC lawyers, American, recommended totally ignoring this body, since they stated it was a well known show business process. Extraneous witnesses would be called, extravagant press leaks used to build up the public image of guilt and in this case raise the righteous wrath of the populous [sic] against the SRC racists. They would parade alleged CIA [agents], such as the pompous Frost, along with every publicity-seeking gimmick possible. It would drag on for 18 months, and nothing could be done to counter it. . . . The hysteric atmosphere created can only be imagined in the context of the infamous Nazi trial of the Jews.

The location of the SRC compound proved a major obstacle for the customs officials, who wanted to track the movement of all goods across the border. But SRC had been using the border to their advantage for years. Untangling the mess was virtually impossible. For example, if Bull had wanted a typewriter for SRC-Q and he found it was two hundred dollars cheaper in Vermont, then a purchase order would be drawn on SRC-US letterhead and the machine would be paid for from a U.S. account. The customs officer at the U.S. gate would be told that the typewriter was for use on the U.S. side. Once through the gate, the machine would be driven to the Canadian side.

The investigation essentially worked on two levels. The U.S. Customs Service was trying to piece together the smuggling operation from documents, which were extracted with considerable difficulty from SRC. At the same time, Curtis and Klinefelter were interviewing everybody they could track down. The only person who was immediately helpful was Jack Frost. He now had his opportunity for revenge.

Once contacted by Curtis, Frost repeated the tale he had rehearsed to the State Department—the story of Frost as hero, rather than villain, damning both the South Africans and Bull as coconspirators. He revealed every detail concerning the arms smuggling that he knew and claimed that he had warned both Bull and the South Africans not to proceed.

"It was clear he was instrumental in bringing the South Africans and Bull together, and it was also clear that when he got cut out of the deal he became the innocent," recalls Curtis.

Frost may have put some flesh on the bones of the story the customs officials already knew, but he also led them directly to the CIA connection, revealing the involvement of John Clancey. Rather than approach the CIA, Curtis went to the Pentagon and tracked Clancey to the marine headquarters at Camp Lejeune, North Carolina. "It was like pulling teeth to get in to see him," says Klinefelter. "When confronted, Clancey never admitted any connection with the case, repeatedly saying, I don't have time to see you guys, or, I don't remember, although he did admit to having heard of Bull and SRC."

Clancey was subpoenaed to appear before the grand jury. The night before his appearance, he met with Curtis and Klinefelter at the Howard Johnson in Rutland. The two men spent the evening watching Clancey drink beer and tell war stories. During the evening, Clancey admitted to having been loaned to the CIA from the marines, but he continued to deny he was a CIA agent. When he appeared before the grand jury the next day, flanked by U.S. Customs agents to guard him from the press, he denied all knowledge of the case. Klinefelter and Curtis wanted to charge him with perjury.

Any further efforts to implicate the CIA in the deal were stonewalled by the Customs Service in Washington, which referred their Washington men to an attorney in the Justice Department. The attorney was supposed to relay the customs agents' questions to the CIA. The questions were never answered. Despite this, Curtis believes that the CIA was not directly responsible for the deal with South Africa. Even though the CIA had wanted to get the 155-mm gun into Angola in 1976, when CIA officials had gone before the Potts Committee for clearance to ship the gun to South Africa, they had been denied permission. Through Clancey, they then approached SRC, which was when they had discovered that Bull already had a signed contract with South Africa. There is no evidence that the CIA had gotten them together. Once the CIA officials found out about the contract, Curtis believes the agency made clear to some government departments that they had an interest in the deal going through smoothly. This had the effect of expediting some aspects of the deal, particularly the approvals granting SRC the use of the Chamberlain munitions plant.

Bill Gray, the U.S. attorney for Vermont, largely shares the view that there was more to the government's involvement. "I was never fully satisfied that I knew everything that I needed to know about the government's role."[5]

In preparation for the discovery phase of a possible trial, Gray was required to search for documentary evidence in all branches of the federal government that might have been involved in the case. In late 1979, Gray traveled to CIA headquarters in Langley, Virginia, to ask for all relevant documents. Once there, he was sent to an empty room, where a low-level functionary who knew nothing about the case brought him files, none of which were of any interest.

"My best guess is that the CIA did not authorize or approve the operation, but that they may have known about it and looked the other way," says Gray. "If that was the case, in the DA's view the CIA would be neither guilty of conspiracy nor aiding and abetting."

The Israelis also refused to cooperate with the investigation in any way. The customs investigation revealed an earlier shipment of refurbished 155-mm gun barrels that had gone from Montreal to South Africa via New York. In theory, these guns would have required an in-transit license, which SRC had never obtained. The barrels had been shipped on board a vessel belonging to the Zim line, which is owned by the Israeli government, and had been labeled as oil-drilling equipment. The customs officials were unable to interview anyone from Israeli Military

Industries or from the Israeli embassy in Washington about the case. Indeed, once they started asking questions, the Israelis used their muscle in Washington, and the customs officials were told to lay off.

Customs also got little cooperation from the Office of Munitions Control, which was reluctant to hand over any documents relating to the case, perhaps because of embarrassment at writing the letter that had allowed Bull to export the rough forgings. In any event, the government lawyers decided that the OMC letter would not be a major obstacle, because it related only to the shell forgings and not to the guns or the radar vans and thus would have had no bearing on any charges for conspiracy or fraud.

As the investigation progressed, SRC's strategy was to claim that the documents required by the Customs Service, such as employee travel vouchers, invoices, and shipping receipts, did not exist. Then, a few days later, after figuring out the line of investigation, SRC would claim that the documents had turned up on the Canadian side of the compound. "I had no doubt that SRC forged shipping and other records on a large scale throughout the investigation," says Curtis.

Toward the end of 1978, Curtis went to the SRC compound for a meeting with Gregory. He was stopped at the guard hut, then was given a pass to see Gregory and waved through. Instead of going directly to Gregory's office in the administration building, Curtis continued on the main road to a records building on the Canadian side of the compound where he hoped he might find some documents lying around. Curtis rifled through some filing cabinets and was on his way out of the building with an armful of paper when six SRC guards arrived and forced him to return the files. Curtis had no search warrant or subpoena and was committing an illegal act, which led to a shouting match with Gregory. Today, the frustration of the case still rankles. Curtis shrugs. "You do what you have to."

One day in August 1979, Klinefelter was called by Bull's private pilot, Judd Glen, who asked him to attend a private meeting with Bull at Highwater that afternoon. Klinefelter explained that he would have to bring Curtis with him. "This sort of meeting was a typical Bull thing. He was really into clandestine shit," says Klinefelter.

Klinefelter called Curtis, and the two men drove to the compound after lunch. They were escorted up to Bull's house. The two customs agents sat with Bull on a deck overlooking the pool while Mimi passed back and forth in a bikini, serving drinks. Curtis drank vodka and tonic, Klinefelter Scotch and water. Klinefelter recalls Bull drinking Chivas Regal.

The customs agents warned Bull that he should not be speaking to them without a lawyer present, but Bull insisted that a lawyer would just complicate the issue. Anyway, he had nothing to hide. The three men talked until 9:00 P.M., by which time they were all on very good terms.

The agents believed that they had gathered enough evidence to have the bare bones of a case, and they certainly knew enough to know when Bull was lying. "Bull sat there for seven or eight hours and lied to Curtis and me," says Klinefelter. "The man just sat there, buddy-buddy, and gave out this spiel."

Despite this cynicism among the customs agents, Klinefelter, who has a genuine liking for most people, found Bull very engaging. "If you had a party going on in a room with fifty or seventy people and Bull came in, within an hour he would be the focal point. He was really a dynamic person."

At the end of the meeting, Bull handed over a copy of a thirty-eight-page handwritten document that he had prepared for his Canadian lawyer, Lambert Toupin, as an explanation of the case and his involvement. It is an extraordinary document, filled with indignation and conspiracy theories and revealing a great deal about the workings of SRC. In it Bull admitted again and again that he did not have the details about key aspects of the business, including the contracts with SRC-I and the negotiations for the South African contract.

Bull argued that the shipments from Antigua to South Africa never took place and, in fact, that all the shells were fired on the island while testing the 155-mm guns. The confusion arose, claimed Bull, because of incompetence by Antiguan port officials, who filled in a number of loading documents incorrectly. In addition, while some SRC employees might have gone to

South Africa, they had been employed by SRC-I and not by SRC-US and had actually been working for PRB and not SRC at all. Finally, even if the shells had been shipped to South Africa, they had been manufactured by SRC-Q and thus did not fall under the jurisdiction of U.S. Customs.

"As far as Antigua is concerned," Bull wrote,

> let me make myself clear. It was never planned as a trans-shipment operation or for any illegal operations. It was a field operation which was loaded with incompetence and in a country where wild rumors, outright lies, bribery etc. apparently flourishes.
>
> My feelings at this time are that we expanded too rapidly into the big European brotherhood, that our control techniques were naive and our shipping [left] much to be desired. However, I don't think the whole matter is accidental; I have a distinct impression that various plots have been made against us, that possibly we have been sucked into things we don't understand. . . . Simply, our world has changed too much for us.

The idea that he was being persecuted by outside agencies in a way that he did not fully comprehend was to become a recurring theme in Bull's life. At this stage, with his world crumbling around him, he was unable to face the fact that he might have been responsible for any of his problems. On the contrary, he chose to lay the blame on others. At this stage, however, he could not decide exactly who or what should be the focus of his enmity.

To the tough customs investigators, the long document resembled the ramblings of a broken and guilty man. As far as they were concerned, none of the alibis stood up and none of the excuses made any difference to their case. For twelve years Curtis has kept the document in a file at his home marked "Bullshit."

Three months later Bull called the agents again. This time they met in a room at the Howard Johnson in Rutland. For three hours, Bull, now clearly concerned by the way the investigation was going, repeated exactly the same arguments he had presented during their drunken session at his home.

At the beginning of 1979, the government lawyers decided to give First Pennsylvania limited immunity in exchange for access to all documents related to the case. Curtis, who believed he had enough evidence to charge and convict several bank officials, resisted the deal, but he was overruled by Washington. The documents laid out the course of the deal like a diary.

The combination of the collapse of the European operation after the death of Severin, the disintegration of SRC in the United States and Canada, and the imminent trial were beginning to take a heavy toll on Bull. He was simply unable to understand the series of catastrophes that beset him. Instead of accepting any guilt, he came to believe that the case and every other setback was all part of some vast conspiracy against him. In conversations with friends and with Curtis and Klinefelter, he would talk vaguely of communists being behind the ploy and speak frequently about his betrayal by the American government.

Bull began to drink a great deal at this time, and he was frequently incoherent during his meetings with the lawyers. The lawyers now made a point of discussing every important issue three or four times to make sure that Bull had grasped the issues. This, of course, added to the pressure and made Bull's drinking worse.

At the time, Bull's major concern was keeping SRC afloat and paying the salaries of his employees. Throughout his business career, Bull had been unable to fire anybody, preferring to pay them out of his own pocket rather than let them go. This was one of the reasons why SRC never made any money, but now that SRC's income had almost dried up, Bull was getting desperate.

In the middle of 1979, he flew to Vienna and met with the senior directors of NORICUM, a wholly owned arms manufacturing subsidiary of the state-owned Voest-Alpine. Bull had sold the South Africans the rights to the 155-mm extended-range artillery, but he had received no royalties on any of the hundreds of artillery pieces that were later sold around the world by

Armscor, which was a constant source of resentment. Nonetheless, he agreed to a similar contract with NORICUM now. In order to put together enough money to pay SRC's bills until the end of the year, he sold the Austrian company the rights to manufacture the 155-mm artillery and market it around the world. It was an exceptionally generous deal to which no sensible businessman would ever have agreed. In just two transactions with NORICUM and Armscor, Bull had sold the results of all his work since the end of the HARP program.

NORICUM was quick to take advantage of his generosity. The company took his basic gun design and within two years was marketing it as the GH N-45. In 1981, 200 of the guns were ostensibly sold to Jordan, but once delivered to that country they were diverted to Iraq for use in its war with Iran. Three years later, NORICUM made a deal with Libya to sell them 150 GH N-45 guns worth $250 million. In fact, the deal had been secretly concluded with the Iranian government, and the guns had been diverted to Tehran after $56 million in bribes had been siphoned through two dummy companies—one in Liechtenstein and one in Panama.[6]

That same year, NORICUM concluded another deal for 155-mm gun barrels for Brazil worth $60 million. These traveled as far as Yugoslavia, where they were diverted to Iran under the original end-user certificate.

At this point, the arms traffic was being detected in satellite photographs taken by U.S. intelligence. The U.S. warned the Austrian government no less than ten times in 1986 that NORICUM was breaking the arms embargo imposed after the outbreak of the Iran/Iraq war, even producing the photographs to back up its allegations. Only after receiving bad press did the Austrian government take any action; several senior NORICUM directors were jailed after a trial in 1991.

As the investigation of Bull progressed, Curtis came under heavy pressure from his superiors in the Customs Service to produce results. For almost two years, the case had been given number-one priority by the Boston office. All Curtis's requests for assistance from customs agents worldwide had also been rated top priority. But Curtis's bosses were becoming anxious to see the payoff. In March 1980, Curtis met with Jerry Niedermeier, one of the prosecuting attorneys, to review the case. They agreed that the government could prepare indictments against twelve people, including Bull, Gregory, and all the employees who had gone to South Africa, Frank Nel, and Patrick Giles, the American lawyer who had helped set up the deal from his London office. In addition, charges could be made against SRC-US, SRC-Q, SRC-I, Colet Trading, and Paragon Holdings.

Over the previous months, Gray, Karaszkiewicz, and Bennett had been jockeying for psychological advantage.

"By early 1980, the government had backed itself into a corner with its investigation," recalls Karaszkiewicz.

The Customs Service was excited about the case, because they saw a chance to bring a great many charges against SRC, Bull, and Gregory and give a big boost to their annual total of indictments, as well as get a lot of favorable publicity. The prosecutor, however, was faced with a situation in which the actual charges that were to be filed were not general charges of illegal shipment of arms to South Africa, but more specifically, of filing false export declarations with the Customs Service, a much more minor violation.

Additionally, the combination of the Office of Munitions Control letter approving some exports and the specter of CIA involvement and U.S. national security interests in Angola created an aura of doubt which could be exploited [by Bull's attorneys] to great effect.

Inevitably, the prosecution saw the arguments rather differently. Gray repeatedly told Bennett that none of this "outside shit" was going to enter into the case because it was irrelevant to the charges that were going to be filed. But that tough stance against the opposition was belied by serious doubts that the prosecution would be successful. Gray knew that Judge James Holden, who had been slated to try the case, was both tough and fair. In fact, Gray actually believed that Holden would require the CIA to be represented at the trial in order to protect Bull's and Gregory's rights as defendants.

"I can see Holden saying to me, 'Mr. Gray, can you assure me that this is every single document from the U.S. government on this case?' and it would have been very difficult for me to make that assurance."

When Bennett approached the prosecution with the offer of a deal, the discussions were short. Both sides recognized that plea-bargaining was sensible: the prosecution because it might have trouble proving its case, the defense because if Bull and Gregory could get away with pleading a lesser charge, then the threat of their being tried for more than two hundred charges, which Gray had been privately threatening, would disappear.

Initially Bennett asked for all charges against the individuals to be dropped in exchange for SRC-US pleading guilty. By now, however, SRC was virtually worthless and in no position to pay a fine. In any event, what Gray wanted was bodies in jail, people who would pay a price for their crimes.

Eventually, both Bull and Gregory decided to plead guilty to a single charge of exportation of munitions without a license, a felony punishable by a prison term of up to two years. The charge had been divided into three components. The two men admitted to exporting (1) at least thirty thousand 155-mm extended-range projectile forgings and components, (2) two 155-mm gun barrels, and (3) one radar tracking system consisting of two vans.

The plea hearing was set for March 25, 1989. Just three days before the hearing, Curtis learned that a deal had been cut behind his back and that his hope of a full trial of all those involved was to be dashed. The day Curtis heard of the planned deal, Mimi was in the Bahamas with her brother, Dr. André Gilbert, and his family, having a few days' holiday. Bull called Mimi from Europe and explained that the grand jury planned to bring indictments against ten SRC staff members, including himself and Gregory, and three lawyers. Bull said that Gregory had lost the will to fight and that he, Bull, planned to plead guilty on one count to protect "his people."

Mimi argued strongly against the guilty plea but failed to move her husband. She then tried to catch a plane from the

Bahamas to Montreal, but there were no flights that day. By the time she reached Highwater, it was too late; Bull had already passed through on his way to Rutland for the hearing.

The exchange between the attorneys and the judge lasted only a few minutes. Judge Holden questioned Bull and Gregory about a possible conflict of interest in having Bennett represent them both. Both men assured him they were happy to be represented by one lawyer. Holden then asked Bull if he pleaded guilty to all three of the items in the charge.

Bull replied, "Your Honor, I have a slight difference with my co-defendant as regards to my willfully exporting [thirty thousand shells] to the Republic of South Africa. . . . I don't think I could plead guilty to that. I think I would be committing perjury if I said I could. Regarding the other two counts—the other two components of the count, yes, Your Honor, they are, I am guilty of both those."

"What did you do in this connection?" the judge asked.

"Well, as the chief executive of the corporation, I approved it. I knowingly let it take place."

"And you knew that—and you did so with the intent to violate the laws of the United States?"

"Yes sir."

Throughout the investigation, Bull had refused to take his situation seriously. When he finally realized the threat it posed, he never admitted that he had done anything wrong. Even as the evidence mounted, he continued to protest his innocence with a mixture of bombast and cunning. On the one hand, he argued that no weapons were sent to South Africa; on the other, he argued that if they had been shipped, then the event had occurred outside the jurisdiction of U.S. authorities. Underlying all these arguments was his conviction that, in the end, the U.S. would somehow come to his rescue.

His lawyers recall that as the case evolved and the trial date came closer, Bull's facade began to crumble, first from the drinking, then as a result of his increasingly obsessive search to blame somebody—anybody—for his predicament.

One of his lawyers recounts that "from the start of [our] relationship, Bull always came to meetings with one or more acolytes in attendance. These individuals were never introduced and would simply sit and listen." The lawyer believed that these people were part of the large entourage who leeched off of Bull's generosity. "A lot of people made a lot of money off of him, so nobody ever stood up to him. The result was that he was told only what he wanted to hear and never confronted with the truth of his own guilt."

The same lawyer describes Bull as "bizarre, very short-sighted. He would say anything if it would bring him an immediate benefit. He was the most arrogant person I ever met, narcissistic with visions of grandeur, brilliant yet strangely childish, a manic-depressive—at one time saying that he had hired the greatest fucking lawyer ever and the next complaining bitterly at the treatment he had received from all lawyers. People didn't like Bull. If you spent some time with him, you'd want to kill him too."

Eventually, the more Bull was forced to confront the reality of the court case, the more he retreated into the fantasy of a conspiracy being plotted against him. When the day finally arrived for Bull to be brought before the judge for sentencing, he was almost incapable of withstanding the blow to his already shattered pride.

T W E L V E

JAIL

BULL'S SENTENCING on June 16, 1980, was something of an anticlimax. The deal had been agreed to by the attorneys beforehand. The only major concern that remained was the kind of sentence Bull would receive.

Mimi had maintained from the beginning that her husband would be let off with a fine. Bull's lawyers, on the other hand, had made it clear from the start that he would probably be sent to jail, given the high profile of the case and the nature of the charges (Bennett had actually done a study of Judge Holden's sentencing patterns and had predicted a sentence of between four and eight months). Bull chose to believe Mimi because, as he did so often in his life, he disregarded the bad news.

Bull arrived at court with Mimi, Marcel Paquette, and Gabriel LaPointe, Bull's friend and a Montreal lawyer. Paquette remembers them pushing their way through the cameras to get into the courtroom, which was already filled with the media and attorneys. Bull appeared to be fairly relaxed and was looking forward to the end of the case so he could go home and start rebuilding his life.

Before passing sentence, Judge Holden read the pleas of mitigation submitted by Bennett. The lawyer had pointed out that

Gregory was a grandfather who was responsible for looking after his grandchildren because his son-in-law was an alcoholic. In addition, Gregory had suffered a torn retina, brought about by the stress of the case. Bennett pleaded for clemency for them both. In Bull's case, Bennett argued that he had given valuable service to the U.S. government and had pleaded guilty to a "very minor licensing violation."

Bennett also argued that the U.S. government had encouraged SRC to help Israel despite the general assumption that Israel would give whatever technology it possessed directly to South Africa. This was a very unusual statement for a lawyer to make, and Bennett must have been absolutely certain of his facts to have made the point at all. He went on to say that neither Bull nor Gregory should be unfairly penalized for the vagaries of government policy, the media attention, or the general bias against South Africa.

The ever-loyal Arthur Trudeau also submitted a letter arguing for clemency, saying that he had been a director of SRC until recently and that he had known Bull for many years and placed him in the "top 2% of the people [I have] known in relation to the caliber of his service to the United States." The judge clearly found these arguments unconvincing, and he sentenced both Bull and Gregory to a year's imprisonment with six months suspended. Bull was ordered to surrender on July 30, 1980, to begin his sentence.

Customs agent George Klinefelter had been watching Bull closely as the sentence was passed and he saw a look of disbelief cross over his face. Bull quickly looked down.

Until the sentence was actually given, Bull had believed he would walk away from the court a free man. He was convinced that his long service to the U.S. and Canada would be taken into consideration, and he had expected just a slap on the wrist. His jail sentence absolutely devastated him.

"It was the toughest day of his life," recalls Paquette. "He was very nervous, tense, pale, and we couldn't talk to him the whole day. Mimi was affected in much the same way, but after a few hours, when she realized that she would have to take over the entire situation—the houses, the children, everything—she carried it off with great strength."

Writing in his own biography, Bull described his opinion of the court's decision:

> Vicious, vindictive manipulation for purposes against the national interest and decency, perversion of revered institutions guaranteeing protection of both the citizens and the countries, were clear. The very essence of the decency of the society all were clearly demonstrated as hypocritical propaganda. No concern for the individual [or] the national interest were evidenced. Rather, the concept of life was shown [to be] one of smart, fashionable arguments to rouse all to passions against the victim. Legal deceit, practiced by US government lawyers, and by most North American lawyers involved, seeking financial reward and advancement to political heights, dominated all.

The thoughts presented in this rambling and largely incoherent condemnation of all who were associated with the case formed the foundation of Bull's final years. He remained totally convinced that he had been framed, even though the court's transcript clearly indicates he had accepted responsibility for at least some of the charges. His disgust with the system was such that he began the fateful move of turning his back on both Canada, the country of his birth, and America, the country he had adopted.

Bull was unable to face the reality of his sentence. Rather than simply arriving at the jail on July 30, he devised a series of increasingly desperate measures to get the case overturned and to stay out of jail.

He volunteered for admission to the Silver Hill Foundation, a private, nonprofit hospital set on sixty acres of land in a pastoral spot in New Canaan, Connecticut. The hospital specializes in substance abuse treatment and adult psychiatric services. Silver Hill prides itself on giving more individualized and humane treatment than other psychiatric hospitals. Each patient is under the care of a licensed board-certified psychiatrist, with whom they meet for three hours a week, which is more than in most hospitals. The buildings are laid out in a campus-style arrangement around the main building, which is designed to resemble an old inn, giving Silver Hill the atmosphere of a rural retreat rather than a hospital.

When Dr. Robert Humphries first examined Bull, he appeared to be deeply wounded, depressed, and unassuming—a beaten man, which the doctor did not consider particularly unusual under the circumstances.[1]

From the beginning, the two men got along well. Humphries discovered that his grandmother lived just down the road from Bull's stepmother in Kingston, Ontario, which gave them an immediate personal connection.

Bull told Humphries how embittered he felt by the sentence, that he had been stretching the law no more than others did, but that he had been convicted because of his prominence and the politics surrounding dealings with South Africa.

"Bull struck me as a former patriot with a strong capacity for turning against a fatherland that didn't reward him," says Humphries.

Bull was hoping that the doctor would say that he was too ill to be sent to jail. But Humphries found that this was not the case. For instance, Bull was never put under a suicide watch during his stay.

While he was at Silver Hill, Bull had written a letter to Bennett immediately after the sentencing, thanking him for doing an excellent job and negotiating such a short prison term. But the prospect of jail still preyed on Bull's mind, and he decided to change his lawyer, firing Bennett and replacing him with Stanley Pottinger of the Washington firm Troy, Malin and Pottinger. Pottinger had just gone into private practice after serving as assistant attorney general for civil rights in the Carter administration, and he was ideally placed to argue what Bull felt had been an essentially political case. The legal team that Pottinger put together found a very different man from the person evaluated by Dr. Humphries, however.

According to Warren Dennis, one of the lawyers working with Pottinger, Bull was in a mental state that alternated between being intensely focused and mentally adrift. In the latter state his conversation would turn mysterious and he would become virtually incomprehensible. Dennis described Bull as being clinically depressed and said that during his legal consultations, he would "exhibit a fatalistic lightheartedness, repeating over and over that 'My life is over' and calling himself a total failure." On more than one occasion Bull threatened in front of Dennis to kill himself.

Hamilton Loeb, another one of the lawyers working on the appeal, says Bull was in "a clear state of disorientation and significant mental distress." Loeb had serious doubts as to whether Bull had been in full possession of his faculties when he entered his guilty plea, and he felt Bull was unfit to go to jail.[2]

These assessments were not supported by Bull's family or friends, who describe him as having been very distressed by the verdict but say that he was certainly aware of what was happening and understood the significance of his actions.

Interestingly, Warren Dennis was under the impression that Bull *had* been put on a suicide watch and had been under twenty-four-hour guard throughout his time at Silver Hill, something that is firmly denied by his doctor. Bull is the only person who could have made such a statement, perhaps to bolster his pretense of mental instability to convince his lawyers he would be in serious danger if he was sent to prison.[3]

Of course, Bull could have been acting, cunningly portraying himself as a manic-depressive to his lawyers and psychiatrist so they would help him avoid his jail term.

The net result was that Pottinger made a submission to the court on July 23, 1980, arguing that Bull's sentence should be reduced or that he should serve his time in a hospital rather than a jail. Pottinger said that Bull had felt a crushing sense of self-betrayal, of being disloyal to the deeply held values of honor and patriotic duty that had been nurtured by his professional life. Incarceration would serve none of the three purposes of sentencing: rehabilitation, deterrence, or retribution.

On August 26, while reviewing the report from Dr. Humphries, Judge Holden said that the psychiatric evaluation did indicate tendencies toward self-destruction and suicide. Humphries had recommended that Bull be sent to Silver Hill for another month of observation, but the judge, who did not believe the report, ordered that Bull begin serving his sentence on August 30 at Allenwood Penitentiary in Pennsylvania.

While he was still in the hospital, Bull became convinced that he had been set up by his lawyer, Bob Bennett. He fired Pottinger and contacted Bill Gibson, yet another lawyer, and insisted that there had been a serious miscarriage of justice. He told Gibson that he had met with Bennett only once before the trial date and that the guilty plea had been forced on him. Bull argued, and Gibson agreed, that there had been a clear conflict of interest because Bennett also had represented Gregory. All the smuggling had been organized by Gregory, Bull said, an accusation that revealed an astonishing disloyalty given that Gregory had stood by him without argument from the beginning of the investigation. However, even Bull's family and friends claimed that Gregory was the mastermind of the smuggling operation and had profited personally from it.

In September, Gibson filed a motion to set aside the conviction and withdraw the guilty plea. It was the last cry of a desperate man. If Gibson succeeded, then Bull would be opting for a full trial, which would probably last at least nine months and cost him $500,000, money that he did not have.

When Bennett heard that a new plea had been entered, he immediately telephoned Gibson for an explanation. Bennett explained that his private meetings with Bull had accounted for approximately two hundred hours of consultations over nearly two years. Gibson was stunned. The other lawyers were outraged and united behind Bennett. Judge Holden threw out the motion, and Bull had to serve his full term, which amounted to only four months with time off for good behavior.

Apparently, Bull had lied to Gibson just as he had lied to his previous lawyers. Bull's family excused his behavior by arguing that he had been under great stress at the time and his judgment was flawed. Others were less charitable. Customs official Larry Curtis said that Bull was simply repeating a pattern of dishonesty that he had demonstrated for many years.

Allenwood is a minimum-security jail with no fence, no gate, and a very relaxed environment. The inmates are all nonviolent white-collar criminals. "It was like being in college," recalls Paquette, who was one of ten people allowed to visit. "If it were not for the uniforms, you would have thought he was back in school."

Bull was given his own room and had a considerable amount of personal freedom. He even helped the prison warden by doing some engineering drawings of a planned addition to the prison building. He was taught backgammon by one of the inmates, an alcoholic who later committed suicide.

In jail, his only real friend was Bosco Ravennovich, a Yugoslavian exile who had been imprisoned for "anti-Tito political activities." Bull and Bosco became very good friends, says Paquette. "Bosco had a good mind and they could discuss intellectual things." After the two men were released and Bosco went to New York to run a parking garage, they stayed in touch and Bosco came to visit both Highwater and St.-Bruno. Bull even started a novel based on Bosco, which he never completed.

Bull was regularly visited by Charlie Murphy, Paquette, Mimi, and other members of his family. They would meet him in the large visitors' room, which was light and sunny, with vending machines lining the wall. Visitors were allowed to stay all day, but despite the unrestricted environment, Mimi hated going to Allenwood. Even now she refuses to drive or fly through Pennsylvania because of the memories that linger from those months.

Jail had a traumatic effect on Bull. For the rest of his life, his obsession with his innocence would occupy hundreds of hours of research and debates with friends and colleagues. He believed that even if he had not actually been the victim of a conspiracy, he had certainly been let down by a number of officials from several U.S. government agencies, particularly the CIA, who had been perfectly aware of the arms traffic to South Africa and had endorsed it enthusiastically.

The confinement, combined with a growing paranoia, made him depressed and claustrophobic. Both problems would plague him long after he was released. Bull would panic, particularly in airports, becoming suddenly afraid of being arrested again. He would also worry that people were following him. Curiously, he also suddenly became allergic to animals.

But jail also provided time for reflection, an opportunity for Bull to consider both the past and the future. He was still unable to accept that he had even been guilty of mismanagement. Instead, he kept shifting the blame to others, and his friends were unwilling to force him to face the truth. Apparently, he inspired loyalty and friendship but not frankness. Bull's family complicated matters by reinforcing his prejudices and bolstering his belief that he was right and the world was wrong.

In prison, Bull's dislike for government bureaucrats and paper shufflers turned to considerable bitterness. But he was not in a position to revenge himself directly on his enemies. Bull was not a violent man, and he could hardly hunt down his accusers. Instead, he decided that, from then on, he would work outside the system that had treated him so unfairly. He would take his talents to the highest bidder, and to hell with the rest of the world.

As far as he was concerned, the American government had failed to stand behind him by allowing the customs investigation to proceed, and the Canadian government had been conspiring against him ever since he had left CARDE nearly twenty years earlier. The jail sentence had put a stain on his reputation that made it impossible for him to work in North America, and there seemed little prospect of either the government or industry giving him any contracts.

Bull decided that he would never work in either the U.S. or Canada again. In any case, there was little to make him stay. SRC-US and SRC-Q had been destroyed by the case. Highwater, the former source of such happiness, was now an empty shell, the buildings deserted and the guns rusting.

Aside from the U.S. and Canada, the place he knew best was Belgium, because of SRC's links with PRB. He visited the country two or three times immediately following his release and decided to make it his home.

Both Michel and Stephen moved to Brussels with their father; Stephen helped on the engineering side of SRC-I and

Michel balanced the books. Mimi did not want to leave Quebec while their youngest child, Noemie-Jane, was still in school. She tried to persuade Bull to stay in Canada, but he was determined to leave. Mimi was to travel to Belgium five or six times a year until Bull was killed. While the family remained remarkably close until Bull's death, the move to Brussels cast Jerry adrift from the anchor of Highwater and Mimi. Without those restraining influences, the darker side of Jerry's character came to the fore. Exile in Brussels meant the end of any ambitions Bull ever had to use his talents for peace. Instead, he decided to make war on the world.

T H I R T E E N

AN INNOCENT

ABROAD

THE SMUGGLING of Jerry Bull's artillery to South Africa had been a shabby business that corrupted everyone involved. At every level, deceit and dishonesty driven by greed and ambition destroyed careers and made liars out of honest men. It was also a triumph for the apartheid regime in South Africa. The case demonstrated quite vividly that while the American government had officially endorsed the United Nations arms embargo against South Africa, unofficially it had actually encouraged arms traffic.

The investigation and guilty verdict marked the end of Bull's legitimate career. From the moment he stepped through the gates of Allenwood, he became a pariah, deserted by colleagues and companies who were reluctant to do business with a man scarred by prison.

At this distance, it is difficult to judge the extent of Bull's responsibility for the arms smuggling. From the start of his career he had always appeared remarkably naive about the world around him. He preferred to do his work, ignore the consequences of his actions, and say what he believed, no matter how arrogant it seemed. In the petty world of science and government contracts, however, such forthright behavior was never welcome, even from someone as talented as Bull.

At no time did Bull maintain that he was acting in an official capacity for the U.S. government. On the contrary, both he and his family maintain that he was always a free agent. As far as they were concerned, everything that took place was perfectly legal and had been acknowledged by the proper authorities.

The most complete investigation of the shipment of arms to South Africa was made by the Subcommittee on Africa of the House of Representatives Committee on Foreign Affairs. Staff members of the committee, chaired by Congressman Howard Wolpe, interviewed more than fifty people involved in the case, including Bull and Gregory. The committee's report was published on March 30, 1982, and its conclusions provide a fair summary of the case.

1. From 1976–78, Space Research Corporation of Vermont broke the US and UN arms embargoes against South Africa by selling and shipping to the South African government approximately 60,000 155-mm extended-range artillery shells, at least four 155-mm guns including three advanced prototypes, technology and technical assistance to establish its own 155-mm gun and ammunition manufacturing and testing capability, and other military equipment. Almost all of the equipment sent to South Africa was acquired in the US, mainly from US Army plants and supply stocks.
2. The SRC/South Africa transactions led to South Africa's acquisition and development of advanced 155-mm artillery systems which have made major contributions to its regional military capabilities.
3. The SRC case shows that while there has been an official US policy of embargoing arms to South Africa since 1963, the relevant US government agencies have thus far failed to adopt procedures to effectively implement the embargo. Had such procedures been in place, the SRC violations would have either not occurred or been promptly detected and halted.
4. The State Department's Office of Munitions Control gave SRC a letter which misapplied its own regulations and thereby encouraged SRC and its financier, the First Pennsylvania Bank, to proceed with their plans to ship arms to South

Africa. The letter indicated that it might be legally possible for SRC to ship unfinished artillery shell forgings out of the US without an arms export license. It also accepted without investigation SRC's tenuous claim that its technology was not of US origin and therefore did not need a license to be exported abroad. The effect of this mistaken letter was to minimize the corporation's legal risks in exporting arms and arms technology to South Africa. Without the letter, the First Pennsylvania Bank would probably not have approved the letter of credit which enabled SRC's use of US manufacturing facilities to produce its shells, and might well have reconsidered the entire project. OMC's mishandling of SRC's questions was part of a pattern of errors and carelessness in dealing with the corporation's arms exports.

5. Acting under loose and ill-defined procedures, the US Army approved two SRC requests to use a government-owned ammunition plant to manufacture 65,000 artillery shell forgings, nearly all of which went to South Africa. The Army made no attempt to independently verify the supposed destination of the shells.

6. According to the preponderance of evidence, it is probable that a US defense consultant who was assisting the CIA's covert action program in Angola—and was under the supervision of a CIA officer—planned with South African government officials shipments of US-origin arms to South Africa for use in Angola. He also informed the South Africans (representatives of Armscor, the state defense production and procurement agency) that they could obtain superior 155-mm artillery from SRC. Much of this planning and discussion took place after the US government had decided not to ship arms for Angola via South Africa and not to respond to an official South African request for 155-mm artillery from SRC. At the very least, this episode suggests serious negligence on the part of the Agency. At most, there is a possibility that elements of the CIA purposefully evaded US policy. Although the probable CIA agent was one channel of information about SRC to South Africa and was subsequently approached by Armscor to act as an intermediary in conclud-

ing a deal with SRC, there were two other channels which
seem even more important.

7. SRC's extensive and long-term violations of the arms embargo were made possible by the absence of a co-ordinated
US enforcement system to detect and prevent such violations. The State Department and the CIA, respectively, did
not follow up on reports of South Africans seeking US-origin
arms from a US citizen or share information on South Africa's efforts to obtain 155-shells from the US government. No
US foreign policy agency monitored the visits of at least
eight Armscor-led arms buyers to the US in 1976–77 or the
often multiple trips of sixteen high officials and technicians
from SRC to South Africa in 1976–78. No US agency was
aware of the role of . . . Israeli third parties in the development of the SRC-Armscor contracts. As news reports began to expose the SRC violations, no US foreign policy
agency felt responsible for investigating the specific allegations being made. After a US Customs investigation was
launched, the emphasis was on the slow, careful construction of a criminal prosecution and not on the detection of
continuing SRC violations and the prevention of future
ones. Thus no co-ordinated action was taken to follow up on
information that SRC had a Canadian export license for
35,000 artillery shells for the government of Spain and that
the shell forgings came from a US munitions plant. As a
result of these enforcement lapses, SRC was able to ship over
32,000 US-forged artillery shells to South Africa, via Spain,
eight to nine months after the initial allegations and four to
five months after the Customs inquiry began.

8. The poor performance of US foreign policy agencies in the
SRC case seriously weakened the Justice Department's
1980–81 criminal case against SRC, the First Pennsylvania
Bank, and their officers and associates. Of particular concern
to government lawyers in a potential trial was the appearance of possible US government authorization of SRC shipments to South Africa. The upshot was Justice's acceptance
of a plea bargain in which only the two top officers of SRC
paid a price—four and four-and-a-half months at a minimum

security prison—for a $19 million illegal arms deal. Although there was some minority sentiment in Justice for attempting more vigorous prosecution, no State Department representatives (and thereby no US foreign policy interests) participated in the decision to accept the plea bargain.

9. The causes of the government's failure to adequately implement the arms embargo were structural rather than accidental in nature. OMC's failures reflected the organization's lack of capacity to adequately enforce arms licensing regulations. OMC officials acknowledged their lack of sufficient technical expertise to make reliable judgments on applications of their own regulations and lack of sufficient staff resources to properly process their workload. The Army's slip-ups were due to loose and ill-defined procedures, some of which have been tightened in the backwash of the SRC affair. At the CIA, a preoccupation with the immediate bureaucratic need to move arms efficiently into Angola through South Africa appeared to supersede the larger US policy of enforcing the arms embargo against South Africa. Finally, SRC's successful implementation of its plans revealed that there is a "non-system" of enforcing the arms embargo in the US government. US foreign policy agencies did not interrupt this scam because collecting information on the embargo's operation was not high on the list of any agency's priorities; procedures for sharing and centrally assessing relevant information did not exist, and—most fundamentally—there was no clear delineation of organizational responsibilities for obtaining relevant intelligence, evaluating it and acting upon it.

10. In order to strengthen the US arms embargo against South Africa (and arms restrictions aimed at other countries), the following steps are recommended:

(a) The Secretary of State should promptly designate a lead office, logically the Bureau of Politico-Military Affairs, to supervise US implementation of arms embargoes and restrictions. The lead office should have a formal, written mission and authority to represent the Department in inter-agency discussions. A Deputy Assistant Secretary of State should be made formally responsible for implementing arms export restrictions. At the time of these designations, the Secretary of State should clearly and vigorously express the rationale for the arms embargo against South Africa and other arms-export restrictions.

(b) Under the aegis of the lead office, the Executive should reassess the current system for implementing US arms-export restrictions.

Following this review, and in consultation with Congress, the Executive should:

delineate formally and in writing organizational responsibilities for implementation, including preventative action;

re-evaluate existing organizational procedures in light of newly-assigned responsibilities;

take steps to ensure that each organization has the resources to do its job;

require increased intelligence collection on illegal international arms transactions and install formal communications procedures to make sure that intelligence is utilized.

(c) Pending completion of this reorganization:

the Office of Munitions Control should be given increased resources in staff and technical training to perform its existing functions;

the House and Senate Intelligence Committee should investigate the possible roles of employees, agents and contacts of the CIA in efforts to evade the US arms embargo against South Africa during the Angola conflict, and in the development of the SRC/South Africa relationship.

The conclusions were little more than suggestions from the committee and were never enacted. However, the committee had uncovered a conspiracy involving the Israeli government, the CIA, and the South Africans. The incompetence of the OMC had made the operation easier, but the deal would have gone through even if OMC had done its job. Bull simply would have bought his supplies from one of the many sources of rough forgings in Europe.

The case represented much more than a simple evasion of the arms-exporting laws or even a violation of a UN arms embargo. When allied to the technology that the South Africans had acquired after they bought SRC-Q, the export of shells, guns, and other equipment gave them a competitive advantage in the arms business.

On the back of its deal with Bull, Armscor had developed a major arms industry. Within ten years, South Africa would be among the top ten arms exporters in the world. They would also have an artillery system that would be far superior to anything else available. If the intention of the UN arms embargo was to isolate South Africa, it was completely undermined by the export of Bull's guns. Armscor used the G-5 to barter for oil in Iraq and the United Arab Emirates, to gain influence in Latin America, and to earn valuable foreign exchange.

When Jerry Bull finally emerged from Allenwood in February 1981, the cynical side of his personality, which had always been subdued by his ebullience, began to play a greater part in his life. Leaner and more fit than when he had entered prison, he apeared almost recovered from the physical effects of his alcoholism. But the one thing that had not changed was his need for money.

SRC had gone bankrupt and had been closed down by the South Africans when their role had been exposed and the South Africans had stolen all the technology they needed. Bull knew that before anything else could happen, SRC had to be bankrolled.

While Bull was in jail he had received a letter from a Chinese government official through an intermediary in London. The letter invited him to visit Beijing as soon as he was able. The government wished to discuss "matters of mutual interest."

Bull had never been to China and had never dealt with the Chinese. He was a firm anticommunist, but with his unsophisticated political understanding he did not associate the Chinese with communism in the same way he did the Soviet Union. At the time, China was being led out of the restrictive era of Mao

Tse-tung by Deng Xiaoping, who had introduced a program of liberalization that included preliminary discussions about bringing some form of capitalism to the country.

After a two-week Caribbean holiday with Mimi, Bull flew to Europe to investigate business possibilities there while Mimi returned to Quebec. Six months later, short of money and with no new business, Mimi and Jerry flew to Beijing. To his surprise, he was treated with great respect, something close to veneration, by the military leaders and scientists he met. He found that the officials were familiar with his work, had read his reports on the HARP program, and had followed with interest his work on new artillery systems. It was all very flattering to his bruised ego. When he was asked if he would do some work for them, he accepted immediately. "Bull was very impressed with the drive of the Chinese and idolized it somewhat," says Charles Murphy.[1]

The Chinese were particularly interested in Bull's long-range artillery for use along their border with the Soviet Union. This area had been in dispute for many years, and there had been a number of border clashes. The Chinese were concerned that the Soviet Union's more effective long-range rocket systems would put them at a serious disadvantage if another confrontation erupted. This was an exact replay of the argument used by the CIA and South African government in relation to the Soviet equipment in Angola and was a testament to the continuing effectiveness of Bull's designs.

The Chinese agreed to an unusual contract that demanded no performance bonds or guarantees, since Bull was so short of cash. Instead, the Chinese supplied an advance of $500,000 in working funds as the first installment of a $25-million contract. Just as unusual for the arms business, the Chinese paid on time, delivering a check to Bull each month.

Later, when Bull was writing his long personal testament, he obtained a letter from the Chinese that explained their involvement:

> We have complete confidence and trust in Dr. Bull. Before [presenting a] contract, we had him and his wife make a lengthy visit to China. Our institute and military had stud-

ied Dr. Bull's work from his earliest publications. We developed aeroballistic ranges in early 1960 based on his work. We made an attempt to duplicate his HARP work, but were not successful. We received all HARP firing reports from the Canadian government as they were issued in 1962, 1963, 1964, 1965, and 1968. After careful scrutiny by our best people, who attended the weeks of lecture we had Dr. Bull present in Beijing in the summer of 1981, a unanimous judgment was made that Dr. Bull was among the most outstanding scientists that ever visited our country. His humanity, dignity and human decency made a lasting impact on us. Before he and his wife left China, we insisted that he sign a protocol to return and discuss a long term contract. In the years of working together, we have never found Dr. Bull to engage in any deceit or misleading actions. He is rigorous in ensuring a fully understood, fully truthful explanation is made on all matters. In effect, our trust was total, and remains solidly so today.

The Chinese gave Bull the confidence (and cash) to set up his business again, this time in Brussels, where he created yet another company, Space Research Corporation after the old, bankrupt U.S. operation. Although he was without Mimi, Bull was joined by his son Michel, who had recently qualified as an accountant, and his son Stephen, who came to help him run SRI.

In 1981, shortly after the Chinese contract was signed, Bull was approached by Sarkis Soghanalian, a Miami-based Lebanese arms dealer, who suggested a trip to Baghdad. Soghanalian explained that the Iraqis were interested in buying some of Bull's artillery. For Bull, the invitation and the prospect for a new deal was a godsend. He traveled with Soghanalian to Baghdad, where the two men met with the Iraqi defense minister. This was the highest level Bull ever reached in the Iraqi government. Contrary to some reports, he never had any secret meetings with President Saddam Hussein; he was generally handled by functionaries in the Ministry of Defense or the Ministry of Industry and Military Industrialization.

The Iraqis had asked Soghanalian to contact Bull because they thought Bull could manufacture guns. When they realized he was actually a designer, they asked if he could modify some of their Soviet artillery pieces to increase their range and accuracy.

Although the contract offer was welcome, Bull was nervous about getting involved with Soghanalian, whom he considered to be a shady character. He decided to sever all connections with him. Consequently, the first attempt by the Iraqis to recruit Bull failed, but they were prepared to bide their time until a better opportunity arrived.

To meet the contract with the Chinese arms manufacturer NORINCO, Bull had to obtain the designs for the G-5 gun, which he had already sold to South Africa and Austria. In the past, this had been a simple matter of raiding the Highwater data base and extracting the information. But the collapse of SRC-Q had left the Canadian end of the operation in a state of chaos, and while Bull was still in jail, much of the technology and equipment had been taken from the site.

After the demise of SRC-Q and SRC-US in 1980, a group of the company's former engineers had decided, with Bull's agreement, to make use of SRC's technology, which was stored on computer tapes in the electronics building on the U.S. side of the compound. About twenty of the employees, including Denis Lyster and John Ward (who had traveled to Schmidtsdrif to train the South Africans in 155-mm technology), formed Phoenix Engineering. At first the company operated at North Troy, inside the American end of the Highwater compound; then, after a year, Phoenix moved to Newport, Vermont, where it is still located.

The company struggled for two years because no Canadian or American firm wanted to have anything to do with the men from SRC. But once Bull had established his relationship with NORINCO, he tried to get Phoenix and PRB interested in marketing the old SRC technology to generate some much-needed income. Bull persuaded Lyster to come and work for him in Brussels for a salary of about $200,000 a year. Then Bull set about filling the new G-5 contract.

Fern Tomashuk, Bull's secretary at Highwater, had established a library of drawings, blueprints, computer programs, and tapes of SRC technology down the road from Bull's house inside the compound. Bull set up a system whereby he would call Fern and she would extract the relevant material and send it to him in Brussels. Bull would find the precise data needed for the Chinese, make his amendments, and then pass the information to Phoenix in Vermont for updating. Phoenix would then send the material back to SRC in Brussels, from where it would, in turn, be sent to Beijing.

In 1982, Phoenix went to the State Department for formal permission to transmit arms technology to the Chinese government and was referred to the OMC. Although nothing was put in writing, the OMC staff appeared to have learned their lesson. They gave Phoenix the impression that if they made a formal request, it would not be approved. Despite the warning, Phoenix went ahead with the deal, and the technology was shipped to Bull, who sent it to China.

Once again, U.S. Customs asked Larry Curtis to investigate, but this time there was no hardware involved, no crates conveniently breaking open, no independent witnesses. Instead, it was a matter of tracking the movements of individuals who may or may not have carried computer tapes and drawings across the Atlantic in their briefcases. Two grand juries were convened, and three different U.S. attorneys handled the case. Curtis was convinced that enough evidence existed to bring charges against Phoenix, Bull, and a number of other individuals. But no one was prosecuted because during the course of the investigation, U.S. government policy toward China changed, allowing some sales of defense technology as part of a general improvement in relations. So, while Bull and Phoenix may have broken the law when the technology was first transferred, in all likelihood it was not a violation a few months later.

The contract with the Chinese was still in effect at the time of Bull's death and had proved to be very successful. Bull had designed a new version of the 155-mm howitzer, which the Chinese named the WA 021 and first displayed at the Asian Defense Exhibition in Peking in 1987. Work had also begun the previous year on a more powerful 203-mm towed gun that was built in conjunction with the Spanish arms company SITECSA. This gun was not tested until November 1990, eight months after Bull was assassinated.[2]

Bull also supplied the Chinese with the plans for a complete manufacturing plant for both the guns and the ammunition so they could start to produce significant numbers of the weapons for their own use and for export. Bull had passed on his knowledge to the next generation of military scientists in China with regular lectures to graduate students at Nanjing's East China Engineering Institute, which specializes in ordnance and ballistics.

For Bull, working with the Chinese proved to be one of the happiest experiences of his life. He was working in a friendly atmosphere, among scientists who clearly respected him. There were no politics, no discussion about the morality of what he was doing, and, above all, no dreadful bureaucracy like the ones that had dragged him down at every other stage in his career.

With SRC up and running again, Bull became even more convinced of his innocence. Receiving a pardon from the U.S. government became an obsession, a point of honor. Among his friends, there was a great deal of tolerance for Bull's little eccentricities: his forgetfulness, his practical jokes, his love of gossip, and his permanent state of disorganization. But his preoccupation with his pardon evolved into something even his friends felt bordered on mental illness.

In 1983, his old friend Arthur Trudeau, now living in retirement outside Washington, D.C., suggested that Bull set down his story on paper, as much for Bull's sanity as anything else. Trudeau hoped that writing the story might prove cathartic for Bull and purge his system of the desire for revenge. In fact, the reverse happened. The book, *A Review and Study of the Case History of Dr. G. V. Bull and the Space Research Corporation and Its Related Companies in North America with Supporting Relevant Documentation*, ran to more than a thousand pages and cited Don Mordell, Bull's old sponsor at McGill, Jan Heymans, the former president of SRC-I and a business associate of Jack Frost, and Carleton Braithwaite, the former general manager of the HARP program in Barbados, as its authors. In fact, the book was written almost entirely by Bull with the assistance of Don Mordell.

Instead of helping to purge his obsession, however, the act of writing down the whole story simply fueled Bull's anger. By the time he had finished the book in the summer of 1985, he had resolved that his campaign for a pardon would be stepped up. Several hundred copies of his book were printed privately and distributed to friends, congressmen, and anyone else he could think of who might be interested in the case. Then he enlisted the help of his long-suffering friends to write letters to Congress and to the president recommending the pardon. All of these efforts were ignored by the U.S. government.

As Bull's apologia was completed, a second opportunity arose that sparked an old ambition.

During their spring offensive in 1918, the Germans had bombarded Paris with an enormous cannon that had a range of more than seventy-five miles. The cannon had caused a sensation at the time. Its shot had reached a height of twenty-six miles, a record that would last until the development of the V-2 rocket during World War II. To a student of ballistics like Bull, the origin and design of the Paris Gun had been something of a mystery. He had done some preliminary research on the subject but without much success, since there were few records in existence and the available writing on the history of ballistics was very unreliable.

After the collapse of HARP, Bull had felt that its true role in the development of artillery and guns had never been fully understood and had gone largely unrecognized. He believed that if he could find out more about the Paris Gun and relate it to his work on HARP, then the project might achieve its proper historical importance.

In 1965, a German woman had visited the Highwater compound, and some of the staff remembered her mentioning that her father had played a role in the development of the Paris Gun. Hans Luckert, the chief aerodynamicist of the Space Research Institute at McGill, agreed to go to Germany to try to find her. Luckert had worked on Hitler's rocket program and had emigrated to Canada in 1950, but he still kept in touch with his former colleagues back home. After months of painstaking research, Luckert tracked down a chauffeur who had worked for the woman who had visited Highwater. When she died, he said, she had left a number of papers to him, including an unpublished manuscript written by the designer of the Paris Gun, Professor Dr. Fritz Rausenberger.

The manuscript showed complex formulas that demonstrated how the shells and the gun had been designed. By running the formulas through a computer model, Bull was able to simulate the design and the performance of the gun. He discovered that he and Rausenberger had been thinking along similar lines, though fifty years apart. Rausenberger had managed to get the gun to fire as far as it did by redesigning the nose cone of the shell, making it narrower and more aerodynamic, something that Bull had done himself on HARP.

Aside from being of great interest to the few ballistics experts who understood the subject, the Paris Gun papers provided exactly the right context for a book on the HARP project. Bull enlisted the help of his friend Charles Murphy, and together they wrote a 246-page book entitled *Paris Kanonen—The Paris Guns (Wilhelmgeschütze) and Project HARP*, which was privately published in Germany in 1988.

Bull wrote most of the book sitting by the pool behind the small house he had bought on the coast of southern Spain. He would travel to the house with Mimi for two-week holidays three times a year. During 1985 and 1986, those times were spent finishing the manuscript.

To the layman, much of the work is incomprehensible, filled with complex equations and graphs. But it is a better-written, more academic and thorough work than his own biography, which he had completed the previous year. Interestingly, *Paris Kanonen* was translated into Chinese, which must have been a major task, an indication of the importance the Chinese attached to Bull's work.

A certain sense of security finally entered Bull's life. The Chinese project was going well; SRC in Brussels was expanding and now had almost sixty employees. He had set down his case for a pardon and, although he had not yet succeeded, he remained hopeful. Most important, he had shown to the world that the HARP program had a rightful place in the history of artillery. The period that had begun with his jail term and the collapse of SRC-Q was actually turning out quite well.

What he had left to prove, however, was that his theories about large guns had any modern application. He remained convinced that the HARP concept was still valid and that the American military establishment had withdrawn its funding for political, not practical, reasons. Nevertheless, even his new friends in China did not seem to think that HARP could really work as an alternative to rockets.

Then a call came from an unexpected quarter that led Bull to believe that perhaps HARP could make a comeback. In November 1985, Bull was invited to attend a workshop in Arlington, Virginia, organized on behalf of the Strategic Technology Office of the Defense Advanced Research Projects Agency (DARPA). The workshop included twenty-three eminent scientists. Only Bull and his assistant, Luis Palacio, had come from outside the United States. Charles Murphy and Arthur Trudeau had also been invited. The purpose of this elite gathering was to discuss intercontinental cannon and orbiter technology.

In opening the workshop, Dr. Fred Quelle from the Office of Naval Research in Boston explained that work was currently being conducted on miniaturized guidance systems that could be inserted into the nose of a 155-mm shell to guide it to its target, using a global positioning system for navigation.

This work was part of a general effort by the military to produce munitions that could be maneuvered once they had left their launcher—"terminally guided" in military language. Quelle said that it was now possible to fire such munitions from a gun without the complex microcircuitry being destroyed by the high G forces. DARPA was interested in exploring whether this system could be used to fire shells across continents, an idea that appeared to present a cheap alternative to more conventional missiles. The missions envisaged for such a system included long-range attacks on bunkers, command and control centers, and airfields; fast-response reconstitution of space assets; and resupply to orbiting platforms.

This, of course, was exactly what HARP had been about. It appeared that, at long last, the American scientific community was coming around to Bull's way of thinking.

In his speech to the meeting, Bull began with a historical overview, guiding his audience through the Paris Gun project and then through HARP. He concluded by proposing that a gun-launched orbiter (GLO) could be the solution to DARPA's problem.

"GLO is a low-performance, fin-stabilized, center-sabot design," Bull said. He added that the GLO could be delivered in either a sixteen-inch or a sixty-four-inch version; the latter could be built with a hardened steel pipe.[3]

After the workshop, Bull was asked to deliver a formal proposal for his GLO system, which he submitted a few months later. Once again he was confident that not only was HARP about to be revived, but as a result he would receive the pardon he'd been seeking. but it was not to be. GLO was shelved, and the pardon never materialized.

F O U R T E E N

PROJECT BABYLON

FROM 1980 to 1989, Iraq spent as much as $80 billion on weapons procurement, a rate of arms purchasing higher than that of France, West Germany, or Britain. The cost reached a peak of $33.3 billion in 1984, but even by 1989 Saddam Hussein was still spending $15 billion on weapons annually.

Understandably, countries lined up to take advantage of the oil revenues that were flowing into the arms market. More than twenty-four nations supplied arms to Iraq. While the Soviet Union supplied 53 percent of the equipment, Western countries rushed to sell to Saddam as well. From Italy, Iraq bought modern frigates and missile boats worth more than $3 billion. From Britain and Holland, Saddam received frequency-hopping radios and electronic equipment. From France, Iraq obtained more than $15 billion of modern weapons systems, including 133 Mirage F-1 fighter-bombers, 140 armed helicopters, 1,000 armored vehicles, 884 Exocet missiles, 20,000 HOT and Milan antitank missiles, and 2,500 air combat missiles. From North Korea and the Soviet Union Saddam bought Scud missiles. From China he ordered Silkworm missiles.[1]

This enormous investment in military equipment meant that, at the outbreak of the Gulf crisis, Iraq had one of the most powerful military machines in the world. The inventory included 4,200 main battle tanks, an additional 5,000 armored personnel carriers, 9,000 artillery pieces and rocket launchers, and an air force with 1,000 aircraft. To man all this equipment, Saddam raised an armed force of 1 million men.

Iraq had achieved this formidable inventory even though all Western nations had agreed not to supply weapons to either Iran or Iraq during their eight-year war. To circumvent this official ban, Iraq had set up a worldwide underground procurement network specifically designed either to buy arms directly from the manufacturers or buy the machinery with which to make them. In theory, to buy arms on this scale should have been impossible. However, Saddam Hussein's arms buyers had created such an intricate network of dummy companies and fake bank accounts that they were easily able to exploit the greed of governments and companies who were more interested in foreign sales and quick profits than proliferation. Iraq's arms buying was a sad illustration of the impotence of most Western governments in the face of the kind of cash that Iraq had been spending in the arms market for more than a decade.

In some cases, Iraq bought the equipment, such as fighter aircraft or tanks, wherever there was a willing seller. For other, more complex, purchases, Iraq tried to buy the equipment through its underground network so that it could manufacture the weapon free of interference from outside governments.

The two most important types of arms were nuclear weapons and the ballistic missiles with which to deliver those weapons. Iraq was a signatory of the Nonproliferation Treaty and officially allowed inspection of its civilian nuclear reactor. However, it had secretly bought all the technology and the raw materials required to make a nuclear device and was on the verge of developing its first nuclear weapon before the Gulf War began.

Where Iraq's military ambitions and Jerry Bull's expertise coincided was in the field of ballistic missile development. In 1982, Iraq, Egypt and Argentina decided to cooperate on the joint development of a new ballistic missile known to the Argentinians as Condor 2. The missile would have a two-stage rocket, have a range of at least 625 miles, and carry a payload of 1,100 pounds, in the form of a nuclear, chemical, biological, or conventional warhead.[2]

Argentina had already developed a Condor 1 rocket with a range of approximately sixty miles, and thus had demonstrated a knowledge of the technology involved. The Egyptians had done some work on guidance systems. The Iraqis had the cash. All three countries perceived a strategic need for such a rocket: Iraq could attack deep into Iran and would not be dependent on future supplies from the Soviet Union or China; Egypt would have a system to match the Jericho missile being developed by Israel; and Argentina would gain considerable status in Latin America, as well as having a weapon it could use to threaten the Falkland Islands, which it still hoped to get back from the British.

If any of these countries managed to manufacture and deploy a ballistic missile system, it would have a serious effect on the world's strategic balance of weaponry and would undoubtedly encourage neighboring countries to acquire their own systems or upgrade their existing capabilities.

To buy the necessary equipment, a network of companies was set up by all three countries, led by Iraq, based primarily in the Swiss canton of Zug. The most important of these companies was Consen, which had offices in Monte Carlo. Other companies, such as Desintek and Condor Projetke, were also based near Zurich. All had personnel recruited from the West German company Messerschmitt-Boelkow-Blohm (MBB), which had been heavily involved in the Condor 1 project.[3]

Iraq had constructed a vast missile testing center called Saad 16 near Mosul in northern Iraq. The complex housed a supersonic wind tunnel and ramps for testing rocket motors. The contract for constructing the complex had been led by the Saad General Establishment (SGE), which works on construction projects for Iraq's State Organization for Technical Industries. SGE employed as prime contractor the Gildemeister company of Düsseldorf, which in turn bought equipment from a wide range of industrial companies, including Tektronix of Beaverton, Oregon, which makes computer graphics terminals and measuring instruments; Scientific-Atlanta of Atlanta, which makes telecommunications and satellite ground station equipment; and Hewlett-Packard, which makes computers. According to Hewlett-Packard, electronic equipment was supplied to MBB, which listed SGE as the end user but described it as "an institute for higher learning."[4]

In fact, during the early eighties these exports had first been sent to Germany and then legally forwarded to Iraq. In April 1987, however, seven nations (the U.S., Canada, France, the U.K., Italy, Japan, and West Germany) signed the Missile Technology Control Regime (MTCR) to curb exports of equipment that might be used to develop missiles or chemical and biological weapons.

Under the MTCR, the signatories agreed not to export complete rocket systems (ballistic missile systems, space launch vehicles, and sounding rockets) and unmanned air vehicle systems (cruise missile systems, target drones, and reconnaissance drones). Also not to be exported were individual rocket stages, reentry vehicles designed for nonweapons payloads, some solid and liquid fuel rocket engines, some types of guidance sets, and arming, fusing, and firing mechanisms.[5]

Behind all the formal language, there was also an informal agreement to share intelligence about any efforts by third world countries to gain access to this type of technology. Even countries that were not signatories to the agreement, such as Switzerland, have since provided information to the seven member nations.

One result of the pledge to share intelligence was that on March 18, 1988, U.S. Customs received information that a California-based aerospace scientist, Abdelkader Helmy, might be one of the links in a chain of Americans who were secretly involved in the Condor project.

Helmy was an Egyptian who had become a naturalized American citizen in October 1987. He worked at the Aerojet General Corporation in Rancho Cordova, California, where he was cleared to handle material classified secret. Helmy was the chief scientist working on the research and development of a new shell for a 120-mm gun.

In March, U.S. Customs watched Helmy meet with another Egyptian and ship two boxes to an address they discovered was that of the Egyptian military attaché in Washington. Suspicious, the customs officials began to tap Helmy's home and office phones and arranged with the refuse collection men for his trash to be put to one side for customs to go through at its leisure. Each week revealed a new haul of incriminating documents, many of them carefully written in Helmy's own hand.

The first investigation of his rubbish revealed two pages of handwritten notes describing how to work with a material called carbon-carbon—an exceptionally tough, heat-resistant material with a low radar signature that is used in the manufacture of rocket nose cones, rocket nozzles, and heat shields on reentry vehicles. All exports of carbon-carbon require an export license. Further examination of Helmy's rubbish revealed drawings that demonstrated how a rocket nose cone could be constructed from carbon-carbon.

Helmy eventually set up a dummy company called Science and Technology Applications that was registered to his home address. By listening to his telephone calls and searching once more through his trash, the customs agents discovered Helmy's bank accounts at the Cameron Park branch of World Savings and Loans. The bank records showed that since December 15, 1987, $1,030,000 had been transferred to the account from IFAT Corporation in Zug, Switzerland. Some of the money had been used to buy carbon composite material and missile nose cones from two California companies, Kaiser Aerotech and Greenleaf Technical Ceramics.

Eventually, enough documents were pulled from Helmy's rubbish for officials to approach his boss at Aerojet. He identified the documents as the complete package needed to build or upgrade a tactical missile system.

Helmy and two assistants had been filling a shopping list sent to them by Colonel Hussam Yossef, an Egyptian who was based in Austria. The flow of requests from Yossef had increased until eventually he was demanding thirty tons of different materials.

Most of the American companies Helmy had approached through his dummy company had agreed to sell him the material with no questions asked. They had no particular reason to be suspicious, since the goods were being sent to an apparently legitimate California-based company and Helmy never suggested that they would be exported.

The Condor project had been closely watched not only by the Americans but also by Israeli intelligence. In the past, when Egypt had attempted to develop its own missile capability, the Israelis had not hesitated to take action. In 1962, when the Israelis discovered that the Egyptians, then led by President Nasser, were building rockets that could be targeted at Israel, they acted immediately. The scientists working on the project had been recruited primarily from West Germany; Mossad, the Israeli intelligence organization, began a campaign of intimidation against them, which included kidnappings, threats, and the posting of letter bombs. The campaign was successful, and all the key scientists left Egypt.

The Condor case was potentially just as serious. If Condor 2 succeeded, both Iraq and Egypt would have the means to attack Israel with ballistic missiles against which it had no defense.

At 3:00 A.M. on May 27, 1988, an empty Peugeot car parked on the street in Grasse, in southern France, was blown to pieces by a remotely detonated bomb. The car belonged to Ekkehard Schrotz, general manager of Consen, the Zug-based company that was coordinating the purchases for the Condor project.

An anonymous call to the Agence France Presse news agency claimed that a previously unknown pro-Iranian terrorist group, the Guardians of Islam, was responsible for the attack as a warning to Schrotz to stop his work for the Iraqi regime. But Western intelligence services believed that the attack had all the hallmarks of Israeli intelligence, and some thought that more attacks would be on the way unless the project was stopped.

The Egyptians also seemed to have concluded that the Israelis were responsible. In a telephone call to Helmy on June 3, a few weeks after the explosion in Grasse, Yossef said that "certain people tried to do away with us. They put something in a company car and it exploded. We suspect the ones next to us because the way the operation was executed by remote control indicates that the country next to us is the culprit."

U.S. Customs decided to act. On June 24, as a box labeled "Personal Items Air Force Club," which in fact contained 430 pounds of carbon fiber for rocket nose cones, was about to be loaded onto an Egyptian air force C-130 at the Baltimore-Washington Airport, customs men arrested three key members of the smuggling ring. Helmy, his wife, Abia, and an associate, Jim Huffman, were charged with exporting materials without a license and money laundering. The Egyptian diplomats claimed diplomatic immunity and left the country two days after the arrest.

Customs officials had completed a successful operation, and the breakup of the ring provided the U.S. government with the perfect opportunity to apply pressure on Egypt, its close and trusted ally, to drop the project.

This pressure appears to have been successful. Egypt backed out of the project, and Argentina, which now had a more moderate government, decided it could no longer afford such an expensive military commitment.

But these setbacks did not in any way diminish Iraq's ambitions to develop its own ballistic missile. The withdrawal of its two other partners meant that more money would have to be spent, but oil revenues were sufficient to cover any shortfall. It was much more difficult to fill the gap left by Argentina's expertise in missile technology and Egypt's access to an efficient network that could gather the vital raw materials.

The loss of Helmy and his knowledge of carbons and nose cone technology was a serious blow to the project. At one stroke, U.S. Customs had removed one of the most vital ingredients of the Condor project. Now, Iraq urgently needed to find a source of both information and hardware. At this point, the Iraqis remembered a meeting in 1981 with an American artillery designer named Jerry Bull who had just been released from jail after smuggling arms to South Africa. They remembered how he had boasted of helping design the Minuteman rocket and how his HARP guns had fired missiles into space, breaking all world records. Perhaps, they thought, this man would have the answers they needed.

After seven years, the Iraqis got in touch with Jerry Bull in November 1987 via their embassy in Brussels with an offer of an all-expense-paid trip to Baghdad for Bull, Michel, and Stephen. Bull, at that point, was well known to them. The Iraqis had excellent relations with the Chinese, from whom they bought large quantities of arms; they had already bought the South African version of Bull's 155-mm artillery.

The offer was well timed—the contract with China was drying up, and SRC-I was once again having difficulty paying its bills. As at the time of the South African contract ten years earlier, the company was virtually bankrupt and urgently needed a new lifeline.

"We were having a lot of trouble, because we were trying to remain on the right side of the law," says Michel.

As part of his new law-abiding policy, Bull checked with the Belgian Foreign Ministry to get some idea about their rules governing deals with Iraq. They were advised firmly to stay away. Despite this warning, business was so bad that Bull felt they had little choice but to explore the Iraqi offer. In January 1988 the trio flew first class from Germany to Iraq on Iraqi Airways and were chauffeured to the Al Rashid Hotel, which later became the headquarters of the international press corps during the Gulf war.

Their hosts were Hussein Kamil, the son-in-law of President Saddam Hussein, and the Ministry of Industry and Military Industrialization. Kamil was one of Saddam's most trusted advisers, the man responsible for overseeing Iraq's nuclear and chemical weapons program as well as the country's international arms-purchasing network. After the Gulf war, Kamil was put in charge of dealing with internal dissidents, including the Kurds. Also in attendance was Amir Saadi, Kamil's deputy, who would become the liaison between Bull and the Iraqi government.

The Iraqis told them that the war would end soon (the cease-fire was agreed to six months later) and that they needed both engineering and defense assistance. They said they were satisfied with the GH N-45 gun, which had been supplied by the Austrians, but would like to have a self-propelled version. They were also interested in any new artillery that Bull might be designing.[6]

During the visit, Bull took the opportunity to give a number of lectures to senior military officials in the defense ministry about the HARP program. He argued that HARP represented a major opportunity for a developing country like Iraq to get into the space race. This was his standard lecture, one that he had given often in China and had bored his friends with on numerous occasions over the years. But this time, his message was well received.

On their own initiative, the Iraqis had been trying to develop a ballistic missile program, particularly a missile to launch a satellite into space. The recent setbacks to the Condor project were likely to delay this program for several years, and the Iraqis were finding it increasingly difficult to obtain the technology they needed.

Iraq's pattern of arms purchases and military development had been to buy a stake in a company or purchase the services of an individual to obtain the required knowledge and then to transfer that knowledge to an Iraqi manufacturer. For example, in the case of their nuclear program, instead of buying all the equipment abroad, the Iraqis bought stakes in a number of companies that made parts for the nuclear industry. Those companies then shipped parts to Iraq, where they were sent to new factories, which put all the bits together with the help of engineers and scientists either trained or hired overseas.

So, while Bull was lecturing the Iraqis about the possibility of HARP, the Iraqis were not thinking only about HARP but also about obtaining access to Bull's design skills and the spinoffs generated from HARP. They already knew that Bull could produce outstanding artillery. Now they understood that he knew about rocketry as well and was offering a proven and apparently cheap solution to their problems.

Martlet 4, the staged rocket that Bull had wanted to produce to fire out of the HARP gun, was a multistage rocket with a significant payload. It would use all the materials and technology of a much larger rocket, such as the Condor. As had been the case with the South Africans, Bull thought he was dealing with the single issue of sending a rocket into space from a gun. But the Iraqis saw Bull as a brilliant Western scientist who was prepared to work for them and supply all the technology required for them to build their own ballistic missile. Once again, Bull would be the source of the design and technology information that would give a developing nation a major military advantage.

In March 1989, Michel flew to Washington to discuss the possible artillery contract with the Iraqis. He was determined not to make his father's mistake of going ahead with a deal without touching all the bases. In a meeting with the Office of Munitions Control, Michel explained that SRC-I had been asked to modify some Iraqi artillery and that there was some interest in his father designing a new artillery system. He made no mention of a possible gun to shoot satellites into space. The OMC advised him that there would be no American objection to the contract provided it was not filled before the end of the Iran-Iraq war.

In April, Jerry Bull returned to Baghdad alone for further discussions with the Iraqis. During that summer, there were also a number of meetings with diplomats from the Iraqi embassy in Brussels. Then in August an Iraqi diplomat came to SRC's offices with a firm proposal. His government wanted to put a satellite into space using a Bull supergun. The program would be called Project Babylon, and the Iraqis would commit whatever funds were required—an initial investment of $20 million was discussed. They expected the gun to be working within five years. After more than twenty years of dreaming, Bull was now about to realize his life's ambition to build a massive gun, a gun so powerful that it would require a barrel nearly five hundred feet long. It would be capable of sending a fifteen-hundred-pound payload into orbit or firing a shell more than a thousand miles. Bull was elated and immediately told Michel and Stephen of his success.

"We clashed from the start," says Michel. "I was sure such a project would have big political problems, and I suggested to my father that we talk about it with the Americans. He said, 'No, they will just sabotage it like they did the HARP program.' "

Later that month, Bull flew to Baghdad again to discuss the

project in more detail. When he returned, he told his sons that the deal had been done. Once again, according to Michel, he tried to dissuade his father from any further involvement with the Iraqis, but without success.

The decision had been made to keep the project secret, which set Bull on a course of confrontation with the intelligence services of the world. He immediately moved from being a small-time arms designer whose work was well known to becoming a man of mystery whose work was understood differently by different people. There was now nobody who knew the full story of the supergun project except for Jerry Bull and his Iraqi backers, and they were not prepared to talk about it. This secrecy would be a key aspect of the project as it developed and came to the attention of the British, American, and Israeli intelligence services. Each agency examined the available evidence and interpreted it differently. Each service, however, looked not only at what was said to be the gun's purpose, but at its long-term capability, a significant difference that would raise the profile of the entire project.

While Bull was busy preparing a detailed proposal for the Iraqis, discussions were continuing about work on more conventional artillery. In November, SRC-I signed a contract with the Iraqis worth $5 million a year to cover work on transforming the Austrian GH N-45 into a self-propelled gun and designing a new and more powerful artillery piece. In both cases, Bull was given considerable freedom to achieve the extra ranges the Iraqis wanted. In gun designs for Western armies, there is a requirement to keep the noise as low as possible to protect the hearing of the soldiers. This did not apply in Iraq; Bull was allowed to design a gun with no noise reduction system at all, which made the gun much more powerful. At the same time, the old problem of sabots flying off the shell once it left the gun barrel and injuring nearby friendly troops was not considered a difficulty by the Iraqi military. They clearly took the view that some dead or deaf soldiers were less important than enhancing their military capability.

The Iraqis promised that they would pay a fixed sum each month in advance, a major concession that ensured they would have almost total control of SRC. Once more, financial necessity forced Jerry Bull to allow a foreign government to take over his operation.

Under the detailed plan for Project Babylon, it was agreed that two guns would be designed and purchased, the first nicknamed Baby Babylon, the second, Big Babylon. Project Bird would be the program to design the space launch vehicle that would be fired from the gun. The first gun would essentially be a large pipe 170 feet long, mounted on rails similar to the test guns at Highwater; it would be used for ballistics trials. Big Babylon was Bull's grand vision. It would have a barrel 500 feet long that, at its tip, would stand 350 feet above the ground. It would weigh 2,100 tons, as much as seven hundred Rolls-Royces. The breech would weigh more than 180 tons; each of four recoil mechanisms, 60 tons. Baby Babylon would be supported by a metal scaffold, Big Babylon by a concrete tower. The breeches would be installed in a giant concrete pit over 100 feet deep. Each projectile would be three feet wide and be powered by a three-stage rocket that would be pushed out of the barrel by a propellant charge more than 20 feet long.

Bull's determination to proceed with the supergun project caused a serious rift in the family. Michel, who had already been in several battles with his father over the running of the company and his father's extravagance, was anxious that the company not be exposed to a political backlash because of its involvement in such a high-profile project. Both he and Stephen argued that the supergun was dangerous and could land them all in trouble. But his father was adamant. They finally compromised with him, agreeing to set up a separate company to run the supergun contract. Both Stephen and Michel wanted nothing to do with it.[7]

Jerry Bull registered a new company, Advanced Technology Institute (ATI), in Athens, Greece. Athens was a useful home for the company since the Greek government was notoriously lax about checking on businesses operating in their country and had virtually no reporting requirements. ATI operations were actually based a few streets away from the SRC offices in Brussels, and a number of the SRC staff members were put on the new project.

The first task facing Bull was to draw up the detailed plans for Baby Babylon and Big Babylon. He hired a British designer, Christopher Cowley, who had trained as a metallurgical engineer. Cowley had been involved with SRC for some months, helping with a number of artillery projects. Michel, who was now running SRC, had decided that he was a disruptive influence and was about to fire him when the ATI option came up. "My word to my father was, don't hire this guy because he's nothing but trouble. He had what I call the Ph.D. syndrome, thinking he knew everything. He was also a prima donna who always wanted to be in the spotlight," says Michel.

As usual, Jerry disregarded Michel's advice and took Cowley with him to ATI. They worked on plans for the two guns together, and by June 1988, discussions were begun with a number of British and other European companies for the delivery of specialized equipment. That same month, the Iraqis approved the plans in outline, and a contract was signed between the Iraqis and ATI.

Bull would soon change his mind about Cowley. In December, he called Michel from Brussels and asked for a meeting in Geneva, a convenient city for them both. When the two met, Jerry Bull did nothing but complain about Cowley, saying that Michel's initial judgment had been right. Upon Bull's return, Cowley left the project.

The supergun deal was the final straw for Michel. Since he had moved to Brussels from Montreal, he had lived and suffered in his father's shadow. As a trained accountant, Michel had some idea of how a company should be run, and he had watched his father ignore his advice and use SRC as his personal preserve.

Michel had tried to bring some financial controls to SRC but had found it almost impossible to rein in his father. Bull had no interest in the business side of the company and felt that he should be allowed to spend as much money as he wanted. He was also fiercely loyal to all of his employees. At the time of the dispute over the supergun, the income from the China contract had diminished substantially; even so, SRC continued to employ the same number of people that had been needed when work on the Chinese project was at its busiest. Michel knew that the Iraqi contract for conventional artillery would not meet the gap between income and expenditure, and he was tired of fighting with his father. The problem he faced was trying to maintain his own financial freedom while continuing to have some kind of relationship with his father. Ironically, Bull came up with the answer, but it proved to be as much of a mistake for Michel as the supergun project was for his father.

F I F T E E N

LEAR FAN: THE
NORTHERN IRELAND
DEBACLE

IN 1988, Jerry Bull had been invited to Northern Ireland by the Industrial Development Board (IDB), which is responsible for encouraging business in the area. The Northern Ireland economy has been struggling for more than twenty years as the Irish Republican Army has waged its terrorist war against the British government. Any business that moves to the province faces the prospect of having its workers intimidated, its premises firebombed. The British responded to the problem by setting up a series of incentives, including subsidies and tax breaks, to make it as attractive as possible for businesses to start up or relocate there.

In 1978, for example, the IDB had negotiated an agreement with American businessman John DeLorean to set up a factory that would manufacture a new "ethical" car made out of fiberglass. After four years, the factory shut down at a cost of $170 million to the British government. The DeLorean car was an ill-conceived automobile that, seen in retrospect, never had a chance of succeeding. Belatedly, the gull-winged car found fame as the time machine in the *Back to the Future* movies.

Ten years later, the IDB was faced with another disastrous investment project. Lear Fan, a company that had been set up to

produce an advanced business jet made from high-technology
carbon composite materials, had a revolutionary concept—an
aircraft for civilians built out of materials similar to those used
for the F-117A Stealth Fighter. While the Stealth needed a fuse-
lage made from composites to lower its radar signature, the Lear
Fan jet would be constructed out of composites because they
were light, were exceptionally tough, and would reduce fuel
consumption. IDB encouraged the idea and originally helped
finance it.[1]

But in 1985, Lear Fan went bankrupt, at a cost of $100 mil-
lion to British taxpayers. Since then, the IDB had been searching
for a buyer who would purchase the 200,000-square-foot plant
set on eleven and a half acres outside Belfast. While there had
been no willing purchaser until 1988, F. G. Wilson (Engineering)
Ltd., a local engineering firm, eventually bought the site for
$1.17 million. Equipment and parts in the factory—including
jigs, tools, molds, and autoclaves—that had been used to make
the composite materials were sold for $702,000.

Shortly after buying the factory, however, F. G. Wilson decided to expand in other areas and notified the IDB that it would
like to sell. According to Michel Bull, the IDB then called his
father and asked him to come to Belfast. The British government
claims that Bull had approached Lear Fan first, which in turn
had alerted IDB, which then contacted Bull. The IDB officials
showed Bull around the factory and gave him a short tour of the
province. Obviously, they were offering him the opportunity to
invest in Lear Fan. They spoke of the aircraft's potential and
their disappointment that the project had collapsed. They mentioned too that large grants would be available to anyone who
brought employment to the area.

To Bull, who was used to dealing with countries such as
South Africa and China, the terrorist problem was not a serious
consideration. He believed, with his usual optimism, that somebody as apolitical as himself would be universally welcomed.
He returned to Brussels inspired by the idea of getting SRC involved in a business other than weapons. He immediately sat
down with Michel and Stephen to discuss it.

"He came back extremely enthusiastic, saying he was going

to finish the Lear Fan," recalls Michael. "He knew we would be keen as well because we were both pilots and could see what the Lear Fan might mean for the civilian aircraft market."

Michel then flew to Belfast and met with the IDB officials. He was also very impressed, recognizing at once an opportunity for SRC to diversify, which would allow him to run a project of his own and give him a chance to demonstrate the business acumen he was sure he possessed.

The family decided to try to take over the company. They needed capital of approximately $13.5 million, of which the IDB promised just under $4 million. Fifty percent of the balance would be put up by SRC; the remainder would come from an outside investor, if they could find one. Companies were approached in France and Canada without success.

On one of Bull's trips to Iraq, he mentioned the project to Amir Saadi, his chief contact in the Ministry of Industry and Military Industrialization, who seemed interested in the scheme. He suggested that Bull contact the Technology and Development Group (TDG) in London. This company, he explained, had made a number of investments for the Iraqi government in Western countries and they might have sufficient funds available to help out a project like this.

According to Michel Bull, the Iraqi involvement was no secret. In fact, he had made a point of telling the IDB officials that the Iraqis had a share of the new company. The family was assured that this would present no difficulty. Similarities between this and the South African deal seemed to be arising, however. The Bulls had approached the official body looking after the legal side of the transaction and had been reassured that they were following the correct procedures. Then, as now, they would find that the officials had a very narrow view and that others would see the Iraqi involvement in a much more sinister light.

The Iraqis insisted that they had no interest in the running of the company and would treat their involvement as a long-term investment; they simply saw some value in the composite-making capability of the factory. After all, they pointed out, composites were a by-product of the oil industry, and the technology might be of use to their petrochemical industry at some time in the future. In addition, the composites would be useful in the Condor missile project, if it ever was revived.

At the beginning of 1989, Michel formed SRC Engineering in Geneva, which would be his own personal vehicle for handling the Lear Fan project. SRC Engineering then took a 50 percent stake in another new company called Canira (after Canada and Iraq) Technical Corporation Ltd. The other 50 percent was owned by the Technology and Development Group.

On March 9, 1989, Michel also formed SRC Composites Ltd. All of its 10 million one-pound shares were owned by Canira. SRC Composites was registered with the Department of Economic Development in Northern Ireland, as was required by law. Then, on May 11, 1989, two new directors were appointed —Namir Al-Naimi, who described himself as an engineer, and Dr. Fadel Jawad Kadhum, who said he was a lawyer. Both were Iraqis and listed their address as 2 Stratford Place, London.

The same month, SRC Composites bought the Lear Fan factory from F. G. Wilson (Engineering) Ltd. for $6.3 million, giving the Northern Ireland company a profit of $3.9 million.

The price paid for the company was more than double what the government's own assessors had believed it was worth a year earlier. The IDB was concerned that they had perhaps made a mistake. To cover themselves, they circulated a memorandum to see if anything further was known about the people who had purchased Lear Fan.

At the same time, Michel Bull had been making inquiries about purchasing a filament winding machine for the new factory. Certain types of these machines are on the list of equipment restricted under the MTCR because they can be used to make light, strong, and heat-resistant composites for the nose cones of missiles.

These two pieces of information came across the desk of the person responsible for monitoring arms proliferation, including the growth of Iraq's arms industry, at the Secret Intelligence Service in London. Closer examination of the Lear Fan deal revealed the degree of penetration that had been achieved by the Iraqis.

Fadel Jawad Kadhum, the chairman of Canira, had also become a director of SRC Composites in May. Kadhum was known to British intelligence as a senior official in the Iraqi government who was partly responsible for Iraq's covert arms procurement network. In addition, he was a director of the Technology and Development Group, which, in turn, was owned by Al-Arabi, an Iraqi government–owned company in Baghdad. TDG had already come to the attention of British officials two years earlier.

Kadhum and TDG had financed the $7.2-million management buyout of TI Machine Tools, a subsidiary of the TI Group. TI Machine Tools was then renamed Matrix Churchill. The company had been operating at a loss for ten years, but the orders placed by the Iraqi government the year after the buyout enabled it to show a profit of $4.2 million that year. Matrix had been attractive to the Iraqis because of its expertise in modern high-speed lathes, which can be used to manufacture artillery shells.

The company exported lathes to Iraq, which allowed the Iraqis to set up a fully equipped factory to manufacture the shells. The MTCR prohibited the export of the software that drove the lathes, rather than the machinery itself. Matrix got around this problem by shipping the lathes separately. Software was then purchased from Japan and shipped to Switzerland, and from there diverted to Iraq. Among the shells that the lathes could manufacture were the 155-mm ammunition that had been created to fit the guns that Bull designed. The ammunition had been supplied by South Africa and NORICUM during Iraq's war with Iran.

By purchasing Matrix Churchill, the Iraqis obtained access to a U.S. subsidiary of the company, Matrix Churchill Corporation of Solon, Ohio. Under Iraqi ownership, the company had expanded beyond America for the first time in its ten-year history with a contract for supplying lathes to a $14-million machine tool factory and a glass-fiber production plant in Iraq. Both factories had a dual-use capability, meaning their products could be used for either civilian or military work. Precision machine tools, for example, could be used in the Iraqi armaments industry, and some types of glass fiber are used in rocket casings.

Matrix also set up Matrix Projects, with an office in Krefeld, West Germany, which was given a $46-million contract to build a die-forging plant for the Nasser State Enterprise for Mechanical Industries, a branch of Iraq's Ministry of Industry and Military Industrialization. The minister responsible was Hussein Kamil, the same man who had welcomed Bull to Baghdad in 1988 and whose deputy had suggested the initial contact with TDG.

The Matrix Churchill deals were financed by the Italian Banca Nazionale del Lavoro. The bank's Atlanta branch advanced more than $3 billion in loans to Matrix and other companies without the authority of the bank's head office. This money was used to fund purchases by Iraq's underground arms-buying network around the world.

With the British intelligence investigation beginning to reveal some alarming connections between the SRC family of companies and the Iraqi government, it seemed likely that some action would be taken. Meanwhile, Michel continued to plan the future of Lear Fan with the assistance of the IDB. As far as he or the officials at IDB were concerned, there was no reason to believe that IDB's involvement in the project would not proceed as planned.

The accountants Peat Marwick drew up a detailed business plan, which was submitted to the IDB, who then told Michel that the new company would certainly qualify for a grant. The IDB wrote to Michel Bull in the summer of 1989, agreeing in principle to the funding. An appointment was made for a formal contract to be signed on August 16.

But on August 14, 1989, D. J. Watkins, the deputy chief executive of the IDB, wrote the following letter to Michel:

> I understand your company has been in discussion with the executives of the Industrial Development Board about the availability of selective financial assistance under the Industrial Development (NI) Order 1982, for a proposed investment in Northern Ireland.
>
> The IDB has been advised in the following terms by the Foreign and Commonwealth Office (FCO):
>
> "The involvement of Iraqi backed companies in the con-

sortium is itself a possible source of concern. Iraq is known to be involved in an advanced ballistic missile development program in co-operation with other countries including Argentina. Composite materials, which the former Lear Fan factory can produce, are used in ballistic missile and other weapons systems. The UK, as a member of the Missile Technology Control Regime, is committed to do all that it can to prevent the proliferation of such missiles. The government would not wish to see public funds being used to assist in the acquisition of sensitive technology which could be relevant to missile development programs in Iraq or in a number of other countries."

Having assessed all the information available to the IDB concerning the company's project and in light of the FCO advice, the IDB has decided to decline to make an offer of selective financial assistance.

In view of this decision, I can see no point whatsoever in proceeding with the meeting suggested for next Wednesday, 16 August.

The letter came as a total surprise to Michel, who had been given no inkling from any of the IDB officials that the project was about to collapse.

"It was a total shock," says Michel. "I tried to talk to or see someone from the IDB, but they refused to discuss the matter on five occasions."

Increasingly frustrated and apparently genuinely baffled by the idea that anyone could have found anything dangerous in the project, he then wrote to the British Foreign Office on September 11:

By letter of the 14th August, our company has been informed that Her Majesty's government had refused to grant the financial support for the investment to be made in our Belfast factory concerning our future products as a subcontractor to the aerospace industry.

This decision, suddenly notified three and a half months after the communication of our Business Plan to the United

Kingdom Authorities and after quite positive negotiations with them, including a provisional decision in principle to support the project, would inflict extremely grave damages; on the other hand, we are convinced that if the Foreign and Commonwealth Office would receive more information, a different decision might be taken, including eventually some guarantees of/or measure of control to answer the fears of the United Kingdom government.

The undersigned ask therefore to be received by the Foreign and Commonwealth Office as soon as possible because of the increasing damage inflicted on us by any additional delay and will attend a meeting of the Foreign and Commonwealth Office at your convenience.

Having been dragged back from the brink of getting involved in what might have developed into a political debacle, the Foreign Office was not about to concede anything. They replied on September 22d: "The Foreign Office position in this matter was made clear in the Deputy Chief Executive's letter to you of 14 August. I do not believe that any useful purpose would be served by a meeting with Foreign Office officials, nor would it be appropriate."

The British decision to block funds for the Lear Fan factory meant that SRC-I could no longer afford its involvement. Michel approached the Iraqis, who also refused to put up any more cash. He had no choice but to try and sell it. In October, only two months after the funding was stopped, Short Brothers, the Belfast aircraft and missile maker, which is owned by Bombardier of Canada, bought the factory for $6.3 million. The fact that Michel was able to sell the factory to Short at such a high price suggests that the government had originally sold it to Wilson Engineering for too little and therefore had lost the British taxpayers a significant sum of money.

The Lear Fan project would be Michel's last venture free of his father's control until after Bull's death the following year. Michel remains both baffled and bitter about the Lear Fan deal. He believes that the IDB encouraged SRC's involvement and then backed away for no reason that he can understand. "We were the scapegoat in a big political game," said Michel, echoing the same sentiments expressed by his father nine years earlier.

However, a study of the Iraqi covert arms-purchasing network in the 1980s suggests that the Iraqis' involvement in the Lear Fan project fit a pattern they repeated with great success all over the world. First, they would buy a share in a company, preferably through corporations that had been established for this purpose in a third country. Then, once in control, they would siphon the technology back to Iraq, where similar factories would be established.

Alternatively, as with Matrix Churchill, the Iraqis would use a front company to buy control of another company that had access to specialist technology. Contracts would then be awarded to the company using covert Iraqi money to finance the deal. All the equipment they acquired would be shipped to Baghdad.

Certainly, the Industrial Development Board in Northern Ireland must bear considerable responsibility for the Lear Fan farce, which could easily have become a source of significant technology for the Iraqi regime. It is difficult to understand why the IDB dealt with Jerry Bull in the first place. Bull was well known as an arms designer with an unsavory reputation, and after the IDB's experiment with DeLorean, one would have assumed that the board would negotiate only with thoroughly reputable people.

Even after the initial approach had been made, there is no evidence that the IDB made the required checks with the intelligence community concerning such a sensitive project, which implies a lack of political and business competence.

The experience left Michel Bull a very bitter man. He had come to enjoy Northern Ireland in the few months he had spent there. He liked the people and was looking forward to making his home in the province. Until the letter from the IDB he was confident that he was on course to prove himself as a businessman in his own right. Yet, having warned his father about getting involved with the Iraqis over the supergun project, it is difficult to understand why Michel thought Iraqi funding for Lear Fan would be any less controversial.

Michel does seem to have believed the Iraqis when they told him that they wanted to get involved with Lear Fan only as an investment. If that is true, then Michel was as naive as his father and was exactly the kind of patsy the Iraqis must have been astonished to find in such large numbers in Western countries.

S I X T E E N

OPERATION BERTHA

DESPITE THE very public involvement of the Bull family with the Lear Fan project and its known involvement with the underground Iraqi arms network, the only information gathered by British intelligence until the fall of 1989 related to SRC's contracts with Iraq for the 155-mm self-propelled howitzer and the new 210-mm gun. But this knowledge had been abandoned to a file marked "For Interest" and nothing further had been done.

In August 1989, Baby Babylon, a prototype of the supergun, had been constructed at a secret site at Jabal Hamrayn, ninety miles north of Baghdad in central Iraq. This was the smaller horizontal gun that was mounted on railway tracks, so that the huge recoil could be absorbed by the gun shunting backward down the line. The gun was a scaled-down test version of the bigger gun that would be built over two years, beginning in 1990. Meanwhile, test firings of Baby Babylon were planned to provide sufficient data to allow for design modifications. As with the gun in Highwater, a complex array of test equipment had been set up in Iraq to photograph the new rocket in flight and to record data of the gun's performance.[1]

Two other guns were also being designed at the same time as Baby Babylon. The first had a bore of 350mm and a barrel one hundred feet long that was capable of being elevated and trained. Some of the pipes that would later be seized in Greece and Turkey on their way to Iraq from the British firm Walter Somers were destined for this gun. Bull had also designed another gun with a 600-mm bore and a two-hundred-foot barrel, which when built could also have been elevated and trained. While this gun was still on the drawing board when Bull was shot, it was clear that Bull had secretly agreed to design large guns in addition to the gun Bull described to his employees as a satellite launcher.

These two new guns, the existence of which has never before been revealed, would have combined the range and payload of Big Babylon with the flexibility of some of his more conventional smaller guns. Leaving aside any possible hazards by Big Babylon, there is no doubt that if these two artillery pieces had been built and worked as Bull hoped, then Iraq would have had an artillery system that would have been several times more powerful than anything else in any army in the world.

The initial firing of Baby Babylon was not a success. The seals between the lengths of tube that formed the barrel blew apart. This delayed the project by several months, and repairs were finally completed at the end of 1989.

Even this failure, which had been widely discussed at SRC, was not picked up by the intelligence community. Presumably no one suspected the Iraqis to be involved in a project as unlikely as the supergun.

In June 1988, Astra Holdings was an ammunition company, positioned to become a major player on the international scene. Under the chairmanship of Gerald James, a former Guardsman in the army and a banker and qualified accountant, the company had expanded rapidly. In fact, Astra had just completed the take-over of the British Manufacture and Research Company (BMARC), a division of the Swiss Oerlikon arms company. Astra's turnover in 1987 was only $31 million, but by the middle of 1988, the company was predicting $225 million in turnover income for the upcoming financial year.[2]

Astra had started out manufacturing fireworks, but under

James it had begun to diversify into ammunition and propellants. In Britain, all ammunition had previously been manufactured by the government-owned Royal Ordnance (RO) factories,
which had become expensive and inefficient. Under the government of Prime Minister Margaret Thatcher, however, the Royal
Ordnance had been privatized and sold to British Aerospace. As
part of the arrangement, the government had given British Aerospace a sweetheart deal that guaranteed them a percentage of
the ammunition orders from the Ministry of Defence. Even so,
James believed he could bid on and win some of the remaining
British contracts while he aggressively pursued foreign orders.

That June, an executive at Paine Webber suggested to James
that he look into the Belgian company PRB, which rumor suggested might be ripe for a takeover. James investigated the company immediately and concluded that it would fit in perfectly
with Astra's long-range plans.

"It had everything we needed to take on Royal Ordnance in
a proper fashion," says James. "It had very good technology that
was ahead of RO, including combustible cartridge technology
[the caseless round] plus the 155-mm extended-range round,
which it was making for SRC."

James discussed the matter with his CEO, Christopher
Gumbley, who had joined Astra from Brocks, another fireworks
company, after working in the Ministry of Defence. The two
men agreed that PRB would be an ideal purchase.

PRB was wholly owned by a company called Gechem, which
in turn was owned by SGB, the huge Belgian conglomerate. In
early 1989, James opened negotiations with Gechem, which said
it was prepared to sell for $72 million. The discussions contin-
ued through the spring, with Gechem gradually reducing its
price.

Then in March 1989, Bull also approached PRB and offered
to buy it. Jean Duronsoy, the head of Gechem, told James that
he did not like Bull and so had turned down his offer.

The negotiations between Astra and Gechem were finally
concluded on July 17, 1989, with a contract for $44 million, a
little over half the original asking price.

Both James and Gumbley now believed they were perfectly

poised to attack not only Royal Ordnance but the major European and American arms manufacturers as well. From the Ministry of Defence's point of view, the growth of Astra and its expansion into Europe was a good thing, since it would produce some competition for the Royal Ordnance, which had a long-standing reputation for incompetence. James and Gumbley soon discovered, however, that all was not as it seemed at PRB.

Although Astra's accountants had been able to go over the books for previous fiscal years, they had not been allowed to see the current order book, which is common practice in the unusually competitive arms business. All negotiations had taken place with Gechem officials, and there had been almost no discussions with the board members of PRB. As Belgian law demands, when Astra took over the company, all the board members were forced to resign. James asked two of the directors to stay on, but both refused.

Then James came across some internal correspondence between PRB executives and senior officials at Gechem that showed that management had been aware of PRB's problems but had deliberately chosen not to tell Astra.

These memoranda also demonstrated that profit forecasts for 1989 had been based on 1988 figures and not on actual numbers for 1989, which had been revised substantially downward. According to one memorandum, "The management anticipates a negative reaction from the new shareholder and does not see how it can manage the shortfall, if this situation is not set right in time."

Later investigations revealed that while PRB was far from making a profit of $3.6 million in 1989, as they believed, it was actually anticipating a loss of more than $20 million. There were also serious gaps in the future order book, which meant that profits would have been down considerably in the years to come.

Both Gechem and SGB rejected any allegations of wrongdoing, claiming that it was up to Astra's management to examine the books properly. By talking to the factory workers and examining the order book, however, the Astra directors soon found out about a very large contract for ammunition for Iraq that had been shipped via Jordan. By itself, the news was not particularly alarming, but then Gumbley spoke to Roger Harding, deputy head of Britain's arms sales department, the Defence Export Services Organisation (DESO), about the deal.

In early September 1989, Gumbley ran into Harding at the Royal Naval Equipment Exhibition in Portsmouth, England. Harding, a large, witty, and immensely experienced arms salesman, had known Gumbley for many years and considered him talented, imaginative, and honest. He had watched with interest Astra's negotiations to purchase PRB. In fact, Harding had been discussing it with Bob Primrose, the director of marketing services at DESO, who had made some cautionary noises about the sale.

Primrose was a liaison between departments in the government—including the Department of Trade and Industry (DTI), the Foreign Office, and intelligence organizations—concerning potential arms deals. He also had an unspecified but important mandate to spot early warnings of potential problems within the industry in which he had worked for more than thirty years.

As it happened, a major scandal was beginning to surface in regard to the $1.4-billion merger between the British company Ferranti International and the American firm International Signal and Control (ISC), run by James Guerin. Ferranti had discovered that there was a shortfall of approximately $450 million in the ISC order book; as a result, Ferranti was in danger of going bankrupt.

The problem arose because a number of contracts, notably with Pakistan, proved to be fake. It also emerged that the U.S. Justice Department had been conducting a secret investigation into ISC because of alleged illegal arms sales to South Africa and Iraq, which was believed to have bought the technology for the Rockeye cluster bomb made by an ISC subsidiary.

News of the scandal, which did not surface until the *Sunday Times* (London) reported it on September 17, 1989, had caused consternation in the Ministry of Defence (MOD). Ferranti was an important British defense company, party to many expensive contracts. While the problems were clearly the fault of Ferranti's management, the MOD wanted to be sure that nothing like it happened again.

In this context, Roger Harding advised Gumbley to look closely at the contracts that PRB might have on its order books. There had been rumors for several years about various countries selling ammunition and explosives to Iraq and Iran while they were at war. In addition to Spain, Italy, and France, Belgium was thought to be one of the countries involved.

"There was nothing specific about PRB that caused me to doubt the deal," recalls Primrose. "It was the moment in time that gave rise to my concern. With Ferranti and all the rumors about arms to Iran and Iraq, we wanted to make sure that Astra was all right. It was a lucky guess, if you like."

At this stage in the takeover, Gumbley had not even seen a complete PRB contract list. The auditors had pored over the PRB accounts covering the previous few years, but the current accounts had to be taken on trust. One clause in the signed contract allowed for a later adjustment of the purchase price if the company did not perform as expected.

After meeting with Harding, Gumbley contacted PRB at once and obtained a full list of their contracts. On September 13, he then met with Primrose in the Ministry of Defence building.

"I looked down the list and one contract stuck out at once. At the time, I was concerned about missiles, and the contract looked to me like an order for solid fuel propellant," says Primrose.

The order showed Jordan as the end user, but this was a front frequently used by the Iraqis. Primrose immediately assumed that Baghdad was the destination. Further examination of the order showed that the specifications were not that of solid fuel for a missile. Instead, the order was for a number of giant sticks of propellant that were designed to fit together to form one enormously long tube. The order appeared to be for two different barrels, with two different gauges that matched no known missile or firing tube.

"We started to question what a stick like that could be used for," says Primrose. "It seemed to fit the profile of a gun propellant, but nobody had ever seen anything like it before. It was unbelievable, but it appeared to be so."

Primrose then wrote a memorandum to a number of government departments advising them of his discovery and asking for advice and further information. He received nothing in return. At the beginning of October, however, James and Gumbley were summoned to a meeting at Stuart House, a Ministry of Defence building in London's West End. In attendance were Primrose and representatives of other government departments, including the intelligence community.

At that time, no one had much to contribute. The officials listened to what the men from Astra had to say. After James and Gumbley left, the officials agreed that all they could do was try to investigate further, none of them really believing that the evidence before them showed that Iraq was building some kind of enormous gun. They obviously had to find out more, but they would be hampered by the fact that the PRB deal was a contract by a Belgian-registered company under Belgian law, and the British authorities had no jurisdiction. Two months later, having scraped together the few bits of hard information they could find, they decided to send a message to the Belgian Foreign Ministry alerting them to the contract and asking them to investigate.

The result was that Primrose drafted a letter that was sent to the Belgian Foreign Ministry in December by the British Foreign Office. The letter alerted the Belgians to the suspicious nature of the PRB contract with Jordan, which the British now believed was actually with Iraq. In response, the Belgian government alleged that they had informed the British Security Service about the supergun contract the previous May. This, of course, was untrue.

Toward the end of December, officials from British intelligence learned that Trebelan, the Spanish arms company based in Vitoria, was forging barrels for the giant gun. They alerted Spanish intelligence, who began to investigate the matter. Then, as so often happens in intelligence work, a lead was discovered in the press. El Mundo, the Spanish weekly magazine, published an article in February 1990 referring to a "supergun" being constructed in Iraq with the assistance of SRC and PRB.

At about the same time, the British were told by the Spanish that Trebelan had been making barrels for the conventional artillery that Bull had designed for the Iraqis. In actuality, the

Spanish company had been manufacturing slide bearings for the big gun, which would help absorb its recoil, as well as enormous steel beams, which would support the five-hundred-foot barrel in its concrete tower. To the amazed investigators, it appeared that some vast project was under way, the scale or purpose of which no one could fully comprehend.

The next piece in the puzzle came from *Middle East*, a British magazine. Alan George, a freelance journalist, wrote an article in the March 1990 issue claiming that Iraq was trying to revive Bull's HARP program. George concluded the article, which was essentially a review of HARP, by saying, "There is no hard evidence that Iraq's interest in HARP has moved beyond initial discussions to procurement. Last summer, however, Bruce Smith, a Canadian who 30 years ago supervised the construction of HARP guns, visited Barbados to assess the condition of the Paragon gun, which is owned by the Barbadian government. He was accompanied by an executive of SRC. Smith is presently a senior executive with the Belcan company of Canada, a subsidiary of PRB."

By then, British intelligence knew that, contrary to George's article, the Iraqis had already established a vast international procurement effort. The article seemed to confirm the *El Mundo* piece of the month before. In fact, it had advanced the information significantly by establishing links between SRC, PRB, the HARP program, Bull, and the Iraqis. At this point, Britain's Secret Intelligence Service (SIS), in concert with U.S. intelligence, coordinated a worldwide alert to locate any equipment that might be going to Iraq.

After months of baffling investigation, the intelligence community now seemed positioned to destroy the carefully constructed underground network that surrounded Project Babylon. Then, information was discovered in Europe that suggested two British companies, Walter Somers and Sheffield Forgemasters, were also implicated in the scheme.

At the beginning of April, a few weeks after Jerry Bull had been killed, SIS was tipped off that a shipment of parts destined for the supergun was about to be sent to Iraq. British customs was alerted and set up Operation Bertha, erroneously named after the massive German gun built in World War I that Bull had documented in *The Paris Guns and Project HARP.* (The gun's real name was Long Max.)

On Tuesday, April 10, customs officers examined a number of crates stored in the warehouse on Quay Seven of Tees Dock, just downstream from the Midlands town of Middlesbrough on Britain's east coast. The crates had been delivered that evening, after regular work had stopped for the night. Eight wooden cylinders, each twenty-five feet long by three feet wide, were marked "Republic of Iraq, Ministry for Industry and Minerals, Petrochemical Project, Baghdad, Iraq." The crates were about to be loaded onto the *Gur Mariner*, a ten-thousand-ton Bermudian-registered cargo ship that was due to sail for the Iraqi port of Umm Qasr. The ship had been chartered by the Iraqi Maritime Organization.

Inside each crate was a smoothbore barrel that had been carefully machined so that it fit perfectly into the next barrel, with the tube tapering toward one end. At first sight, it appeared that the intelligence information had been correct and officials had found a very large gun. But the customs officers wanted to wait until an expert from the Ministry of Defence could confirm their findings and until the formal documentation could be submitted. The shipping documents they had matched the labels on the crates. Before the Ministry of Defence man could appear, however, news of the find leaked to the press. On Wednesday night, the customs men moved in. By nightfall, they had no hesitation about proclaiming their discovery as a gun.

"We are considering the possibility that the gun was manufactured in Britain for the Iraqis," said a spokesman. "It is capable of firing a nuclear shell, or anything else you wanted to put on top of a one-meter shell, and could easily hit Iran or any other Middle East trouble spot."

After the raid on the company premises of Sheffield Forgemasters, customs officials raided another company, Walter Somers of Halesowen, West Midlands, the maker of high-technology heavy forgings. They also claimed they had been supplying forgings to an Iraqi petrochemical project. Both companies claimed that the forgings were steel pipes and had no military application.

After the initial excitement, there was considerable skepticism about the gun. The Ministry of Defence was openly suspicious and private briefings to journalists suggested that it was not a gun at all, that such a huge gun could never be built, and even if it was built it could never be fired. Army artillery experts and weapons designers were also dubious, but customs insisted that it was right. On April 12, a MOD ballistics expert visited the Middlesbrough dock and after a five-hour inspection said that the pipes could indeed be a gun barrel. But he too was not completely convinced, unable to comprehend a gun of such size or the military purpose in building it.

The companies who had been raided were now open to prosecution for illegally exporting weapons, and they mounted a vigorous defense. The company that had made the pipes, Sheffield Forgemasters, claimed not only that the pipes were for the oil industry but that the company had received permission to export them from the Department of Trade and Industry. Phillip Wright, the chief executive of Sheffield Forgemasters, protested his company's innocence:

> If this thing is part of a gun, then we, the DTI and many other people have been victims of the biggest con job in the history of arms manufacture.
>
> It sounds to me like something out of a sci-fi fantasy. I do not believe it is part of an enormous gun. We have done everything above board, legitimately and with full clearance from the DTI.
>
> There is no precedent anywhere for a gun of the size they are talking about. It's mind boggling to even consider. It is like something out of a best seller to suggest now we have been conned into producing the barrel of a giant gun. If they did manage to get all the other necessary components, I wouldn't stand within a mile of the thing if they tried to fire it. It would blow itself to pieces.

Documents discovered at the companies provided evidence that a massive shipment of pipes was already under way. Over the next week, trucks were stopped in Greece and Turkey on their way overland to Iraq. On board were more steel pipes described by shipping documents simply as "tubing."

Meanwhile, Walter Somers and Sheffield Forgemasters were marshaling their defenses. As it turned out, there had been numerous conversations between the companies and various British government departments regarding the proposed exports. On June 17, 1988, Bryan Cookson, the managing director of River Don Castings, a subsidiary of Sheffield Forgemasters, called the DTI from the Brussels office of SRC to ask if exports of steel tubes were permitted. The call came before any warning flags had been raised regarding Lear Fan, Condor, or even Iraqi's massive illegal procurement network. Cookson was told there were no restrictions on the exports he described.

Then, on July 7 and 8, another Forgemasters director called the DTI to check on the rules controlling the export of petrochemical industry equipment to Iraq. The director was told to send detailed specifications of the contract, including the plans, which he did. Walter Somers made a similar inquiry about its contract the following month, and the deal was again cleared by the DTI. Walter Somers got in touch once again with the DTI after the death of Jerry Bull; even then, no warnings had been sounded by the British government.

Perhaps the most damning accusation came from Sir Hal Miller, the British Conservative member of Parliament, who said that he had been in touch with DTI and MOD officials about the contracts on three separate occasions—in 1988, 1989, and 1990—after a director of Walter Somers had contacted him. According to Miller, the director had said that the specifications for some of the parts the Iraqis were demanding did not match their stated use. Miller also claimed that he spoke to a member of British intelligence whose name and affiliation he refuses to disclose. In every case, officials raised no objections to the deal. The DTI has confirmed that a conversation took place; the MOD has said that there was a conversation but the Ministry cannot find any record of it. There is absolutely no evidence to support Miller's allegation that he spoke to a member of British intelligence.

The DTI now says that the companies never sent the blueprints of the pipes and, if they had, their export applications would have been treated differently. This is clearly a specious argument. SRC's involvement in the contracts was known, and the only work they had done was designing weapons. SRC had no history of working on petrochemical projects, so the fact of Bull's involvement should have caused some concern. Exactly the same arguments apply to all the companies involved. It is difficult to believe that men with considerable business expertise, some with long-term associations in the arms industry, did not run checks on SRC before they agreed to the deal.

In fairness, the DTI was not familiar with the latest intelligence, and neither the intelligence community nor the MOD was made aware of the petrochemical contract. In addition, the DTI employs ninety-four staff members to vet seventy thousand export applications a year. Partially as a result of being overlooked, the deal was allowed to proceed. It was precisely this kind of bureaucratic fumbling that had allowed Iraq to build up such an effective military machine in the face of international arms embargoes.

Faced with contradictory evidence, customs officials had to prove that the companies and individuals involved had knowledge of Project Babylon. In short, they needed hard evidence. One of the first leads they received was a tip that a model of the supergun had been made by a British company and that a celebratory cake had been baked to mark its completion. An immediate search ensued for both the model maker and the baker. Customs officials traced the model to Amalgam Models in Bristol and learned that they had been commissioned by Christopher Cowley, the troublesome British designer who once worked for Bull. He had asked for a scale model of the supergun for display at the Baghdad Arms Fair at the end of April 1989. The model makers had kept photographs of the model itself, which they handed over to customs officials. The baker was also found, but he had not kept a picture of the cake, which had been made to look like the gun.

The full scale of the Iraqi plot was finally being revealed. In May 1990, West German customs seized seventeen crates of equipment in Frankfurt that were destined for Iraq. The equipment had been manufactured in Belgium by a hydraulics company called Rexroth that was a division of the German company Mannesmann, one of the world's largest producers of steel pipes. The company had been told that the Iraqi order was for the petrochemical industry.

At the same time, the Swiss impounded a consignment of machine components destined for Iraq, and the Italians impounded a consignment of ninety tons of hardware. These seizures led the Italians to raid a company called Società della Fucina located in Terni in Umbria, which in turn led them to arrest Aldo Savegnago, the engineer who had been hired by Cowley to be project manager. Savegnago admitted to the Italian police that he had coordinated the plants producing equipment for the Babylon project in the U.K., Italy, and Switzerland. He said he had been approached by Bull's Advanced Technology Institute (ATI) in late 1988 and was asked to draw up plans for Babylon. On behalf of ATI, Savegnago visited Von Roll, a Swiss company in Berne, ostensibly to order to order hydraulic cylinders for a forging press. A later raid by the Swiss on the same company revealed what appeared to be the recoil mechanism for Big Babylon.

Meanwhile, the precarious financial position of PRB was underlined when it went into liquidation in August 1990, the month that Saddam Hussein invaded Kuwait. Astra, too, had become a shadow of its former self and is struggling to restore its tarnished image to this day.

Obviously a massive effort had been made by the Iraqis to smuggle the equipment they needed to build Bull's supergun. In many respects, the network mirrored the one used by the Iraqis to obtain technology for the Condor rocket and nuclear program. The difference on this occasion was that Jerry Bull, a single individual, and one company, ATI, had been at the center of the web.

S E V E N T E E N

THE RIDDLE OF

BABYLON

SINCE THE discovery of the supergun in 1990 and the admission of its existence by the Iraqis in July 1991, there have been repeated allegations that Western intelligence agencies had full knowledge of the whole operation and, for some reason, had decided to ignore it. Some of those involved, including members of Jerry Bull's family, have maintained that the deal was no secret and that everyone must have known about the gun. There have also been suggestions that Bull himself alerted British intelligence about the project. None of these allegations are true.

It is very rare indeed that the kind of intelligence coup one finds written about in spy novels actually happens. Most intelligence work is the simple gathering of raw data. To trawl for specific information, an intelligence agency has to be charged with a specific task. Contrary to popular belief, resources are strictly limited. The reputation for omnipotence is encouraged, not by the reality of daily work, but by the all too rare exceptional incident.

In the case of the supergun, there was a general order in a number of agencies in the United States, Britain, and other European countries to monitor arms transfers to foreign countries. Iraq was known to be developing a nuclear and ballistic missile capability, and some attention was being paid to prevent the transfer of technology to the area.

However, it is a measure of the ineffectiveness of this monitoring effort that by the time Iraq had invaded Kuwait in August 1990, the regime had developed a chemical and biological capability, had test-fired a ballistic missile, and was on the verge of developing a nuclear capability. These advances had been achieved during the 1980s, when there was an international embargo on arms sales to the country. By the time the supergun contract was in force, the war between Iran and Iraq had ended and Western countries were once again lining up to sell arms to Baghdad.

The supergun fell through the cracks. The effort to destroy the sophisticated underground network that the Iraqis had established in order to buy Bull's equipment did not begin until the fall of 1989. For several months after that, as the full picture began to emerge, there remained two undercurrents that hampered the investigation. First, a significant credibility gap existed between the evidence that was coming in to the intelligence community and defense ministries and those agencies' professional assessment. In other words, people simply refused to accept what the evidence was telling them.

The Bull gun, which was more than four times larger than anything that had even been previously considered, was simply too big to grasp. In addition, from the start of the investigation, all the memos and papers referred to a gun, not a launcher. The assessments that were written by ballistics experts and others tried to answer the question *If it's a gun, what is it for?* No one in either Britain or the United States who was involved in the early stages of the investigation could find a military use for such a weapon. Therefore, people simply did not believe that a weapon was actually being constructed.

Because of this credibility gap, the analysts looked for another explanation of the evidence. As is usual with many unexplained phenomena in the Middle East, the answer was Israel. As 1989 turned to 1990, the consensus was that all this talk of a supergun had been, in fact, a massive Israeli disinformation campaign designed to make Iraq a laughingstock and focus the attention of Western governments on Iraq's illegal arms-buying network. In the bewildering world of intelligence, where so little is as it seems and the most obvious explanation is always suspect, the Israeli solution was seized upon by some as the perfect answer. That it was completely wrong was discovered only after Jerry Bull had been murdered.

Even after determining all the players in the game—Britain, Italy, Spain, Turkey, and Greece—some doubt still existed about the idea of the supergun itself. Several experts have suggested that the supergun was simply a huge gun designed to send a shell larger and heavier than a family car more than a thousand miles into the atmosphere. This shell, it has been argued, could have been loaded with a chemical or nuclear weapon and used to devastate Iraq's enemies, particularly Israel. In defense of this argument, reports during the Gulf war suggested that the gun had been fired at Israel and that it was a priority target of allied aircraft. Both of these stories were untrue.

During the Gulf war Iraq clearly demonstrated that it already had the capability to attack Israel with Scud missiles. This proved to be an effective terror weapon but was of little military value, in part because the Iraqis never loaded the missiles with chemical weapons. The Scuds also proved to be very inaccurate, making it difficult for the Iraqis to hit strategic targets with any reliability. Nonetheless, the Scud threat occupied more than a third of the allied air capability through the entire air phase of the war, which prolonged the air campaign longer than had been expected.

In firing the Scuds, the Iraqis showed a sure understanding of modern artillery tactics and the threat posed by air strikes and by enemy counter battery fire from both rockets and artillery. The most effective tactic they used is known as "shoot and scoot." This tactic demands that after a missile is launched, the launcher and its crews "scoot" from the area within sixty seconds. In today's world of artillery, where counter battery fire can be ordered and delivered with great accuracy within seconds, such tactics are essential.

If it had been completed, the supergun would have had a barrel more than 500 feet long, supported by a concrete tower

350 feet high. It would have been immovable and constructed to fire from only one position. To test the weapon's capability, it would have been necessary to fire several ranging shots before the real mission was launched. Each firing of the gun would have produced a flame nearly 300 feet long that would have been instantly visible to any number of satellites flying overhead.

The signature of the shell immediately after launch would have been similar to that of an intercontinental ballistic missile, and so it would have also been picked up by several satellites designed to provide early warnings of such systems. If the shell was fired during a time of conflict, then it is likely that surveillance aircraft would be in the air; they too would detect both the signature of the gun firing and the shell in flight. Consequently, it is extremely doubtful that the gun would have had an opportunity to carry out a ranging shot. It is thus certain that the gun would have been very inaccurate.

During the HARP program, the loading of a single Martlet rocket into the sixteen-inch gun required several men working more than two hours. Loading the Iraqi gun, which was much bigger, would have taken perhaps as long as eight hours. Though the gun would have been very powerful, its practicality was questionable. It would have been clearly visible and able to fire only two or three rounds a day.

Even if it had no military utility, the gun could certainly be used as a satellite launcher. In fact, whenever Bull spoke about the project, he referred to it as a satellite launcher, which is how he—and the Iraqis—had always envisioned it.

Saddem Hussein wanted to be the leader of the Arab world —economically, politically, and militarily. The ability to launch satellites would place him in a league by himself in the Arab world, where status is as important as substance. It would increase his military capability significantly, allowing him to use surveillance satellites to spy on every country in the Middle East, including Israel. In addition, he would be able to sell access to the launcher and information from the satellites to other developing nations, which would produce both revenue and influence. In any case, the intelligence community in Britain and the United States, as well as the Bull family and Bull's great friend, the formidable ballistics expert Charles Murphy, all believed that the Iraqis had bought a satellite launcher, not a gun.

But even if the satellite launcher had never worked, the Iraqis' investment in Jerry Bull would have been worthwhile for Bull's considerable knowledge of ballistics and rocketry alone. To launch a satellite, Bull would have had to design a multistage rocket, made of the latest composite materials, which would be capable of traveling more than a thousand miles into space. To be fired from the barrel of a gun, the rocket would have to be able to withstand enormous pressure. The Iraqis had been trying for over a decade to gain access to modern rocket technology, including basic designs and plans for guidance and propulsion systems. The supergun was meant to fulfill the original purpose of the Condor project—to provide a long-range delivery system.

At the same time, the Iraqis had come close to developing a nuclear capability. Before the Gulf war, opinions in the intelligence community had been divided about when Iraq would have a nuclear device, with some arguing that it could be as early as 1992. Certainly, if Iraq's covert nuclear program was allowed to continue, a nuclear weapon would be the result.

There is no particular evidence that Bull was actually involved in designing ballistic missiles for the Iraqis. In fact, this was not his field, and he had never shown any real interest in the subject. Bull's personal history suggests that he was once again an innocent dupe of the Iraqis, his only real concern to see his passion for the HARP program vindicated through the construction of the world's biggest gun. But to the Iraqis, Bull was an outstanding source who could produce for them a possible satellite launcher and much of the missile technology for which they had been searching. But, as happened so often in Bull's life, the situation was not as simple as the satellite-launcher theory or Saddam's determination to gain missile technology might suggest. According to Western intelligence sources, correspondence between the Iraqis and SRC referred to the gun as "a long range strategic bombardment system for the bombardment of distant targets." There was also discussion of "the adequacy of the HE [high-explosive] payload providing sufficient lethality."

This kind of correspondence makes clear that Bull was doing

more than simply designing a satellite launcher. Both Big Babylon and Baby Babylon had a different and more sinister purpose.

While it is clear that Big Babylon made little sense as a gun
to Western intelligence analysts, to Saddam sitting in Baghdad
and to his enemies in Tel Aviv and Tehran, the Bull project
looked very different. Big Babylon was being constructed in a
mountainside in Iraq with the body of the gun concealed in an
enormous cavern. When it was fired, it would indeed produce a
massive signature that could make it instantly visible to satellites. But neither Israel nor Iran have such reconnaissance capability.

During the Gulf war, the allied coalition forces showed that
precision bombing could reduce even the most protected bunkers and well-defended military sites to rubble. But such bomb-
ings required the use of the most modern munitions, including
laser-guided bombs and cruise missiles that follow computer
maps generated from satellite imagery. Such weapons are not
readily available to either the Israelis or the Iranians. It is perfectly possible that if the big gun had been used against its
neighbors rather than a country such as the United States, it
could have survived long enough to do damage.

If the launcher was used to fire shells rather than satellites,
it is possible that the United States would have shared appropriate intelligence information with the Israelis, but this is not
something the Jewish state could have relied upon. Instead, they
recognized that once the gun was in place and ready to fire they
would be vulnerable to an attack from a new weapon against
which they would have only a limited defense.

The only people who can describe the true purpose of Big
Babylon are Jerry Bull, who is dead, and the Iraqis, who are not
talking. The consensus in the intelligence community is that
Big Babylon was very probably both a satellite launcher and a
gun. It is known that Bull was committed to using the gun for
satellites; he told both family and colleagues of his intentions,
and there is every reason to believe he welcomed the opportunity to realize his life's ambition of firing a satellite into space
using a gun of his own design.

The Iraqis, on the other hand, were determined to build not

just the most powerful military force in the Middle East, but a force with prestige armaments that would enhance that power. Big Babylon would have perfectly suited Saddam's grandiose ambitions. Whether Bull knew that the gun was going to be used for more than just launching satellites is not known, but he must have had a good idea that Iraqi intentions were not entirely peaceful.

If Bull was unsure about Big Babylon, he can have had no such uncertainty about the purpose of the two enormous artillery pieces he had designed for the Iraqis. These two guns, one with a barrel one hundred feet long and a bore of 350 mm, the other with a two-hundred-foot barrel and a bore of 600 mm, would have been the largest artillery pieces in the world. According to Bull's own designs, both guns could be elevated and trained, which would make them very accurate and far more dangerous than Big Babylon. Both would have brought Israel well within range of Iraq.

According to correspondence found among Bull's papers after his death, he referred to "improving the lethality" of the guns. There must have been no doubt in his mind that he was constructing weapons of war, weapons so powerful that they would have given Iraq the ability to attack all of her neighbors, including Israel, Saudi Arabia, Iran, and Turkey. Even some European countries would have come within range of the artillery, which could fire shells loaded with chemical, biological, and perhaps eventually nuclear weapons.

The debate about the ultimate purpose of Big Babylon is unlikely to be resolved. As a satellite launcher it could have brought Saddam Hussein and Iraq into the space age; as a gun it could have done some damage but would have had little serious military purpose. The guns in the middle range, however, were a different matter and posed a very serious threat to the security of a large number of countries.

In 1953 Bull had said, "War will never occur until a nation planning aggression thinks it can win. As long as the nations desiring peace can maintain better weapons than the nations desiring war, there will be a deterrent to aggression. Then they are not weapons of war, but weapons of peace."

These idealistic sentiments sounded good coming from a young man starting out on his scientific career. Today, they read like the naïveté of many young scientists who make such statements before confronting the harsh realities of life. As Bull's career soured, he appears to have compromised all the high ideals with which he set out. Just before his death he had designed two new artillery systems of almost unimaginable power that could not remotely be described as "weapons of peace." On the contrary, they would have allowed Saddam to wage war using weapons of a destructive power never before seen.

Perhaps Bull hoped that Big Babylon would be the monument to his genius and the other guns were the price he accepted to realize his life's ambition. Perhaps he had become so bitter that he simply no longer cared about consequences, only results. Whatever the reasons for this final folly, Bull misjudged the international response to his partnership with the Iraqis. Instead of designing and building the biggest guns in the world, he was brutally, even clinically, murdered, a victim of a world his ego and his innocence never allowed him to understand.

In the months before his death, Bull was under enormous pressure, and he became even more obsessive than usual. He believed that he was being followed, that his apartment had been broken into on a number of occasions, that his belongings had been searched.

The Iraqis had set up a tight schedule for the supergun contract, so it is difficult to judge just how valid Bull's fears may have been. The evidence he supplied of the break-ins—books that had been moved, a videotape that had been rewound—was suspect coming from a man who conformed to the image of a disorganized scientist. He lived in a mess and rarely ate properly unless the food was cooked for him. His apartment was a shambles unless someone came in to clean it. His work environment was no more orderly; his desk at SRC was always piled high with papers and books. His personal filing system consisted of a bulging briefcase, which he carried everywhere, papers spilling out of all the pockets. In such an environment, it would have been hard to discriminate between signs of someone searching his apartment and the results of the absentminded scientist mislaying his own possessions or forgetting how things had been left.

At this time, Bull had been working hard to obtain a pardon for his conviction of smuggling arms to South Africa. Bolstered by the evidence he felt he had gathered in preparing his lengthy and autobiographical defense statement in 1985, he was totally convinced that he was on the brink of a breakthrough.

Central to his argument was the belief that he had been the victim of some unfathomable conspiracy that had resulted in his prison sentence. Immediately after his conviction, Bull had argued with both family and friends that he had been "let down" by the American government and that the CIA had failed to stand by him after he had been arrested. Over the years, this sense of betrayal had hardened into a conviction that the evidence against him had been fabricated and that the conspiracy had been orchestrated by people he did not know. And now the conspirators were active against him again, he said, which made him all the more determined to prove his innocence.

Meanwhile, Mimi had been trying to get her husband's Canadian citizenship back. In December 1989, she finally extracted a promise from the Canadian government that if Bull returned to Canada, he could apply for a passport and one would be issued. She called Bull with the good news, and he agreed to fly back to Canada. He had actually bought his ticket and was about to board the aircraft when he changed his mind and refused to go. He later told his family that returning to Canada and reapplying for citizenship would be a recognition that the Canadian government had the right to take it away in the first place. He refused to give the government that satisfaction and decided instead to fight on for his pardon.

The same month, Bull had received some information regarding his pardon that was very encouraging, though he would not disclose the nature of it to his family. His trip to America in February 1990 allowed Bull to spend time with Mimi in New Orleans and then go to Washington for a few days to follow his quest for evidence.

While he was in Washington, Bull met with William Gill, a lobbyist whom he had hired to work on the pardon. He also spent a day with Donald de Kieffer, a Washington lawyer, whom he also consulted about the pardon. De Kieffer had been recommended by Gill and was an interesting choice for Bull to have made. In 1978, when the South Africans were taking over SRC, de Kieffer had been hired by the South African government as a Washington lobbyist during the Muldergate Scandal, when it was discovered that the South African government had been secretly funding a worldwide propaganda campaign. Since then, de Kieffer has gained considerable expertise as a specialist in international trade legislation and sanctions.[1]

Jerry "Bull was very interested in examining the possibility of getting a review of his case," recalls de Kieffer. "There was also an extended conversation about the facts of the case at the time."

De Kieffer is naturally cautious about saying exactly what passed between him and his client, but it is clear that he was slightly baffled when Bull's rumpled figure appeared in his office. Bull spent eight hours recounting in exhaustive detail the story of a case that happened more than ten years earlier. Reluctant to dismiss him out of hand, de Kieffer asked for more information: says de Kieffer, "We were not able to conclude from our conversation whether he had any basis for an appeal. We told him that we needed additional information and we gave him a list of what was needed."

On his return to Brussels, Bull said that he had also met with someone who told him that if he had not pleaded guilty at his trial, he would have been killed. While this piece of information distressed him, he was elated to have confirmation of his suspicion that a plot existed in the first place. He never, however, discussed the identity of his source.

Bull had told his son Stephen that he was "that close" to learning the full details of the CIA's involvement in the smuggling of arms to South Africa. In a separate conversation with Charles Murphy, he said he had uncovered evidence that the shells that U.S. Customs proved had been shipped from Canada to Antigua and then on to South Africa, had, in fact, never left Canada.

At this stage in his life, Bull was prepared to believe anything and anybody who tended to support his conspiracy theory.

He was showing the signs of a man obsessed: his thousand-page autobiography written with the help of Don Mordell, the letter-writing campaign he organized among his friends, and the conversations with anyone who would listen about the merits of his case.

Into this complex tale, Bull wove the additional element of Joseph Severin, his friend and the former head of PRB. Bull believed that Severin's death in 1978 had been the start of his difficulties; after that, PRB had stolen his designs for artillery and extended-range ammunition. For years, Bull had been seeking revenge on PRB and SGB, the conglomerate that owned it. He called Christopher Gumbley, who had suffered similarly at the hands of PRB, after the Washington trip.

Gumbley resigned from the board of Astra on March 13, 1990—nine days before Bull was killed—after being arrested for giving a BMW to a friend who worked in the contracts department of the Ministry of Defence. The two men were old friends, and Gumbley says that it was simply a generous gesture to a man who had been kind to him when he had hit hard times a few years earlier. The MOD official worked in a department that was of no use to Gumbley, so his story might have been true. (However, at his trial in 1991, the jury did not believe him and he was jailed.)

When Bull heard the extent of Astra's and Gumbley's troubles, he called Gumbley at his home in Nottingham and offered him lunch in Brussels, where, he said, they could discuss matters of mutual interest.

Gumbley, who had never met Bull, was curious about him and agreed to the meeting. He asked Harry Cranz, Astra's Austrian agent, to come along so that he would have a witness to whatever Bull had to say. The three men spent much of the day together; over lunch, Bull brought up his reason behind the gathering.[2]

Bull explained that he was convinced that the people at Gechem and SGB were crooks. He told Gumbley that officials at SGB were responsible for the murder of Severin, who had not fallen down the stairs, as people believed. He had been murdered and his death had been made to look like an accident.

Gumbley, a short, almost spherical, businessman with no

knowledge of the strange world that Jerry Bull had come to occupy, was astonished at the turn in the conversation.

Bull complained that he had formed a joint company with PRB to make money and that the death of Severin had meant that he had never received the cash and that PRB had walked off with all his designs for new artillery and ammunition. He added that he also had tried to buy PRB but had been turned down. Then Bull said he had enough evidence against SGB to force the company to compensate Astra for the shambles with PRB.

According to Gumbley, Bull said, "I will do anything to get those bastards in SGB. If you sue them for personal loss, I will pay your legal expenses—as much as it takes for as long as it takes."

Gumbley was astonished at this extraordinary offer to bankroll a very expensive legal action from a man he had just met. He stammered his thanks and his acceptance, and the two men agreed to meet again the following Thursday. About 6:00 P.M. that evening, Gumbley left SRC's offices for the airport. Once there, he called Gerald James, the former chairman of Astra, to tell him the news. According to James, Gumbley said, "Would you be able to get to Brussels next Thursday?"

"Why?" James asked.

"Bull does not like SGB and he has got enough on them to make life pretty hot."[3]

By the time Gumbley had flown out of Brussels, Bull was dead. For the next few months, Gumbley lived in fear of his life and consistently denied ever having met Bull. He was convinced that Bull's death was directly related to their conversation and that Bull was killed because he knew something about some powerful people in Belgium. Gumbley has no idea what Bull knew, only that it was enough to get him killed. He was sure that if he spoke about the meeting, he too would be assassinated.

Both Gumbley and James are men whose careers as international businessmen collapsed shortly after their involvement with PRB. Neither of them is fully able to comprehend the reasons for the disaster that overtook them. Almost overnight, the company they had nurtured and led to considerable success was near bankruptcy. Gumbley was facing a jail sentence; James was out of work and suing Astra for compensation.

In their search for an explanation, they have concluded that they unwittingly became involved in a conspiracy involving the British Security Service and arms deals with Iraq. They believe that Bull had information on PRB that, if revealed, would have shown extensive British involvement in the arms trade with Iraq. They also believe that because Astra had bought PRB, they too were at risk, since they had examined the books that revealed the arms trade.

For these reasons, Gumbley and James think that British intelligence is responsible for killing Jerry Bull, that he was gunned down before he could provide concrete support for Gumbley's court case against Gechem, including the extent of the British government's involvement in the illegal arms trade with Iraq.

This theory is possible but unlikely. The involvement of British companies in the arms trade with Iraq is well known and has been documented by the media. It may be that hidden layers to their involvement exist that have not been exposed, but it is hard to imagine just what removing these layers might uncover that would be enough to cause the death of Jerry Bull. In other countries, such as West Germany and France, where illegal arms deals have been exposed, no ministers have resigned or governments fallen.

It is also difficult to contemplate any senior official in the very bureaucratic British intelligence community authorizing the assassination of an American national on the soil of a NATO ally. Indeed, there is no mechanism in British intelligence for authorizing such a killing; without official sanction at the highest level, no agent would have agreed to carry out the mission.

There was speculation at the time of Bull's death that he had been killed by the Iraqis because he had fallen foul of the merciless Saddam Hussein, but no evidence exists to support this conclusion, and there is a considerable amount of evidence to contradict it.

Project Babylon had been proceeding well, and the Iraqis had already invested several million dollars in it by the time Bull was killed in March 1990. Stephen Bull was actually in Baghdad at the time, overseeing the project, and he claims there was no sign whatsoever of any change in the normally excellent relationship between SRC and the Iraqis. In addition, although the Iraqis show great ruthlessness in dealing with their own people and have no hesitation in killing troublesome Iraqi exiles, they do not have a record of killing foreign nationals, especially those who have given such good service to their country. If they did, their military-industrial complex, which relies in large measure on the willing participation of foreign scientists, would swiftly grind to a halt.

The Bull family, who for the ten years since the trial had listened to Jerry Bull railing against the conspirators who sent him to prison, believe it was neither the Iraqis nor the British but the Americans who killed him. In particular, the family blame the CIA, which they believe was responsible for setting up the original arms deal with South Africa. The CIA's record in this area is not completely clean; however, in recent years it does not have a record of murdering businessmen or even dealers in the illegal arms industry. Instead, the CIA seems to spend a great deal of effort attempting to bring them to trial.

The family cite as evidence for their theory Bull's claim that he had finally found evidence to support his long-standing suspicions of a conspiracy. The strongest argument in favor of this theory is that the evidence Bull had been purportedly gathering for over a decade is missing.

Jerry Bull was an inveterate memo writer who would constantly scribble notes to himself because he was so absentminded. Yet after he was killed, his family could find no trace of any file relating to his pardon.

"We know he had been running this investigation, and we did not find anything among his papers relating to it," says Michel. "This is extremely odd. He was a memo writer and kept records of everything. Yet here was something very dear to his heart, and he apparently kept no record of any kind after all those years of work looked like coming good. It's very odd indeed."

Friends of Bull's, such as Charles Murphy, find the CIA argument hard to accept. Murphy believes that the CIA had lost its appetite for such activities and is too restricted by congressional limitations and presidential findings to consider anything so obviously illegal.

It seems unlikely that anyone in the intelligence community today would care about something that happened fifteen years earlier—and care enough to kill Jerry Bull—and thus it seems unlikely that the CIA was responsible. The CIA's involvement in the arms deal was not exactly a secret, so what threat could Bull have posed?

In the key period when Operation Feature was being launched in Angola and the South Africans were being supplied with arms and the contacts were being opened with SRC, George Bush was the director of the CIA. If there remain buried in the CIA archives details of some secret aspect to this operation, a secret so terrible that if Bush's role in it ever became public it could threaten the United States presidency, then the CIA would indeed be capable of assassinating the parties involved. However, enough disaffected CIA agents have emerged from that period to tell their stories that it seems likely that such a dark secret, if one exists, would have emerged by now, even in the form of an unproven accusation.

After all the suspects have been lined up, the Israelis appear to be the ones with the most compelling motive to kill Bull. They had already demonstrated their willingness to take extreme action against those involved in the Condor project when they blew up the car of one of its key people. The Israelis had also killed a scientist working on Iraq's nuclear program, and Israeli intelligence almost routinely murders members of the PLO whom it considers to be a particular threat.

There is no doubt that the Israelis have both the expertise and the disregard for international law to do the job. But why would they have bothered?

The supergun was not a serious threat to the security of Israel. Even though the Iraqis planned to bury it in a mountainside and the Israelis had no satellite surveillance capable of detecting its position, there is considerable doubt in the scientific community that the gun would ever have proved effective as an offensive weapon. The test-firing of Baby Babylon showed that Bull was pushing the limits of what was actually possible to achieve by bolting a number of metal tubes together to fire a single rocket or shell. While Baby Babylon had been repaired, Big Babylon was much larger, and even a single firing might have destroyed the whole structure. There had been repeated failures of the breeches and the barrels during the HARP program, and it is likely that such failures would have been repeated during the Babylon project. A single failure in Big Babylon would have set the project back months, perhaps years.

If the Iraqis had planned to use Big Babylon as a bombardment weapon, similar to the way the Germans used the Paris Gun, it would have been a failure. It would have taken several days of rapid fire—which in supergun terms is one shot every few hours—to produce a fall of shot that could be relied on to hit Tel Aviv or Jerusalem. Even if the Israelis were unable to locate the gun itself, they could launch retaliatory strikes against Iraq that would have made Saddam pay a heavy price for each shot fired from the supergun.

The single most important disadvantage of Big Babylon was that it was a fixed weapon that could not be elevated or traversed. Once in place it would only be able to fire along a single track, with the only variables being the amount of propellant and the weight of the shell, which would change the range.

There would have been no such restriction with the two smaller weapons, with barrels of one and two hundred feet, that Bull was creating for Iraq. According to Bull's designs, these two guns could have been elevated and traversed, making them much more dangerous weapons. But here, too, there is some doubt that the designs would have worked and, if they did, about how effective they would have been.

Bull had clearly convinced the Iraqis that his designs could produce an effective artillery system. But Saddam would have had to build several guns, perhaps dozens, to give them any real tactical value in a war. The guns would have been inaccurate, would have required several ranging shots before being able to hit their targets, would have had a very slow rate of fire, and would have proved mechanically unreliable. To ensure some degree of reliability, Saddam would have had to build large numbers of them. It would have been an immensely costly program, more expensive than buying modern and accurate ballistic missiles from China, North Korea, or the Soviet Union.

In any event, Iraq already had powerful weapons including Scud missiles, that posed a much greater threat to Israel than any version of the Bull guns. Other projects, such as Iraq's program to produce genetically engineered weapons, had proceeded without any interference from the Israelis. Given the weight of this evidence, it is difficult to understand just why Bull was singled out for elimination.

However, the Israelis were quick to claim credit for Bull's assassination, even releasing alleged details of how it had transpired. According to a report on PBS in February 1991, the killing was carried out at the end of an intelligence operation lasting several months and involving more than eighty people. The Israelis claim that Bull received two direct warnings that he ignored, after which two hit teams arrived in Brussels.

> One team waited outside his apartment building while another was outside the office as Bull was picked up to be driven home. Only days before, his prototype gun had been tested in Iraq. . . . And the moment he leaves the office, they click on the closed-circuit matchbook, indicating that he left the office and that they are following him. . . . The moment he entered the apartment, two clicks. And while he is going up to the sixth floor, the team that was in the apartment building waiting in ambush is rushing to the sixth floor through the emergency staircase, not using the elevator. Jerry Bull and the team appeared together at the entrance to his apartment. One guy opens fire, five shots. You don't hear any noise. The only thing you would hear is a "Phut! Phut!" kind of noise and they are gone. . . . The hit team was driven to the train station in Brussels and took the first train out of town to Germany.[4]

There are several problems with this colorful scenario. First, if Bull had received two warnings from Israeli intelligence, this normally garrulous man had never told his family about them. In fact, he believed that the Israelis, people he had done business with for many years, knew about the project and didn't care.

Second, the prototype gun had not been tested a few days before he died, but a few months earlier, and the test had been a failure. The test itself was hardly an incentive to kill Bull.

Third, no intelligence agency reveals how it operates without a motive, and it only does so if it has a very important reason, or it swiftly becomes ineffective. Consequently, the fact that the Israelis have been keen to talk about their role is in fact a strong argument against their being involved.

If the Israelis did kill Bull, their reasoning remains unclear. Bull was, after all, an American citizen, and the Israelis have never been known to kill an American, for fear of upsetting their supporters in the U.S. Also, Bull was living in Belgium, a Western country with which Israel has good relations that could have been seriously jeopardized if the mission had gone wrong.

The only logical explanation is that Israeli intelligence analysts misunderstood Project Babylon. Intelligence agencies are trained to look at capabilities—what something *could* do, rather than what it was intended to do. It would have been possible for the intelligence analysts who look at worst-case scenarios to build up Jerry Bull and his guns into a potent threat. All the guns might work, they might be fitted with chemical or nuclear shells, and Israel would be unable to retaliate in time to prevent the devastation of large areas of their country. None of these assessments may have seemed *likely*, but they were possible, and it could be argued that killing Bull would immediately resolve the problem. But such extreme action against an American citizen does not seem justified unless the Israelis overestimated the nature of the threat posed by Bull's guns. Or if they had another motive for killing him.

In the past few years, as the Arab nations surrounding Israel have bought more sophisticated weapons from the growing number of suppliers, Israel has come to believe that in another Middle East war, a fourth victory against the Arabs is unlikely. They rightly believe that the technology gap, which served them so well in the 1967 and 1973 wars, has narrowed so that there is little qualitative difference between themselves and their enemies. Israel now has American fighters, but so does Saudi Arabia; Israel has effective helicopters, but so do all her neighbors; Israel has the nuclear bomb, but Libya, Syria, Iran, and Iraq have chemical weapons and the means to deliver them. There may still be a qualitative gap that gives Israel some advantage, but this too is narrowing.

Bull was a threat to the Israelis because of what he knew *and* because of what he represented. He was yet another arms dealer who was feeding at the Arab trough, ready to take oil money in exchange for modern weapons. Killing Bull would not only have stopped the supergun project, it would also have served as a warning to all the other dealers operating in the underground arms bazaar that trading with Israel's enemies is a dangerous business.

Exactly who killed Jerry Bull is still a mystery and likely to remain so. The Belgian police are keeping the file open, but they have virtually given up investigating the case and privately acknowledge that it will never be solved.

As far as the Western intelligence community is concerned, they do not care who did the job, only that it got done. Bull, they argue, was an amoral merchant of death who, in effect, died by his own hand, and the world is a better place without him. Nonetheless, his old friend Marcel Paquette says that Bull was convinced he had "a good star" that protected him in some way.

"Jerry had one motto that he lived by all his life," said Paquette, " 'There is no tomorrow.' "

Perhaps this is the most charitable epitaph that Jerry Bull will ever have.

E I G H T E E N

T H E L E G A C Y

WHEN THE air phase of the Gulf War began in the early hours of January 17, 1991, the allied air forces had a list of priority targets. Among them were strategic sites such as airfields, command and control bunkers, and facilities where chemical or nuclear weapons could be manufactured.

The intention of the campaign was to destroy Iraq's industrial and defense infrastructures and to demolish Saddam Hussein's fighting capability. Aircraft from the allied air forces simultaneously launched missiles and dropped bombs on factories all over Iraq and directly attacked Saddam's military machine.

One of the first priorities given to the air force, however, was the destruction of the conventional artillery guns designed by Jerry Bull. The same satellite capabilities that had allowed the CIA to confront the Austrian government with evidence of NORICUM's smuggling of Bull artillery to Iran in 1986 had allowed the Americans to detect the movement of Iraqi artillery to the front line. As part of their reinforcement of the front following the August invasion, the Iraqis had brought forward all their long-range artillery, the best of which were the 155-mm guns that had been shipped from South Africa and Austria.

The allies knew that the Iraqi artillery had a greater range than anything available to the coalition, except for the multiple launch rocket systems. Simple intelligence analysis before the air phase started suggested that Iraq had two principal methods of launching chemical weapons: by bombs dropped from aircraft and by artillery. Both systems had been used during the Iran-Iraq war and Saddam was likely to repeat the pattern if given the opportunity.

Within a week, the allies had established air superiority, which gave them total control of the skies. While Iraq still had several hundred aircraft hidden at more than sixty-eight airfields around the country, the threat they posed had been reduced considerably. There remained the residual threat that Saddam would order all the available aircraft to surge in a single strike against the allied ground forces. If Saddam had chosen to arm two hundred aircraft with chemical weapons and launched all of them at once against the allies, it is almost certain that some would have broken through. But he chose to keep his aircraft on the ground or send them to Iran.

The artillery presented a different problem. In the month prior to the air phase of the allied campaign, U.S. intelligence had detected a significant increase in the activity at various chemical weapons plants in Iraq. At Fallujah, Samarra, and Akashat, factories were working twenty-four hours a day, seven days a week, and allied intelligence believed that more than a hundred thousand artillery shells filled with chemical agents had been shipped to the front line. This later turned out to be untrue.

At this stage of the war, these chemicals posed no serious threat to the allied forces. While some reconnaissance units were probing forward across the Saudi-Kuwait border, these patrols went largely undetected. The body of the allied ground forces was spread in a 250-mile-wide arc at least 25 miles south of the border, well out of range of Iraqi artillery.

However, the longer the air phase went on, the closer the allied forces had to move to the border, which brought them within easy range of Iraqi artillery. The allied war planners were concerned about the window of vulnerability that would occur after the coalition forces came within range of the Iraqi artillery but before they had brought their guns within range for counter battery fire. It was exactly the same problem that had faced the South Africans in 1974 and that had led to Operation Feature. If Saddam's forces struck while the allies were nearing the Iraqi border, the chemicals could be expected to hit the allied ground forces and cause large numbers of casualties. But if the Iraqi commanders waited until the assault had actually begun and the allies had come within range of the smaller artillery pieces, then there was a reasonable chance that the chemicals would do as much damage to the Iraqi forces as to the allies.

It was critical, then, for the allied forces to destroy the G-5 and the GH N-45 artillery pieces, since these were the only artillery that could hit the ground troops at long range. A month of continuous air attack ensured that the Bull artillery was destroyed. When the allied ground forces finally attacked late on the night of February 23, not a single artillery shell loaded with chemicals was fired at the allied forces.

To confront Saddam's enormous military power, the allies amassed a huge force in the Gulf region. In many respects, it was the most powerful military force ever seen in action, and the war proved to be an excellent proving ground for all weapons and tactics on land, sea, and in the air. The Gulf war will shape not only the future of warfare, but the future of specific weapons and the arms business for decades to come.

In the first three days of the Gulf war, 40 percent of the targets were destroyed by the F-117A Stealth Fighter, which made up only 2 percent of the allied aircraft in the war zone.[1]

In a war that produced its full share of astonishing statistics, this illustrates perfectly what the conflict was all about: the triumph of technology on and above the battlefield. The Stealth Fighters were able to fly deep inside enemy territory, night after night, and remain completely invisible to Iraqi radar and any Iraqi fighters that tried to intercept them. The U.S. Air Force claimed that at no time in the course of the war were any of the forty-eight Stealth Fighters detected by the Iraqis.

For many years, war planners have debated the virtues of technology over those of the humble soldier. High-technology weapons are expensive and soldiers are relatively inexpensive; all military planners have to strike a balance between the two. The United States, with its post-Vietnam obsession with casualty figures and the constant need to reassure the public about how painless war can be, has firmly opted to fight a high-technology war whether it be on the central front in Europe, in Panama, or in the Gulf.

The war played to America's strongest military suit. Instead of fighting an enemy who rarely sought a direct confrontation, as in Vietnam, or an enemy who would not fight by the rules, as in Grenada or El Salvador, the U.S. battled Saddam, who opted to sit in the desert in full view of his enemies. This war gave the Americans the opportunity to do what they do best: gather massive firepower and use it ruthlessly.

From the outset, Saddam Hussein had completely misunderstood the nature of modern warfare with its emphasis on air power and deception and mobility on the battlefield. Instead of giving his forces flexibility and freedom to maneuver, he chose to build an Iraqi Maginot line, which was intended to stop the allied advanced in the same way he had managed to stop the Iranians for eight years. As a result, his troops became prisoners in their own bunkers and trenches, victims of the most intense bombing campaign ever seen. In the course of the war, 110,000 sorties were flown by the allies with a loss of only forty-nine aircraft.

Unlike every other conflict in history, this was a precision air war. Tomahawk cruise missiles confounded their critics by flying over Baghdad and hitting their targets precisely. Laser-guided bombs, infrared heat-seeking missiles, and other delivery systems also proved their worth. Even the Apache helicopter, which had been dismissed by its critics as ineffective, was successful in destroying tanks and other armored vehicles.

These precision weapons allowed the allies to keep civilian casualties to a minimum. Never in a conflict on the scale of the Gulf war have so few civilians been killed or injured. The allies have set a benchmark against which the conduct of all future wars will be measured. No longer will war simply be about winning, irrespective of the cost. Military planners will have to accept that civilians are not legitimate targets if they are at all interested in maintaining a position on the moral high ground.

While strategists and tacticians will argue for decades over the subtleties of the war, lessons will be learned from it by countries both rich and poor, advanced and emerging. To be successful in a modern war, an armed force needs the best technology available, and plenty of it. This basic tenet may not be new, but the ambition of a growing number of countries to achieve such a high-technology solution by using weapons of mass destruction—conventional and unconventional—makes today's world an infinitely more threatening place than it was for previous generations.

The war also taught hard lessons to a number of the countries involved. Despite huge investments in modern military equipment, both Saudi Arabia and Kuwait were essentially impotent in the face of the massive Iraqi assault.

The Israelis, for the first time in history, were forced to stand back and allow themselves to be struck again and again by Iraqi Scud missiles without retaliating. Instead of meeting force with force, as the Israelis have always done, they had to turn to the United States for protection, relying on U.S. supplied and manned Patriot missile batteries to meet the Scud threat. It may have been politically expedient to do nothing, but the reality was that Israel could do nothing militarily that was not already being done better by the allies. A country that had almost bankrupted itself to maintain a top-notch military found itself helpless against a neighbor armed with an effective modern weapon.

The Iraqis, despite their massive investment in matériel, were unable to withstand the allied assault and suffered one of the most ignominious defeats in recent military history.

But this is not just an issue of modern artillery being sold to Saddam or even of the willingness of people like Bull to sell new, more powerful weapons into the ever-hungry arms market. Rather, Bull and his inventions are merely symbols of a greater problem: the failure of the international community to halt the spread of weapons throughout the world, and the seemingly endless cycle of proliferation that is a hallmark of the arms business.

It would be comforting to assume that those countries directly affected by the war have learned that however great the investment, no weapon can buy security. It would also be comforting to assume that dictators who aspire to conquest, the next generation of Saddams, have learned a lesson from the Gulf war and will decide to pursue their ambitions by means other than arms.

But history does not suggest that any country or leader can be counted upon to draw such peaceful conclusions from war. On the contrary, for Saudi Arabia, Kuwait, Iraq, and Israel, the single lesson learned is that more arms, not less, are needed for their nations to be secure.

Before the dust of the war had settled, business was booming in the arms world. Teams of arms salesmen from the United States, Britain, France, West Germany, and other minor-league producers all flocked to the Middle East to tout their wares. They found plenty of willing buyers.

Egypt has made clear it would like to buy Hawk missiles, M60 tank upgrades, and F-16 fighters. Israel wants portable battlefield navigation systems, upgrades for the F-15 fighter and the M109 artillery piece, and more Patriot missiles. The United Arab Emirates would like some Abrams M1A1 tanks and Patriot missiles, and so would Bahrain and Turkey.

By far the biggest buyer will be Saudi Arabia, which is already in line to receive a $15-billion arms package including F-15 fighters, Apache helicopters, Abrams M1A1 tanks, AWACS radar planes, Patriot missiles, multiple launch rocket systems, Seahawk helicopters, and Bradley Fighting Vehicles.

In addition, the United States, Britain, and France will need to replenish their stocks that were expended in the war. When the procurement decisions are made, those weapons that performed best in the Gulf are the ones that will be bought. All future research and development will concentrate on those areas that proved their worth: lasers, microcomputers, standoff systems, Stealth technology.

The development of new weapons can no longer be done in

isolation; it is simply too expensive. Increasingly, cooperative ventures are becoming commonplace among countries that cannot afford to invest alone in developing new systems. If there is to be an emphasis on high-technology systems in the future, and there surely will be, then such ventures will be essential.

New weapons mean that large numbers of second-generation weapons will come on the market and be sold to developing countries, while manufacturers seek rich customers who can afford to buy the new systems, thereby reducing the unit cost and increasing profits.

Within that cycle, there is an additional force driving the proliferation of conventional arms after the Gulf war. Defense contractors who supplied the allied forces can now market weapons that have been tested and proved in battle. At a time when defense budgets are being reduced and contracts are being cut, exports could make up the shortfall for manufacturers who would otherwise be forced to shut down production lines and lay off workers. These contractors have little interest in arguments about the morality of the arms business; they are only concerned with maintaining the bottom line and satisfying their stockholders.

On the other side of the defense equation, the Soviet Union's equipment performed very poorly in the war. Their top-of-the-line tank, the T-72, was hopelessly outgunned by the older and less powerful American M60; their artillery and counter battery fire were no match for the allied equivalent; and their aircraft were shot down in every single engagement with the allies. Shortly after the war, the official Soviet news agency, Tass, quoted one Soviet colonel as saying that huge numbers of their armored vehicles, tanks, and artillery pieces were absolutely useless.[2]

While the political future of the Soviet Union remains uncertain, military officers have acknowledged that immediately after the war ended, the Soviet high command began an urgent review of equipment currently in service or planned for the future. The Soviets may have difficulty selling some of their weapons on the arms market, but they will certainly try to do so as new equipment comes on-line.

The real challenge facing the world in the aftermath of the Gulf war and the cold war is how to break out of the arms cycle that has ensured the continued proliferation of ever more advanced weapons.

President Bush has made it clear that he saw the Gulf war as an opportunity to build a new world order. While the exact terms of this new world order have never been fully articulated, the major Western allies have understood it to mean that the U.S. will lead the way in breaking out of the arms race that has dominated so much of international trade since the end of World War II.

At a press conference on March 1, 1991, at the end of the week that saw the allies victorious in the Gulf, President Bush declared, "Let's hope that out of all this, there will be less proliferation of all kinds of weapons, not just unconventional weapons."

The previous month, in testimony to Congress, James Baker, the U.S. secretary of state, promised he would mount a major nonproliferation effort in the Middle East, calling for extremely intrusive measures of inspection and verification.

President Bush reinforced this commitment in his address to the joint session of Congress on March 6, 1991. The speech was a celebration of victory and an opportunity for the president to set out his vision of the much vaunted new world order. He identified four key areas that required immediate attention, emphasizing that action was needed on all if any were to succeed.[3]

> First, we must work together to create shared security arrangements in the region. Our friends and allies in the Middle East recognize that they will bear the bulk of the responsibility for regional security. But we want them to know that just as we stood with them to repel aggression so now America stands ready to work with them to secure the peace.
>
> Second, we must act to control the proliferation of weapons of mass destruction and the missiles used to deliver them. It would be tragic if the nations of the Middle East and Persian Gulf were now, in the wake of the war, to em-

bark on a new arms race. Iraq requires special vigilance. Until Iraq convinces the world of its peaceful intentions— that its leaders will not use new revenues to rearm and rebuild its menacing war machine—Iraq must not have access to the instruments of war.

Third, we must work to create new opportunities for peace and stability in the Middle East. On the night I announced Operation Desert Storm, I expressed my hope that out of the horrors of war might come new momentum for peace. We have learned in the modern age, geography cannot guarantee security and does not come from military power alone.

Fourth, we must foster economic development for the sake of peace and progress. The Persian Gulf and Middle East form a region rich in natural resources with a wealth of untapped human potential. Resources once squandered on military might must be redirected to more peaceful ends.

The United States has a unique opportunity to build on the goodwill generated by the Gulf war. There is a chance that for the first time in recent memory, the world will actually listen when the United States speaks, but the president will have to produce something more concrete than fine words.

Just how the four-point master plan will translate into action is unclear. What is clear, however, is that existing measures to deal with the spread of unconventional weapons have failed.

By 1991, twelve developing countries—Iraq, Burma, China, Egypt, Ethiopia, Iran, Israel, Libya, North Korea, Syria, Taiwan, and Vietnam—were known to have chemical weapons. A further eighteen countries—Afghanistan, Angola, Argentina, Chad, Chile, Cuba, El Salvador, Guatemala, India, Indonesia, Laos, Mozambique, Nicaragua, Pakistan, Peru, the Philippines, South Africa, and Thailand[4]—have been trying to obtain chemical weapons and may have succeeded.

Generally, this chemical capability has simply not been passed to these countries by one of the superpowers. On the contrary, all nations have acted responsibly in trying to control the passage of chemical stocks from one country to another.

(There have been instances of the Soviet Union supplying limited stocks to countries like Egypt, Ethiopia, and Syria, but this has been the exception rather than the rule.) Instead, the developing countries have had to acquire their own capability, usually illegally, but frequently with the complicity of Western companies and governments that turn a blind eye to a useful source of export earnings.

In 1985, plans for a chemical weapons plant at Rabta in Libya were drawn up by the West German firm Imhausen-Chemie, which was having financial difficulties at the time and needed the cash from the Libyan contract. Imhausen commissioned plans for the plant from the Salzgitter steel company, which is owned by the German government, telling them that the project was for a pharmaceutical plant in Hong Kong.

To maintain this fiction, raw materials for the plant were shipped by Imhausen to a Hamburg firm, Pen-Tsao-Materia-Medica, which had been set up by Imhausen's founder, Dr. Jurgen Hippenstiel-Imhausen. Pen-Tsao was supposed to ship the goods to its Hong Kong subsidiary, but they went instead via two Belgian firms to Tripoli.[5]

The Japanese Steel Works did much of the construction at Rabta with workers imported from Thailand through a Thai firm called Supachok. By 1988, the plant was producing nerve gas casings at the rate of ten a day from steel supplied by other West German companies. British and American intelligence had been watching the project closely and by the summer of 1988 were convinced that once the plant was fully on-line, the Libyans would be able to produce between twenty-two thousand and eighty-four thousand pounds of nerve agents a day, making Rabta the largest chemical weapons plant in the third world.

For some months, private inquiries were made to the West German and Japanese governments. The Germans denied all knowledge of the affair and carried out no investigations. The Japanese claimed that the Rabta plant was a desalination complex, which seemed unlikely, since the nearest sea was sixty miles away.

On September 14, 1988, the U.S. State Department went public with some of its evidence, while selected pieces of further evidence were leaked to the media. And yet, neither the Japanese nor West German government was prepared to do anything about it. Eventually, even the West German government was shamed into action, and Chancellor Helmut Kohl set up a special commission to investigate.

The inquiry discovered that the West German intelligence services knew about the Libyan chemical weapons plant as early as 1980 and had identified Imhausen's involvement in 1985. However, the report said that under existing German law, none of the firms appeared to have done anything illegal. This suggests that according to the German government, any company can transfer deadly technology to a dangerous dictator and remain inside the law.

By the beginning of 1991, U.S. intelligence officials were saying that the Rabta complex was operating as a production line for chemical weapons and that construction had begun on a massive underground storage facility in the desert near the factory. Exactly who is building the underground facility is not known.[6]

To try to curb such blatant abuses, in March 1985 the U.S. secretary of state, George Shultz, called for new efforts to prevent the spread of chemical weapons. The Australian Department of Foreign Affairs took the initiative and invited a number of Western industrialized nations to a meeting at the Australian embassy in Paris in June 1985. The first meeting had representatives from Australia, Canada, Japan, New Zealand, the United States, and the ten member nations of the European Community. The Australia Group, as it became known, meets every six months and has drawn up a list of chemicals that are commonly used in the manufacture of chemical weapons.

As of this writing, the group has expanded to include Norway, Portugal, Spain, Switzerland, and the European Commission. It has identified eleven precursor chemicals that now require export licenses from member states, and a further thirty-nine have been placed on a watch list that members hope will give early warnings of a country's intention to go into the chemical weapons business.

The problem with the Australia Group's initiative is that it is dependent on its members for monitoring the transfer of chemicals effectively and prosecuting violators. There is no standard of enforcement to which every member must adhere and no way of penalizing those members of the group who ignore the agreement or other nations who simply export the raw materials without concern for the group's reaction.

In the middle of the military buildup in the Gulf in November 1990, President Bush vetoed a bipartisan bill in Congress that would have imposed sanctions on companies exporting raw materials that could be used to make chemical weapons. The administration said that the bill was unsatisfactory because it did not allow the president to waive the terms in the interests of national security.

After the veto, the administration drafted its own bill, called the Enhanced Proliferation Control Initiative, which increased the number of precursor chemicals that would be subject to export controls from eleven to fifty. The new measures included criminal penalties for violators. However, business interests argued that the initiative unfairly penalized American companies and opened the door to foreign competitors who did not suffer from similar restrictions.

Many of the items on the new list are used to make a wide range of products such as plastics, pharmaceuticals, and fertilizers. For example, one of the chemicals can be used to remove hair from hides before tanning, but with some modifications, it can also be used to make nerve gas. Lobbyists for the chemical industry argued that by restricting the export of such dual-use chemicals, the U.S. was unfairly restricting American industry.[7]

Then, on February 20, 1991, the Senate passed new legislation that required the president to impose sanctions on countries and companies developing or using chemical weapons. The bill, the Omnibus Export Amendments Act, was slightly modified from the one the president had vetoed the previous year to allow Bush to delay the imposition of sanctions against foreign companies to give the host country an opportunity to take action.[8]

This is a useful step in the right direction and points the way toward a new control agreement. The Germans, at last pricked by conscience, have begun work on a new program of export controls. At present, companies can export defense equipment only if a special permit is granted. But companies frequently get around this by exporting a seemingly inoffensive product to a nonthreatening nation, where the raw material is swiftly converted to military use and then reexported.

The German economics ministry is in the process of examining new legislation that will make a senior board member of each company personally responsible for its exports. Breach of the law would mean that the individual, as well as the company, would be subject to criminal prosecution.

The message from these two preliminary attempts at new arms control measures have a common theme: behind the moral principles must lie tough criminal sanctions that make individuals responsible for their acts. But even if this is accomplished, addressing the spread of conventional and chemical capabilities without dealing with other layers of proliferation is of little value.

Chemical weapons may be the poor nation's equivalent of a nuclear bomb, but this has not prevented a number of those countries from attempting to acquire nuclear capability as well.

In 1968, the nuclear nonproliferation treaty (NPT) was signed and come into force in 1970. The NPT was designed to keep the number of states with nuclear weapons stable at five: the United States, the Soviet Union, Britain, France, and China. The treaty calls for those who have nuclear weapons not to ship the equipment or transfer the technology to other countries that would use them to develop nuclear weapons. As a carrot to support the agreement, those countries that sign the NPT will be assisted in developing peaceful nuclear programs.

One hundred and forty-three countries have ratified the NPT, but some of the most important have so far failed to do so. France and China, two existing nuclear-weapons states, indicated in 1991 their intentions to comply with the NPT, as did South Africa. Others have refused to sign, such as Israel, India, Pakistan, Brazil, and Argentina. But just who has or has not signed seems to have made little difference in the spread of nuclear weapons.[9]

India, which has refused to sign the NPT, developed a nuclear capability in the early 1970s and has actually tested a nuclear device. This encouraged Pakistan, another nonsignatory, to develop its own nuclear weapon. After more than fifteen years of development, it is on the brink of succeeding.

From the start of Pakistan's nuclear-weapons program, Western intelligence agencies have monitored the underground purchasing network used to buy the raw materials and the technical knowledge. However, during the critical phase of research and procurement, the United States, which under the terms of the treaty should have tried to stop the program, did very little to pressure General Zia, Pakistan's leader, to do so. On the contrary, aid to Pakistan had increased steadily until a new $4.02-billion six-year aid package was agreed upon in July 1987. The reason the U.S. took such an apparently relaxed attitude was the war between the Soviet Union and Afghanistan. Zia's support was critical to the U.S. effort to force the Soviets out of Afghanistan; all weapons and cash to the Afghan mujahedin passed through Pakistan.

The U.S. campaign was successful, and on February 15, 1989, the last Soviet soldier left Afghanistan. Under special legislation passed by Congress, the U.S. president was obligated to write a letter to Congress each year stating that Pakistan did not possess a nuclear weapon. Failure to write the letter would result in aid to Pakistan being cut off automatically. In 1990, when President Bush finally wrote the letter, Pakistan lost its aid from the U.S. The action came too late and is a perfect illustration of how political expediency (in this case the war in Afghanistan) can produce deadly consequences.

In January 1991, British and French intelligence agencies received information that the Pakistani government had sold two small tactical nuclear devices to Saddam Hussein in Iraq. While Saddam had his own nuclear program, no one thought he had developed a nuclear bomb. The fact that Pakistan might actually have passed on such a device caused something close to panic among the allies. Fortunately it turned out to be a rumor, and Saddam did not release a nuclear weapon in Kuwait. But the rumor was salutary warning of just what might happen in the future.

One of the forces driving President Bush in the prosecution

of the war against Iraq was the recognition that Saddam was expected to develop a crude nuclear device by the end of 1991. Iraq, which was one of the early signatories of the NPT, had been pursuing an aggressive program to obtain a nuclear weapon for over twenty years. In 1981, the Israelis bombed what they claimed was a nuclear reactor and enrichment plant in Osiraq, Iraq. Since then, Iraq has redoubled its efforts to build a nuclear bomb, using its extensive international underground purchasing network. Switzerland, Germany, and Britain, which have all signed the NPT, were active sellers of nuclear-related equipment to Iraq. German scientists spent long periods of time at Iraq's nuclear-testing sites, helping Saddam build the centrifuges necessary to enrich uranium to weapons-grade strength.[10]

But even after Iraq's invasion of Kuwait, Germany had not fully addressed the problem regarding the transfer of nuclear technology. The government announced that it was terminating all exports of nuclear or military nature. The ban applied to an A group of weapons and military goods and a B group of nuclear materials and isotope-separation technology. However, dual-use technology was not included in the ban, so a loophole for arms acquisition still existed for Iraq to exploit.[11]

Western governments now accept that Israel and South Africa, neither of whom are signatories of the NPT (although South Africa recently promised to sign), have a nuclear capability. Pakistan almost certainly has a nuclear bomb, and there have been repeated but unconfirmed reports that Pakistan has agreed to share its nuclear technology with Libya. Other countries such as North Korea, Taiwan, and Brazil have been working to develop nuclear weapons as well.

In the face of such proliferation, Western nations (unlike the Soviet Union and her allies) have been unwilling to address the failure of the NPT. Some progress was made at the fourth five-year-review conference of the NPT in Geneva during August and September 1990. Suppliers of nuclear materials, such as Germany and Japan, agreed to make these supplies conditional upon an agreement made by the recipient state to adhere to international safeguards. In addition, new measures were taken to improve the inspection capacity of the International Atomic Energy Authority (IAEA).

Iraq, as a signatory to the NPT, had its nuclear plant inspected regularly by the IAEA. However, neither the nuclear-materials factories nor the centrifuge plant for enriching uranium has had its operations inspected by anyone.

But even in those countries where the development of chemical and nuclear weapons has failed, the acquisition of ballistic missiles has not. In testimony to Congress, U.S. defense secretary Dick Cheney has warned that before the end of this century, at least fifteen developing countries will be able to build and deploy ballistic missiles. Of those, eight will either have or will soon have a nuclear capability. Scud missiles are currently in use in Syria, Egypt, Iran, Libya, Yemen, North Korea, and Iraq.

The CIA predicts that by the year 2000, at least six countries will have missiles able to fly nearly two thousand miles, with three other nations able to hit targets thirty-five hundred miles away.[12]

In the areas of nuclear, chemical, and ballistic missiles there are some controls, even if they do not work as they should. But there is a new generation of weapons on the way that will make all these weapons seem relatively ineffective and needlessly expensive.

Genetic engineering has allowed scientists to understand how certain hereditary information is passed on from generation to generation through our genes. This understanding has allowed scientists to begin the duplication of certain types of genes.

The potential for military use of genetically engineered organisms is frightening. Scientists could produce a whole new generation of biological weapons that would make war accessible to anyone with the genetic technology.

The purpose of warfare is to conquer the enemy by destroying his ability to wage war, by occupying his territory, or both. During the Gulf war, the precision weapons employed by the allies, which allowed bombs and missiles to hit their targets with pinpoint accuracy, received considerable praise. Yet the allied coalition killed as many as two hundred thousand Iraqis and destroyed not only the country's ability to wage war but much of its industrial infrastructure as well. The war would have been less costly in money, lives, and manufacturing capability if the allies had a weapon that was even more precise.

No commander wants to kill his enemy; he simply wants to make sure his enemy does not kill him while he achieves victory. Genetic engineering would allow scientists to isolate particular toxins, to refine them and give them a very specific life. Such designer agents could be used in an artillery shell that would explode over an advancing force of infantry. Each load of agent might cause acute vomiting in each soldier, making him unable to advance, or it could cause such instant and severe depression that none of the soldiers would be prepared to fight. Alternatively, a cruise missile could dispense an agent over a port or industrial center that would make all the civilians unconscious for twenty-four hours, disrupting reinforcements at the front and allowing an aggressor to capture vital territory virtually unopposed.

This kind of technology is available today, and for the past ten years Britain, the United States, and the Soviet Union have been studying the possibilities of designer agents as weapons of war. While Western governments are insistent that such work is taking place in the West only for defensive purposes, U.S. intelligence is convinced that the Soviets are well advanced in their preparation of genetically engineered weapons.

It is axiomatic in the arms business that what the superpowers develop one year, other countries will research the next. Developing nations have recognized that chemical weapons, combined with ballistic missiles, can be cheap, powerful, and accessible alternatives to nuclear weapons. Genetic weapons would be even cheaper.

Before the Gulf war, the Iraqis had established the Al-Kindi Company for serum and vaccine production in Baghdad; they also had started a joint venture with Jordan and Saudi Arabia to establish the Arab Company for AntiBiotic Industries and the State Company for Drug Industries. They announced that Iraqi biotechnologists were building a biological research station in the southern marshes that would incorporate a genetics research laboratory.[13]

Currently, there are no conventions, treaties, or other agreements that address the threat posed by genetically engineered weapons, partly because the science has emerged too recently for governments to understand fully the need for controls on the transfer of genetic technology. In addition, the difficulties encountered by attempting to reduce the proliferation of chemical and nuclear weapons has discouraged the superpowers from further attempts to limit other weapons.

Slowing the arms race has been a goal of successive world leaders for decades. All have failed. Instead, weapons at every level of conflict have spread, becoming more terrifying. More important, perhaps, the number of arms manufacturers has increased significantly in the past decade, bringing into the market new companies and countries that see the arms business as a method of generating valuable foreign earnings and political influence. The Iran-Iraq war provided an outlet for many of these newcomers, and the competition was fierce.

Obviously, new systems are needed for policing the arms business at every level. In situations where governments have relied on the morality of their own companies to obey the law or when countries have relied on other countries to behave decently, they have been disappointed. In almost every instance where there has been some form of arms control agreement, countries and companies have ignored the terms for either political or financial reasons.

It is no longer enough to expect governments or companies to behave reasonably. They have not done so in the past; there is no reason to expect they will do so in the future. A new plan is needed to deal with arms proliferation at all levels. It will be up to the Western nations, led by the United States, to come up with a course of action.

As a first step, the United States should persuade close allies such as the United Kingdom and Germany to voluntarily restrict exports of weapons to developing nations.

At a meeting of the seven leading industrialized countries in London in July 1991, it was agreed that the United Nations would be asked to keep a register of all arms transfers so that the leading nations could then withold aid from poor countries deemed to be spending too much on arms. The summit declaration also called for strict guidelines about what arms could be sold and to whom they could be sold and restrictions on the sale of weapons to regions of tension.

This is a useful first step on the long road to effective arms control measures, but it is difficult to see just how this system will work. Both the Stockholm International Peace Research Institute and the London-based International Institute for Strategic Studies keep a detailed list of overt arms transfers; the UN list will simply complement these.

Those countries most responsible for serious arms proliferation—such as Iraq, Saudi Arabia, and Libya—do not benefit from Western aid and are therefore not susceptible to that form of pressure. In fact, the strategic interests of the major powers are best served by keeping such countries well supplied with modern weapons.

The apparent confusion in the policy was made clear at the end of May 1991 when President Bush announced a new arms control initiative for the Middle East. The president said that the five permanent members of the UN Security Council, which alone are responsible for 85 percent of the arms sales in the Middle East, had agreed to a freeze on the sale and manufacture of missiles like the Scud and to a program to eliminate all weapons of mass destruction in the region, as well as a voluntary restriction on the sale of conventional arms.

The day after this announcement, U.S. defense secretary Dick Cheney offered Israel ten more F-15 fighters and $200 million in research money for a new missile system. This generous gesture did little to convince the Arab countries that American policy in the region was concerned with their interests and must have acted as a disincentive for any country in the region to voluntarily participate in arms control measures.

While the major arms producers are trying to make new working arrangements among themselves, the third world arms producers believe that the real purpose of any new deal is simply to carve up a smaller market at their expense. These countries will resist any attempt to set up what they describe as a cartel, and they are determined to continue to sell their products to whichever country has the cash to pay for them.

It is clear that the voluntary arrangements are not going to work unless they become wider in scope. And the fine words need to be backed up by a tough enforcement policy that penalizes countries and companies that break the new rules. The major arms producers, led by the United States, should create new legislation with the purpose of prosecuting those companies that do not follow the guidelines. Only by directly attacking individual companies and their directors will there be penalties strong enough to break the greed that motivates arms dealers to act without regard for consequences.

But the fact remains that the growing competition in the arms market has made the superpowers almost irrelevant. If the major powers agree to curb the weapons trade, other, less scrupulous countries will be happy to fill the orders. Indeed, the relative significance of the major powers as weapons suppliers is steadily being reduced by this competition. For example, the U.S. share of the Middle East arms market has fallen from 36 percent in 1982 to less than 30 percent in 1987, with much of the difference being made up first by European suppliers, then by Latin America countries, South Africa, and China.

The arms control net clearly needs to be widened. Arms producers in South Africa and Brazil, for example, should be asked to join a voluntary agreement. If they refuse to do so and continue to sell arms, then sanctions should be imposed. Such an ambitious policy has little prospect of surviving the elastic morality of day-to-day political decision making. But the world is uniquely receptive to such vigorous action. The United States has provided unprecedented leadership in defeating a tyrant whom all countries involved in the war had helped to support and arm. Even though Eastern European countries will be looking to use arms sales to bolster their shaky economies, the West is in a powerful position to apply pressure on them to resist temptation. Imaginative use of aid and technology transfers, upon which all the Eastern European countries are now dependent, could force them to reduce their arms exports.

If new arms control politics do emerge from the Gulf war, then Jerry Bull will have left a legacy beyond even his dreams. Instead of making weapons to wage war in ever more destructive ways, the example of Jerry Bull's dangerous ambition should serve as a warning to the world against the proliferation of arms.

LIST OF ABBREVIATIONS

ABM	Antiballistic Missile
ADL	Arthur D. Little, Inc.
AMC	Army Materiel Command
APC	Armored Personnel Carrier
ARMCOM	Armament Command (U.S. Army)
Armscor	Armaments Development and Production Corporation (S. Africa)
ASAT	Antisatellite
ATI	Advanced Technology Institute
BMARC	British Manufacture and Research Company
BOSS	Bureau of State Security (S. Africa)
BRL	Ballistics Research Laboratory
CARDE	Canadian Armament Research and Development Establishment
CCC	Canadian Commercial Corporation
CIA	Central Intelligence Agency (U.S.)
CTI	Canadian Technical Industries
DARPA	Defense Advanced Research Projects Agency (U.S.)
DESO	Defence Export Services Organisation (U.K.)
DOD	Department of Defense (U.S.)
DRB	Defense Research Board (Canada)
DTI	Department of Trade and Industry (U.K.)
FCO	Foreign and Commonwealth Office (U.K.)
FNLA	National Front for the Liberation of Angola
GLO	Gun-Launched Orbiter
GPS	Global Positioning System
GWS	Great West Saddlery Company
HARP	High Altitude Research Project
IAEA	International Atomic Energy Authority
ICBM	Intercontinental Ballistic Missile
IDB	Industrial Development Board (N. Ireland)
IRA	Irish Republican Army
ISC	International Signal and Control
MBB	Messerschmitt-Boelkow-Blohm
MDT	Memorial Drive Trust
MiCom	Army Missile Command (U.S.)
MOD	Ministry of Defence (U.K.)
MPLA	Popular Movement for the Liberation of Angola
MTCR	Missile Technology Control Regime
NASA	National Aeronautics and Space Administration

NATO North Atlantic Treaty Organization
NPT Nonproliferation Treaty
OMC Office of Munitions Control
PENCO First Pennsylvania Bank
PRB Poudrières Réunis de Belgique
RO Royal Ordnance (U.K.)
SADF South African Defense Force
SDI Strategic Defense Initiative (Star Wars)
SGB Société Générale de Belgique
SGE Saad General Establishment
SIPRI Stockholm International Peace Research Institute
SIS Secret Intelligence Service (U.K.)
SRC-B Space Research Corporation—Barbados
SRCI Space Research Corporation International (Brussels)
SRC-Q Space Research Corporation—Quebec
SRC-US Space Research Corporation—United States
SRI Space Research Institute (McGill)
SS Security Service (U.K.)
TDG Technology and Development Group
UNITA National Union for the Total Independence of Angola

N O T E S

INTRODUCTION

1. International Institute for Strategic Studies, *Military Balance, 1990–91.* (London: Brassey's, 1991), 100–122.
2. *The National Interest,* Winter 1990–91, 3–10.
3. *The New York Times,* August 13, 1990.
4. *Time,* February 11, 1991, 34–35; *U.S. News & World Report,* February 18, 1991, 36–37.
5. *Los Angeles Times,* September 18, 1990.
6. *Financial Times,* September 12, 1990; *The Washington Post,* October 12, 1990.
7. *The Sunday Times* (London, December 2, 1990. The Sunday Times Insight investigative team did a major exposé of British arms exports to Iraq that is the definitive study on the subject.
8. *The Washington Times,* March 23, 1988; *Financial Times,* March 23, 1988; *Daily Telegraph,* March 23, 1988.
9. *The National Interest,* Winter 1990–91, 3–10.
10. *The New York Times,* January 19, 1991; *The Washington Times,* November 12, 1990.
11. *The Sunday Telegraph,* September 12, 1982; *The Washington Post,* September 27, 1982.
12. Interviews with Dr. Charles Murphy and Michel Bull, 1990 and 1991.
13. Details of the murder of Jerry Bull were covered in a number of newspaper articles at the time, particularly in the Toronto *Star,* March 24, 1990, and March 31, 1990; *The New York Times,* April 20, 1990; the Montreal *Gazette,* April 1 and April 3, 1990; *The Washington Post,* April 5, 1990; and the Vancouver *Sun,* March 31, 1990. Additional information comes from interviews with the Belgian police, the Bull family, and a businessman who was with Bull on his last day.
14. Panégyrique à la mémoire du Dr. Gerald Vincent Bull, par ses enfants, March 31, 1990.
15. Interview with Belgian police, April 1990.
16. Interview with Michel Bull, February 1991.
17. *The Middle East,* March 1990, 17.

CHAPTER 1

1. The most detailed article on Jerry Bull's early life appeared in *Maclean's,* March 1, 1953. I have drawn heavily on this and have

also talked to the Bull family to fill in the gaps. Additional details on his career can be found in Mordell, Heymans, and Braithwaite, *Case History of Dr. G. V. Bull.*

2. Interview with Marcel Paquette, August 1990.

CHAPTER 2

1. Bulkeley and Spinardi, *Space Weapons*, 10–11.
2. Ibid., 12.
3. Lee, *War in Space*, 13.
4. Interview with Charles Murphy, July 1990.
5. Interview with Reed Johnston, March 1991.
6. Mordell, Heymans, and Braithwaite, *Case History of Dr. G. V. Bull*, 41.
7. Correspondence obtained from the McGill University archives.
8. Interview with Charles Murphy, February 1991.
9. Interview with Charles Murphy, July 1990.
10. *Canadian Weekly*, March 2–8, 1963, 3–7.

CHAPTER 3

1. Hastings, *The Korean War*, 403.
2. Interviews with Charles Poor, July 1990, and Charles Murphy, July 1990.
3. Mordell, Heymans, and Braithwaite, *Case History of Dr. G. V. Bull*, 29.
4. McGill University, *Project HARP Description and Status* (Montreal; McGill University, 1962), 1–3.
5. *The Montreal Star*, March 1962, Volume 16, 170.

CHAPTER 4

1. Accounts of the Barbados part of the HARP project appear in the *Barbados Daily News*, March 26, 1962; *The Montreal Star*, 1962, Volume 16, 170; *The Montreal Star*, March 27, 1962; and *The Montreal Star*, March 26, 1962.
2. *Canadian Weekly*, March 2–8, 1963, 3–7.
3. Department of Mechanical Engineering, *Annual Report, 1961–62* (Montreal: McGill University).
4. *Canadian Weekly*, March 2–8, 1963, 3–7.

CHAPTER 5

1. Jahn, *The Problem Solvers*, 204.
2. Interview with Charles Murphy (the student, not the head of BRL), August 1990.
3. Interview with Charles Murphy (of BRL), December 1990.
4. Interview with Marcel Paquette, August 1990.
5. Interview with Michel Bull, February 1991.

6. *The Montreal Star*, June 19, 1963.
7. *Newsweek*, July 15, 1963, 54; and the *Toronto Financial Post*, November 16, 1963.
8. Bull and Murphy, *Paris Kanonen*, 208.

CHAPTER 6

1. Mordell, Heymans, and Braithwaite, *Case History of Dr. G. V. Bull*, 60.
2. Ibid., 62.
3. Interview with Charles Murphy, January 1991.
4. J. W. Wright, C. H. Murphy, and G. V. Bull, "Profiles of Winds in the Lower Thermosphere by the Gun-Launched Probe Technique and Their Relation to Ionospheric Sporadic E," *Space Research VII* (Amsterdam: North-Holland Publishing Company, 1966), 113–22; J. W. Wright and L. S. Fedor, "Comparison of Ionospheric Drift Velocities by Spaced Receiver Technique with Neutral Winds from Luminous Rocket Trails," *Space Research VII* (Amsterdam: North-Holland Publishing Company, 1966), 67–72.
5. Interview with Charles Murphy, December 1990.
6. *The Montreal Star*, December 21, 1965.
7. *McGill News*, September 1967, 11–12.
8. Montreal *Gazette*, April 10, 1967; and *The Montreal Star*, March 7, 1967.
9. *McGill News*, September 1967, 11–12.
10. Interview with Charles Poor, July 1990.
11. Interview with Marcel Paquette, August 1990.
12. Interview with Charles Murphy, January 1991.

CHAPTER 7

1. Jahn, *The Problem Solvers*, 121–22; in addition, a number of interviews took place in 1990 and 1991 with current and former employees of Arthur D. Little. In particular, Jean de Valpine, the head of the Memorial Drive Trust, was extraordinarily helpful.
2. *The New York Times*, October 23, 1990.
3. Interview with Reed Johnston, March 1991.
4. Interview with Jere Lundholm, October 1990.

CHAPTER 8

1. Interview with Charles Murphy, January 1991.
2. Ranelagh, *The Agency*, 312–22.
3. Interview with Charles Poor, July 1990.

CHAPTER 9

1. A more detailed account of this relationship appears in James Adams, *The Unnatural Alliance* (London: Quartet, 1984).

2. Mohamed El-Khawas and Barry Cohen, eds., *The Kissinger Study of Southern Africa* (Westport, Conn.: Lawrence Hill, 1976), 101–16.

3. Stockwell, *In Search of Enemies*, 19–22; and Ranelagh, *The Agency*, 608.

4. Jeffreys-Jones, *The CIA and American Democracy*, 206.

5. Prados, *President's Secret Wars*, 338–47.

6. *World in Action*, October 20, 1980. Unless otherwise stated, the information contained in this section comes from these prime sources: House of Representatives Committee on Foreign Affairs, Subcommittee on Africa, *Enforcement of the United States Arms Embargo Against South Africa*, March 30, 1982; Mordell, Heymans, and Braithwaite, *Case History of Dr. G. V. Bull*; a pioneering investigation by William Scott Malone and Sam Hemingway of the *Burlington Free Press*; a handwritten, thirty-eight-page defense of the smuggling by Jerry Bull dated July 20, 1979; interviews with the customs agents involved in investigating the case and interviews with lawyers who both defended and prosecuted Jerry Bull; and court documents relating to the trial of Jerry Bull. Additional information was supplied by the Bull family and friends.

CHAPTER 10

1. Unless otherwise stated, the material for this chapter comes from the sources cited in chapter 9, note 6.

2. Interview with Marcel Paquette, August 1990.

3. Ad Hoc Panel Report on the September 22 Event, Executives Office of the President, Office of Science and Technology Policy, Washington, D.C., undated; *Aviation Week and Space Technology*, August 11, 1980, 67–72; *Science* 29 (August 1980).

CHAPTER 11

1. Interviews with both Larry Curtis and his deputy George Klinefelter, 1990 and 1991.

2. Document submitted to Bull's lawyers, July 20, 1979.

3. Interview with Michel Bull, January 1991.

4. Interview with Kirk Karaszkiewicz, July 1990.

5. Interview with William Gray, August 1990.

6. The NORICUM affair is detailed in *The Washington Post*, February 2, 1991; *Basta*, January 29, 1988; *Wochenpresse*, March 4, 1988; *Daily Telegraph*, April 5, 1990; Associated Press, January 20, 26, and 27, 1988; *Guardian*, February 27 and 28, 1989.

CHAPTER 12

1. Interview with Dr. Robert Humphries, August 1990.

2. Interview with Hamilton Loeb, July 1990.

3. Interview with Warren Dennis, July 1990.

CHAPTER 13

1. Interview with Charles Murphy, July 1990.
2. *International Defence Review*, January 1991, 13.
3. *Proceedings of the Intercontinental Cannon and Orbiter Technology Workshop, November 1–5, 1985*, prepared for DARPA/STO, 1400 Wilson Boulevard, Arlington, VA. 22101.

CHAPTER 14

1. Timmerman, *The Poison Gas Connection*, 3.
2. Details of the smuggling operation come from documents supplied by the United States District Court, Eastern District of California, Sacramento. In addition, the case was reported by the *The Washington Post*, June 25, 1988, August 20, 1988, and November 1, 1988; and *The New York Times*, September 1, 1988. The BBC program "Panorama" broadcast a report on April 10, 1989. The author received briefings from intelligence sources in May 1989 and August 1990.
3. *Defence*, May 1989, 305–6.
4. *The Washington Post*, May 3, 1989.
5. *Jane's Defence Weekly*, April 22, 1989, 696.
6. Interview with Michel Bull, January 1991.
7. A great deal has been written about the supergun affair, some of it revelatory and much of it inaccurate. I do not have access to all the government files, but I believe that this is the most accurate account to date of the progress of the investigation. In assembling the details, I have drawn on some published sources and have checked the information with the government agencies involved. Where individuals are quoted, it means that I have interviewed them.

CHAPTER 15

1. The Lear Fan project was written about extensively in the press, including the *Irish Times*, February 15, 1988; the *Times* (London), October 11, 1989; *The Financial Times*, September 25, 1989, and October 24, 1989; and the *Observer*, September 28, 1989. Other information was obtained from officials in the Northern Ireland Office, from other British government officials, and in interviews with Michel Bull in January, February, and March 1991.

CHAPTER 16

1. See chapter 14, note 7.
2. The fortunes of Astra were closely followed in the financial press, particularly *The Financial Times* and *The Daily Telegraph*. For the circumstances surrounding the takeover of PRB, except where

stated, I have relied on interviews with the participants conducted in 1990 and 1991.

CHAPTER 17

1. Interview with Donald de Kieffer, February 1991.
2. Interview with Christopher Gumbley, October 1990.
3. Interview with Gerald James, September 1990.
4. "Frontline," February 11, 1991.

CHAPTER 18

1. Interview with senior U.S. Air Force officer, March 1, 1991.
2. *The Wall Street Journal*, March 4, 1991.
3. *The New York Times*, March 7, 1991.
4. Elisa D. Harris, "Chemical Weapons Proliferation in the Developing World," in *Brassey's Defence Yearbook* (London: Brassey's 1989), 67–88; Harris, *New Threats*, and *The Washington Times*, February 19, 1991.
5. A more detailed account of the Rabta affair appears in Adams, *Engines of War*, 240–46; see also Timmerman, *The Poison Gas Connection*.
6. *The New York Times*, March 7, 1991.
7. *The Washington Post*, February 27, 1991.
8. *The New York Times*, February 22, 1991.
9. Barnaby, *The Invisible Bomb*, 143–49.
10. Spector, *Nuclear Exports*, 21–26; and *The New York Times*, November 5, 1990, and November 12, 1990.
11. *Nucleonics Week*, August 9, 1990.
12. *The Wall Street Journal*, March 4, 1991.
13. *The New Republic*, February 4, 1991, 18–20.

B I B L I O G R A P H Y

Adams, James. *Engines of War.* New York: Atlantic Monthly Press, 1990.

Barnaby, Frank. *The Invisible Bomb: The Nuclear Arms Race in the Middle East.* London: I. B. Taurus, 1989.

———. *Weapons of Mass Destruction: A Growing Threat in the 1990s?* London: Research Institute for the Study of Conflict and Terrorism, 1990.

Beit-Hallahmi, Benjamin. *The Israeli Connection.* New York: Pantheon, 1987.

Brzezinski, Zbigniew. *Power and Principle.* New York: Farrar, Straus & Giroux, 1983.

Bulkeley, Rip, and Graham Spinardi. *Space Weapons: Deterrence or Delusion?* Cambridge, Mass: Polity Press, 1986.

Bull, G. V., and C. H. Murphy. *Paris Kanonen—The Paris Guns (Wilhelmgeschütze) and Project HARP.* Herford and Bonn: Verlag E. S. Mittler und Sohn, 1988.

Carter, Jimmy. *Keep Faith.* New York: Bantam, 1982.

Cordesman, Anthony, and Abraham R. Wagner. *The Lessons of Modern War.* Vol. 2, *The Iran-Iraq War.* Boulder, Colo.: Westview Press, 1990.

de Villiers, Les. *South Africa: A Skunk Among Nations.* London: International Books, 1975.

———. *Secret Information.* Capetown: Tafelberg, 1980.

Ford, Gerald. *A Time to Heal.* New York: Harper & Row, 1979.

Gelb, Norman. *The Berlin Wall.* New York: Times Books, 1987.

Harris, Elisa D. *New Threats: Responding to the Proliferation of Nuclear, Chemical and Delivery Capabilities in the Third World.* Aspen, Colo.: Aspen Strategy Group, 1990.

Hastings, Max. *The Korean War.* New York: Simon & Schuster, 1987.

Jahn, E. J., Jr. *The Problem Solvers: The Inside Story of Arthur D. Little, Inc.* Boston: Little, Brown, 1986.

Jeffreys-Jones, Rhodri. *The CIA and American Democracy.* New Haven: Yale University Press, 1989.

Kissinger, Henry. *Years of Upheaval.* New York: Little, Brown, 1982.

Lee, Christopher. *War in Space.* North Pomfret, Vt.: David & Charles, 1987.

Macdonald, Callum. *Korea: The War Before Vietnam.* New York: Free Press, 1987.

McWilliams, James P. *Armscor: South Africa's Arms Merchant.* London: Brassey's, 1989.

Mordell, Don, Jan Heymans, and Carleton Brathwraite, *A Review and Study of the Case History of Dr. G. V. Bull and the Space Research Corporation and Its Related Companies in North America with Supporting Relevant Documentation*. Privately printed.

O'Ballance, Edgar. *No Victor, No Vanquished*. Novato, Calif.: Presidio Press, 1979.

Ostrovsky, Victor, and Claire Hoy. *By Way of Deception*. New York: St. Martin's Press, 1990.

Perlmutter, Amos, Michael Handel, and Uri Bar-Joseph. *Two Minutes over Baghdad*. London: Corgi, 1982.

Piller, Charles, and Keith Yamamoto. *Gene Wars*. New York: Beech Tree Books, 1988.

Prados, John. *Presidents' Secret Wars*. New York: William Morrow, 1986.

Ranelagh, John. *The Agency: The Rise and Decline of the CIA*. New York: Simon & Schuster, 1987.

Ray, Ellen, William Schaap, Karl van Meter, and Louis Wolf. *Dirty Work 2: The CIA in Africa*. Secaucus, N.J.: Lyle Stuart, 1979.

Sims, Nicholas. *Reinforcing Biological Disarmament: Issues in the 1991 Review*. London: The Council for Arms Control, 1991.

Spector, Leonard. *Nuclear Export: The Challenge of Control*. Washington, D.C.: Carnegie Endowment for International Peace, 1990.

Stockwell, John. *In Search of Enemies*. New York: Norton, 1978.

Timmerman, Kenneth R. *The Poison Gas Connection*. Los Angeles: Simon Wiesenthal Center, 1990.

United States Arms Control and Disarmament Agency. *World Military Expenditures and Arms Transfers, 1989*. Washington, D.C.: U.S. Government Printing Office, 1990.